African BREW

For Shawn and Helen, because without them this book would never have happened.
And for Kevin, who would have loved to have read it.

Lucy Corne and Ryno Reyneke

ACKNOWLEDGMENTS/THANKS

Huge thanks to SAB for their assistance with the book, particularly to Jessica Yellin, Denis da Silva, Kate Jones, Laurie Conway, Lauren Steytler, Reto Jaeger and Anton Erasmus.

We'd also like to thank the various chefs who provided recipes for the book out of a sheer love of beer and a desire to explore the world of food and beer pairing.

We would like to individually thank a few people who went above and beyond in accommodating us while researching – to Denis and Debbie Corne, Ian Cook, Garth and Mirabelle Cambray, André de Beer, Chris Heaton, Jonathan and Michelle Nel, Richard and Bridget Pote, Patrick and Goedele van den Bon, Ditte Humphrey of Kowie River Guest House, Soka Mthembu of Zulu Experience and to ArgusCarHire.com for providing car hire for the main section of the trip.

Finally, we cannot begin to express our gratitude to all of the brewers and their families across South Africa, who showed unrivalled hospitality and offered help and support throughout the research and production of African Brew. We raise a glass to you all.

SAB
The South African Breweries   **argus**carhire.com®

Published in 2013 by Struik Lifestyle
an imprint of Random House Struik (Pty) Ltd
Company Reg. No 1966/003153/07
Wembley Square, 1st Floor, Solan Street, Gardens 8001
P O Box 1144, Cape Town 8000

Visit **www.randomstruik.co.za** and subscribe to our newsletter for monthly updates and news.

10 9 8 7 6 5 4 3 2 1

Publisher: Linda de Villiers
Managing editor: Cecilia Barfield
Editor and indexer: Joy Clack (Bushbaby Editorial Services)
Designer: Beverley Dodd
Text by: Lucy Corne
Photography by: Ryno Reyneke
Illustration on pages 22–23 by: Helen Vaughan
Stylist: Brita du Plessis
Proofreader: Janice Whitticom (Bushbaby Editorial Services)

Reproduction by Hirt & Carter Cape (Pty) Ltd
Printed and bound by 1010 Printing International Ltd, China

ISBN 978 1 43170 289 3

Contents

INTRODUCTION

LUCY'S STORY

I was always a beer drinker. And when I say always, I almost mean it – I can even remember, as a small child, asking my dad if I could have "the froth" from his post-dinner beer. The university years brought the usual drinking exploits and a particular habit that would make a true beer lover cringe – that of adding a tot of lime cordial to my pint of lager. Ironically, although I was born and grew up in the UK – not 50 km from the British brewing mecca of Burton-upon-Trent – it took a Canadian to introduce me to the joys of sipping on a traditional English ale. Thanks to that Canadian – now my husband (see how beer brings people together?) – I was suddenly introduced to this amazingly varied world, where beer came in all manner of colours, strengths and flavours.

Beer took us around the world, the presence of a brewery – be it large or small – often dictating which towns would make it onto our travel agenda. We sipped on English bitter in Bangkok, bought a crate of cut-price Dashen lager in Gondar, Ethiopia, rediscovered rural England through its pints, and spent a fascinating afternoon in a North Korean brewpub when our guide needed a place to dump us for the afternoon without fearing we might wander off. It was also in Korea, South Korea this time, that I fell in love with the hop, thanks to a flourishing homebrewing community with a penchant for big, bold American beers. One sip of the flagship brew from the founder of the country's homebrewing club and I was forever hooked – the name of that beer? Death by Hops.

My beer-fuelled travels would eventually lead us, happily, back to South Africa in 2010, a country we had explored from tip to tip four years earlier, tasting every beer we could find along the way. On returning we could see that things had changed;

that things *were* changing at a rapid and tremendously exciting rate. In a new city with just a sprinkling of friends, we sought out the place that we knew we would find a group of like-minded, open-minded and open-armed people – our local homebrewing club. It was through the SouthYeasters that I met Ryno, a meeting that would lead to the book that you have in your hands, *African Brew*.

RYNO'S STORY

It was my father-in-law who first exposed me to the possibility of brewing. Colin Vaughan had been brewing kit beers for a while when he invited me to a homebrewing festival a few years ago. A whole new world was opened up to me as I was blown away by the diversity of flavours on offer and how helpful everybody was with information about brewing.

I quickly purchased a kit beer and, after one brew, I was hooked. I loved the challenge of creating a tasty beverage out of the simplest of ingredients. I spent hours on the internet researching all the different variants of brewing, educating myself on how to make even better brews. In no time I had made my own all-grain system and was brewing as many variations of beer as I could think of. For someone who has always had a passion for food, making "liquid food" was a natural progression.

It was my wife, Helen, who inspired the concept of this book. After listening to my endless talking about beer, making beer and having to taste (she still is my "taster" and I trust her taste buds before I do mine), one day she said "it is time you married your passion and profession and published a book."

I met Lucy at a SouthYeasters Summer Festival where I proudly presented my homebrewed creations for the first time to all who would taste them. After reading a few articles Lucy had written, I knew I had found the right person to write my vision of what is happening in the brewing industry in South Africa today. Little did I know how large the revolution was becoming out there, with breweries opening all over the place at a constant rate by like-minded people as passionate about beer as I am.

It has been an incredible journey and I have been humbled by the dedication of each and every one of the brewers I met while researching and photographing *African Brew*.

THE *AFRICAN BREW* STORY

With a shared vision and a few false starts, we set off to start research on the book in April 2012. You might laugh at the idea of "research" and yes, it did involve tasting a lot of beers, but there was much more to it than that. We went to find the stories behind those beers and were met by smiling brewers displaying a selflessness, humility and unpretentious hospitality that characterises the beer world. Our journey taught us more about brewing, tasting, pairing and packaging. It took us along new alcoholic lines, down the avenues of mead and sorghum beer. It took us to seven of the nine South African provinces (the Northern Cape and Limpopo don't yet have any craft breweries); it took us to dusty *dorpe* and vast cities – it even took us into people's homes for dinners and tastings. We quizzed the brewers and we picked the brains of SAB, without whom this book would never have got off the ground.

Beer is sweeping the nation, with bars stocking a greater range of beers than ever before, breweries sprouting up every month, beer festivals taking over the country's social calendar and restaurants cottoning on to the idea that beer, like wine, can be a perfect partner for food. *African Brew* brings a taste of South Africa's burgeoning beer culture into your home and we hope that it will also take you out of your home to do a little literal tasting in some – or all – of the breweries featured in this book.

> **TICKEY BEER**
> The former South African coin, known as a tickey, was worth three pennies and its name was used to describe a particularly popular beer in the nineteenth century.

THE BACKGROUND

HOW BEER BEGAN

"Someone left the cake out in the rain." This oft-ridiculed lyric in the much-recorded pop song "MacArthur Park" was supposedly referring to lost love, but it so easily could have been a line about the origins of beer.

OK, so that would perhaps be oversimplifying the issue – and might not be entirely gastronomically accurate – but the basic premise is sound. Historians generally trace the first sip of beer back to around 10 000 years ago – before that we were happily getting drunk on mead, and perhaps some rough-around-the-edges wine. The beer too, would have been a little, shall we say, rustic. Like so many great discoveries, beer was a fortuitous accident and while a cake might not have been involved, the inane "MacArthur's Park" line isn't too far from the truth. In fact, a widely accepted theory is that beer basically evolved from a spoiled loaf. It was the ultimate cloud with a silver – or should that be amber – lining: one minute you're mourning the loss of your lunch, the next you're feeling pleasantly tipsy after eating it regardless. Quite how it happened is something of a mystery. Some say that damp grain – grain which had already begun to ferment – might have been quickly cooked up to save it going to waste; others believe a loaf itself might have got damp (left out in the rain perhaps?). Either way, there was grain, there was yeast and there was water. There was also a bunch of very happy people whose new hobby was most likely leaving their loaves lying around whenever the elders predicted a shower.

Drinking a wet loaf can't have been an easy feat, and early beers are thought to have resembled porridge as much as liquid. Ancient Egyptian drawings often depict noble folk sipping from out-sized straws designed to suck the moisture from the thick slurry of wet bread or boozy porridge sitting at the bottom of the urn.

Exactly who came up with beer first is another point that is up for debate, though it's quite likely that more than one group stumbled upon the idea at the same time. Is it a coincidence that this also coincided with man's transition from a hunter-gatherer existence to sticking around in one spot and turning to agriculture? Not according to a lot of anthropologists, who believe that it was this magical, mood-altering beverage that convinced our once roaming ancestors to stay in one place waiting for their grain to grow. In other words, beer is responsible for civilisation.

Early beer history is certainly shrouded in uncertainty – perhaps people were too busy enjoying their new-found nightcap to bother recording it – but once we reach 1700 BCE, things start to make it into the official history books. The oldest beer recipe was written by the Sumerians, inhabitants of a region of Mesopotamia (modern-day Iraq and around), almost 4 000 years ago. Not only is the recipe – in the form of a hymn to the goddess Ninkasi – the oldest reference to beer brewing, it is also the oldest known recipe in the world, proving just how attached people were to their beer even back then. The hymn talks about a type of bread, known as *bappir*, made with honey and dates and later soaked in water to then be blended with other soaked grains before being left to ferment.

In the ancient civilisations – Egyptian and Sumerian specifically – beer pervaded almost every aspect of society. It was treated as a medicine, used in religious rituals, offered to the gods from whence it surely must have come. It was also used as currency, with speculation that the workers who built the pyramids were paid in beer, which might help explain how they managed the gargantuan structures without modern machinery. Some people claim to speak fluent French or Chinese after a couple of pints, others can achieve impossible architectural feats. The first large-scale breweries were also to be found in Egypt, though the country's love affair with fermented grain would come to an end with the arrival of Alexander the Great in 322 BCE. The Greeks, too embroiled in their own tryst with the grape, looked upon beer with disdain and reintroduced Egypt to wine. It would be the start of a millennia-long rivalry between beer and wine, with strong opinions on either side that are still held today. This same attitude was introduced to Britain when the Normans invaded from France in the eleventh century, bringing their penchant for wine along with them – until then the English were happily drinking their ales. Actually, for the most part, they continued doing just that for several centuries. Wine was largely reserved for the upper echelons of society, perhaps because, while it afforded a similar pleasant feeling to that enjoyed with a tankard of ale, it did not constitute a meal – something which beer could.

As in early civilisations, it was women in England who traditionally brewed beer. Most were essentially forerunners to today's legion of homebrewers, but for a gifted few, brewing was a rare chance for women to earn honest money. Professional brewers were known as ale wives and until the Middle Ages they ran the alehouses throughout England. A simple flower would be their undoing, with the ingredient that many beer lovers today consider borderline sacred spelling the end of women's reign over beer production: the hop.

Hops were already being used in beer in small pockets of Europe – largely in the monasteries that were home to many of the continent's earliest breweries – but it wasn't until the early twelfth century that the flower's preservation properties became widely known. A Benedictine nun, later known as St Hildegard, extolled the virtues of *Humulus lupulus* in a natural history text. Until then beer had been flavoured with *gruit*, a combination of various herbs and spices, but once the word got out that hops could do a better job, *gruit's* days were numbered. The spice mixture didn't go out without a fight though, largely due to the Catholic Church making a healthy chunk of change from the *gruit* industry. But hops did a far better job of making beer last longer and their use quickly caught on across Europe.

England was bent on resisting the use of hops and many of the ales remained unhopped for centuries – during this time the term *beer* was used to describe a malt-based alcoholic beverage with added hops while *ale* referred to the unhopped version, though these definitions have now faded into antiquity. Suddenly though, with the advent of hops, beer could be kept for longer, making it

ALES WITHIN ABBEYS

You've probably heard of monks brewing beer in Belgium, but the small European country is not the only place to enlist their holy men to the brewing ranks. In fact, it's widely agreed that Europe's earliest commercial brewers were monks, with monastic breweries situated throughout France, Switzerland, Germany, England and the Netherlands during the Middle Ages. Their reasons for brewing were threefold – first, it guaranteed that passing pilgrims would be able to find refreshment behind monastery walls. Water was a sketchy beverage in those days and the fact that beer-making demands that the water be boiled made it an altogether healthier – not to mention tastier – alternative to plain H_2O. Secondly, selling beer helped to raise a few extra coffers to keep the monastery ticking over and, finally, keeping some for themselves helped the monks through times of strict fasting. Germany's strong Doppelbock beer was actually devised by monks as a meal in a glass, reserved for fasting periods when virtually no solid food could pass their lips. Today, monastic brewing is mainly practised in Belgium and it's still possible to visit a handful of breweries found within monastery walls.

more viable to brew in much larger batches. Now there was real money to be made from beer and men wanted a piece of the brewing action. Women lacked the funds to invest in storage areas and gradually the job that had always belonged to them morphed into a male-dominated profession.

Thanks to a generous dose of war, poverty, hunger and disease in the 1600s, brewing took a bit of a hit and in many European countries it once more became an endeavour practised in the home. Thankfully, fortunes improved and the start of the eighteenth century saw a revival in commercial breweries. As if to mark the resurgence, a new beer style was born in the now thriving city of London – the porter. The origins of this dark and roasty beer are the subject of much speculation and debate, but whether or not it was named for the porters carrying their wares between London markets or not, one thing is for sure – it took the city by storm. This new, hearty beer helped drive the industrial revolution, just as the industrial revolution drove the brewing world in new and exciting directions. Suddenly beer production was steam-powered, leading to a vast increase in production, and since factory work was a thirsty business, consumption moved along similar lines. Major advances were made in malting, making one of beer's base ingredients easier to produce on a mass scale and considerably more productive. Once this technology reached German shores, they mastered it and used it to perfect an underground beer style that had been slowly emerging.

When I say "underground", I don't mean that it was niche or kept secret from the authorities, though it might well have been both. The beer style born in a cave was quite literally developed underground and would one day become as far from a niche beverage as you could possibly get. As well as placing restrictions on the ingredients allowed in beer, Germany's early sixteenth-century beer purity law, the Reinheitsgebot, also imposed a ban on summer brewing. Since its pronouncement, brewers had been working on ways to produce year-round beer that was drinkable whatever

A BREAKAWAY BEER REPUBLIC

If there's one country that has never followed trend or tradition when it comes to brewing, then diminutive Belgium is it. While Germany was passing doctrine on what could and could not appear in a recipe for beer; while Britain was bickering about whether hops or *gruit* made a better addition to ale, Belgium carried on doing its thing, chucking fruit, herbs, flowers and whatever else they fancied into their brewing vats. This anything-goes, almost hippieish attitude to brewing eventually gave rise to some of the most unusual and varied beers out there, all stemming from a brewing culture built by holy men. Other "factions" of monks were already brewing but the Trappists – the monks that are most famous for brewing – didn't start until the middle of the nineteenth century. In 1919 a law banned distilled spirits from being sold in the country's bars, leaving a vacuum for those looking for a little kick in their booze. The brewers stepped in and satisfied the thirst with bigger, bolder beers with a considerably higher alcohol content than those found in most other brewing nations.

the weather on brew day. Decades and centuries passed and the yeast – critters that usually preferred temperatures of 18–24 °C – morphed to cope with the cooler temperatures beneath Bavarian ground. Beers made with this hardy yeast had to be kept in the caves for some time to allow them to mature, and took their name from the German word meaning "to store" – *lagern*.

The hot liquor tank from the former Mariendahl Brewery (c. 1880) is now housed in the museum at Newlands Brewery in Cape Town.

This beer – a crisper, clearer version of the soupy ales people were used to – quickly caught on in Europe, but while many were making lager-style beers, it is Bavarian brewer Josef Groll who is widely credited with perfecting it. Headhunted by the Bürger Brauerei in Bohemia (now the Czech Republic), Groll crossed the border in 1842, armed with a bagful of Bavarian lager yeast. When combined with the local Saaz hops and the latest advances in pale malt, the yeast helped to create what is credited as the world's first clear, golden beer, which became known for the town in which it was first brewed – Plzen. Alas, for some reason the brewery failed to patent its much sought-after beer and the refreshing style was quickly replicated around the world. Half a century later, the Bürger Brauerei (now called Plze ský Prazdro) decided to make a point to global pilsner drinkers that they came up with the recipe first, bestowing it with the moniker "original pilsner" – in German, Pilsner Urquell. Lager-beers quickly swept the globe, with notable pockets of resistance being England, Ireland and Belgium. Today, a century and a half later, over 90 per cent of the world's beers are modelled on Groll's recipe.

Beer – most of it lager – was now being enjoyed throughout the world, though in 1920 Prohibition brought the American brewing industry to its knees. Alcohol in all its forms became illegal and the booming beer business – there were around 4 000 breweries counted in 1873 – collapsed. Prohibition would eventually be repealed 13 years later, but by then the face of American brewing had changed and it would take more than five decades and an army of homebrewers to change it back. Before Prohibition, American lager already had its own personality – German settlers had brought their brewing techniques, but turned to the locally accessible crop of corn to counter the harshness and haze lent by the available American barley. It was a full-flavoured pale lager that was as close to the German original that local ingredients would allow,

BEER FACTS, BEER FICTION

- Ancient Babylonian king Hammurabi allegedly took beer so seriously that there were strict punishments for anyone behaving badly where beer was concerned. Some state the offence as brewing undrinkable beer, some say it was pouring short measures, others claim that cutting the price of beer in a tavern was the crime, but all agree that the punishment was drowning. Whether beer was the medium in which the wrong-doers were drowned is disputed, though it's unlikely the despot would waste his precious booze drowning miscreants.
- The first British settlers to reach American shores weren't full-on puritans. In fact, when the *Mayflower* made landfall in 1620, it missed its mark somewhat. The ship was supposed to hit the shore of what is now New York, but since the beer had run out on board and they were left in need of water, a new destination was chosen and they landed instead in Massachusetts.
- Probably the biggest ever beer catastrophe happened in London in 1815. After a rupture in a brewing vat, beer swept through the parish causing a booze tsunami that destroyed a couple of houses and a pub. Eight people died and over a million pints of beer was lost.
- Of all the adjuncts and extras added to beer throughout the years, perhaps the most grotesque is *lant*. *Lant*, an Old English word meaning stale urine, was said to be added to beer in some European pubs in the seventeenth and eighteenth centuries to strengthen it ... In the 1980s, the practice of adding pee to beer reared its head again, though claims that Mexican brewery workers were peeing into vats of Corona bound for the USA were later found to be made up by a Heineken distributor in Nevada.

but after 13 years of abstinence – and a bit of boot-leg beer – people's tastes had changed. A new generation emerged who had most likely never tasted beer, while their older counterparts had developed a taste for soft drinks and beer needed to change to suit their palates. Add to that new laws limiting the alcohol content of beer and what emerged was a mild-flavoured though admittedly thirst-quenching brew that would be unrecognisable to the German brewers who first brought lager to these shores.

Consumption rose, but the number of breweries decreased as they merged or closed, leaving less than 90 breweries by the late 1970s, almost all of which were churning out a similar product. Then in the 1980s things began to change as microbreweries started to open with increasing frequency. This thirst for a greater range of beers echoed a similar movement in the UK, but it's probably fair to say that it was the American craft beer boom that transformed the global beer map. In a pattern that has repeated itself across the world – throughout Europe, East Asia, Australia, New Zealand and now South Africa – the revolutionaries behind these unusual, full-flavoured and very varied beers were largely homebrewers who had long been creating beer on a tiny scale to quench their thirst for variety. Today there are over 80 styles of beer recognised by the BJCP (Beer Judge Certification Program) a US-based scheme that accredits judges and sanctions beer contests. It is an exciting time to be a beer lover, with experimentation rife, flavours bolder than ever and a variety the like of which has never been seen before. We are living, quite simply, in an era that can only be described as the Beer Renaissance.

THE BIRTH OF BEER IN SOUTH AFRICA

As in world booze history, beer in South Africa was predated by another fermented beverage – mead. The Khoisan used "honey wine" (simply honey and water, fermented with yeast found naturally in the honey) in many of their religious practices, calling the drink !karri. The drink was made by various other groups in South Africa too, including the Xhosa,

---

STUDIES IN BEER

When the now-renowned Reinheitsgebot listed Bavarian beer's permitted ingredients in 1516, the essential element was conspicuously absent. At least, it is conspicuous now, but at the time no one understood that yeast was the magical ingredient that turned sweet, malty water into the wondrous liquid that is beer – it just happened naturally. It wasn't until Louis Pasteur published his book *Études sur la bière* in 1876 that the processes behind the pint became known. As well as working out the secrets of fermentation, the world's best-known beer scholar wrote probably the first list of off-flavours and their causes. He also came up with a way to fend off the bacteria-borne diseases in beer and would give his name to the process – pasteurisation.

---

who called it *iQhilika* and the Tswana, for whom the beverage was known as *khadi* (for more on mead, see page 145). As well as mead, tribes that had migrated from Central and East Africa made a drink that is still popular throughout South Africa today – sorghum beer. It seems that sorghum beer brewing in South Africa had its roots in a much older beer tradition, with later explorers noting that the strainers used by the Zulu people were incredibly similar in design to those used in ancient Egypt (for more on sorghum beer, see page 243).

Traditional beer was a common subject for Europeans chronicling South Africa back in the nineteenth century, with particular attention paid to the many ceremonial uses of the beer and above all to its lack of potency. Missionary Robert Moffat was perhaps in search of a stronger brew throughout his time in South Africa, as he often commented on the low alcohol content of sorghum beer. "It would require one to drink several gallons to produce the effects like ale or spirits" he once noted in his diary, later commenting again that it "possessed of very little of an intoxicating nature".

Aerial view of Newlands Brewery c. 1920.

Following in this theme, an early twentieth-century quote from Zulu historian Father A.T. Bryant perhaps sums up what the early Europeans thought about the local brew. "This native beer, though wholesome, does not appeal strongly to most Europeans; which is understandable, seeing that the normal alcoholic content can hardly be more than two per cent. The beer is a pinkish liquid … and to the European, it has the flavour of highly diluted ale mixed with sorghum meal." Of course, by the time he was experiencing the joys – or otherwise – of sorghum beer, Europeans had long since reached South African shores and there was a thriving trade in "clear beer".

It's well-known that Jan van Riebeeck wasted little time in planting vines when he arrived at the Cape of Good Hope in 1652. But in fact, the first wines were produced in 1659, two years after his first, albeit not very successful, brew. Not only were brewing supplies on one of the first shopping lists he sent back to The Netherlands after landing at the Cape, but in fact the fleet that brought Jan here also carried a fair supply of barrelled beer on board. It was inevitable that Jan and his crew would quickly turn into homebrewers when they hit African shores, considering the solid beer culture alive in their native land. And when you think of the reason for the Dutch landing in South Africa in the first place, the settlement couldn't very well continue for long without a brewery of some sort. Cape Town, as it would eventually become known, was established as a refreshment station, there to help restock supplies on boats headed to the East, and what kind of refreshment station would it be if it couldn't replenish the on-board booze supply of passing ships? They were quite wrong, but those early round-the-world travellers thought that beer helped stave off scurvy, so it was a vital commodity to have in the hold. Cape Town quickly became known as the "Tavern of the Seas" and it would have been a pretty paltry tavern without a steady supply of beer.

Once Van Riebeeck had secured the various ingredients needed to attempt a brew, with corn as the base grain, he was missing just one element – a brewer. The arrival of Pieter Visagie, an Antwerp sailor, was a turning point for the Tavern. He arrived with brewing knowledge and soon set up what was South Africa's first "clear beer" brewery near the Liesbeek River. In 1658, after a false start or two (the 1657 brew never fermented), he brewed South Africa's first pint, which Van Riebeeck recorded as being "delicious". The country's first brewhouse was built in 1659 and South Africa's long and tumultuous love affair with beer began.

It was far from plain sailing though. Ingredients were tough to come by, attempts to grow hops in the area failed and one shipment was allegedly lost in transit when a ship cook, mistaking the hop flowers for veggies, turned the lot into what must have been the most unpalatable salad of all time. Despite the lack of hops, brewing took off, with people starting to brew unhopped beer in their homes. The first licenced brewer, Jan Martensz de Wacht, set up shop in 1664, with a decree to "brew as much Cape beer of malt and hops … as the Honourable Company shall see fit".

By now Jan van Riebeeck had left the Cape, but the brewing legacy he had started continued with a new beer, known as "Mom", appearing in 1666. It was a heavy brew that had first emerged in Germany at the end of the fifteenth century. Alongside this grew another branch of brewing, one that was both cheaper and easier to produce. Sugar beer was composed of bran, black sugar and hops and became a popular homebrew. It presented great competition to Company beer, and its production was quickly – if not very effectively – regulated. Only orphans and widows were permitted to sell sugar beer, but many settlers continued brewing it profit, to the detriment of the Company's revenues, and its sale was later banned entirely.

Beer's popularity in South Africa was to take a hit towards the end of the seventeenth century, with the arrival of the Huguenots. Wine was already being produced with varying levels of success, but the French settlers brought with them greater winemaking knowledge and, as the quality

THE ORIGINAL BREWERS

Historically, beer was made by women, whether it was in Europe, Africa or anywhere else. Although brewing is a largely male-dominated world today, female brewers are increasing in number. African beer history is dotted with female protagonists, worshipped, one way or another, for their feisty spirit. Here's a trio of the most memorable:

Mbaba Mwana Waresa

This is one of the most-loved Zulu goddesses and not because she's associated with agriculture, rain or rainbows. She is associated with all of those things, but she is also credited with the invention of beer and with passing her brewing knowledge on to the Zulu people.

Cockney Liz

Although female barmaids were common during South Africa's gold rush era, few were recorded as frequently as one known simply as Cockney Liz. When she moved to Barberton (Mpumalanga), she gained fame and popularity as a straight-talking barmaid and talented entertainer. She later went on to own bars in the region – perhaps thanks to her habit of auctioning herself to the highest bidder each evening. Her name lives on in a hotel in the town.

Aunt Peggy

Journalist Casey Motsisi's much-documented Shebeen Queen might have been a fictional character, but that doesn't mean there wasn't a large helping of truth behind her ways. A composite of various tavern bosses of the time, she showcased the much-loved traits of the Shebeen Queen – most notably an ample bosom, a devotion to her customers and a fiery, no-nonsense spirit.

improved, beer sales decreased. People were still drinking beer, but many were making it at home, perhaps feeling that their own concoctions were as drinkable as the beer available for purchase. Simon van der Stel brought in regulations barring people from selling imported beers and "Mom" in a bid to save the Company's profits from further damage, but perhaps a better plan to boost their business was the appointment of the Cape's first qualified brewer in 1696. Rutgert Mensing proved himself quickly when he chose a site for his brewery that still plays a large role in brewing today. His knowledge of beer-making meant that he understood the importance of water and he was allotted 30 morgen of land in his chosen spot – near the spring in Newlands. People perhaps rejoiced at his apparent expertise a little prematurely, since it was three years before he produced any beer on his estate, known as Papenboom.

Mensing's foray into the world of Cape brewing was largely a disaster and although his family attempted to keep his brewing monopoly going after his death, they were even less successful. Brewers came and went but the beer stayed much the same – an inferior brew, due in part to lack of expertise but more so to the lack of quality raw materials available. Imported beer was sought after and local production suffered, not aided by the Papenboom brewery burning down in 1773. All-in-all, while the early settlers enjoyed beer, they hadn't excelled at producing it and while the arrival of the British in 1795 was unwelcome in many ways, at least they brought some ale with them. Imported beer quenched the collective thirst for a while, but when the British arrived en masse in 1820 there was a healthy number of beer drinkers – and luckily a few brewers – in their ranks. Soon breweries began to pop up not just in and around Cape Town, but further afield in Grahamstown, Somerset East and throughout Settler Country in what is now the Eastern Cape.

Sorghum beer – also sometimes made with corn – was still the drink of choice for the African population and there are many mentions of the brew being offered as hospitality to visiting

Europeans, especially by the Zulus. Zulu chief Dingane was particularly noted for his love of beer, with American missionaries observing that he enjoyed beer for breakfast and counted on numerous deliveries of it throughout the day. Beer also played its role in the Weenen Massacre, when it was used to distract Piet Retief and his men before Dingane's fatal attack took place. For the Europeans though, it was "clear beer" that they sought, and back in the Cape the foundations for what was really the country's first beer boom were being laid.

In 1820, Jacob Letterstedt had set up the Mariendahl Brewery, named for his wife, in what was unarguably the cradle of South African "clear beer" – Newlands. Letterstedt's brewery survived the tide and although others launched and failed, it was clear that brewing had finally arrived in Cape Town, with an 1854 census noting 13 breweries in the city.

The cooper trade – one that has all but died out today – also flourished, with close to 60 barrel-makers known in the region in the middle of the nineteenth century. Around this time, taverns and breweries began to sprout up in the Natal region, and beer made its first foray into the hinterland, with licenced "drink wagons" serving as mobile pubs. Breweries at this time sold only ales, with beer menus reading much like they would at a traditional British pub today. Many of the brewers were indeed British, but it was an ambitious young man from another European country that would have a long-lasting effect on the South African beer landscape.

Anders Ohlsson, a Norwegian by birth, arrived on Cape shores in 1864, two years after the death of the Cape's other Scandinavian brewing mogul, Letterstedt. A career in importing goods from Sweden followed, but in 1881 Ohlsson realised that there was money to be made in brewing and he bought land in Newlands. Here he built his first brewery, Anneberg, but Ohlsson obviously had greater things in mind and he set about building up a beer empire. In 1888 – a notable year in South Africa's brewing history – Ohlsson made

his first move, taking over the Cannon Brewery and the Newlands Brewery, both located in the same suburb. A year later, Ohlsson added to the empire, leasing – and later buying – the late Letterstedt's Mariendahl Brewery.

Ohlsson's arrival on the brewing scene was perfectly timed, for the golden era of South African brewing was about to begin. Prospecting, be it for gold, diamonds or whatever other mineral, was thirsty work and as gold fever hit the Witwatersrand so did a thirst for gold of a drinkable kind. The 1880s saw a wave of taverns springing up around the newly-established Johannesburg and a spate of breweries opening to keep the diggers' thirst at bay. Kimberley's brewery trade never blossomed due to water shortages in the region, though there was one failed brewery that would have a long-lasting effect on the South African beer trade. Charles and George Chandler, brothers from England, started making beer in diamond country in 1884. The brewery didn't last, but Charles had his heart set on brewing and he moved to the Witwatersrand where his beers were welcomed in the dusty world of gold prospecting. His brewery – first known as the Wiltshire Brewery after his home county in England, but later taking the still-remembered name of Chandler's – flourished while others came and went. Another soon-to-be famous name soon arrived on the Pretoria scene, with the Lion Brewery opening its doors in 1891.

One more name that would be forever immortalised in South African beer history was to enter the fray in this landmark decade of brewing – Charles Glass. Glass had been brewing for British troops in India and wanted to set up a brewery on the Witwatersrand with his wife, Lisa. He sought and secured financial backing and the husband-and-wife brewing team quickly got to work, though their role in the brewery was short-lived. After a couple of years the backers bought Glass out, but they did keep the quickly established logo, a logo that would give its name to the brewery and would live on to the present day. The emblem in question was simple in its design – a picture of three castles.

In 1888 – the same year that the Glass family began brewing in Johannesburg and that Ohlsson was building a beer monopoly in the Cape – important developments were taking place around Durban, with the arrival of an English teenager with ambition, Frederick Mead. The 19 year old did a quick and competent assessment of the brewing industry in the area, noting the state of local equipment and the quality of the beer, and concluding that there was scope for another player to enter the market. In 1889 he established the Natal Brewery Syndicate in Pietermaritzburg. Mead later went on to buy the Castle Brewery, with the two merging under a new name – South African United Breweries. Mead sought further backing from diamond mining magnate Barney Barnato and businessman Sammy Marks and the company was re-christened again, this time with a name that would stick and one day become internationally recognised – South African Breweries. SAB, as it would later become known, was officially founded in 1895. With the new Castle plant in Johannesburg ready, SAB brewed the first lager beer in Africa and Castle Lager was introduced to the local market in 1898.

The Anglo-Boer War would halt production in breweries across the country and while some weathered the storm, others closed to never re-open. Imported beers started to arrive again, but because the quality of beer brewed in South Africa had improved considerably, imported beers were now considered a luxury rather than an essential. There were still breweries dotted around the country, but for the vast majority their days were numbered. The number of beer drinkers diminished with the withdrawal of troops and there was a global trend towards business mergers – a trend that was echoed in the South African brewing world. Smaller breweries were swallowed up and two brewing giants arose – SAB and Ohlsson's, with a smaller player still hanging on to a few loyal beer drinkers. A north-south lager divide emerged, with those in Cape Town preferring pints of Lion (Ohlsson had bought the Pretoria brewery in 1902) and Jo'burg dwellers lapping up the Castle. As

SAB expanded into the Cape, there was talk of the two merging, but as discussions broke down the breweries became rivals, each one employing new marketing techniques to get their beers noticed.

One area where they did work together was in hop production and, in 1935, hop farming kicked off in George – the region with a climate similar to that of the world's major hop-growing regions. Brewers in South Africa had dabbled in hop production for decades, but it was the hop famine created by the 1914–18 U-boat Campaign that made South African beer producers realise that they needed to become self-sufficient when it came to ingredients. Maltsters had long been operating at the Mariendahl Brewery and until demand picked up, small-scale maltings were enough to keep the industry ticking over. In the 1970s, the large maltings plant at Caledon opened, but first the beer industry would have another problem to deal with.

South Africa's beer history closely mirrors that of the United States, with a late nineteenth-century boom and then steadily decreasing numbers of breweries. And as in the US, politics would play a part in the temporary decline of beer consumption. South Africa's prohibition era did not spell a total halt to alcohol production as it did in the States, but the 1928 ban on black South Africans drinking "European liquor" did harm the brewers' profits. Of course, the damage would have been much more serious if not for the advent of a phenomenon inextricably linked to South Africa's beer history – shebeens. While "Shebeen Queens", that is the women who ran the illegal drinking dens from their homes, did produce a fair amount of alcohol themselves, there was also a healthy trade in bootleg booze. In fact, the number of people still purchasing beer from SAB was so great that it spelled a production faux pas once prohibition was lifted in 1962. SAB, anticipating a sharp hike in demand, invested in new equipment and stepped up production in anticipation of the day when beer would be legally available to all. Since many of the "new" customers were actually already drinking lager, albeit illegally, much of the stockpiled beer ended up being thrown away.

When South Africa emerged from prohibition, beer drinkers found themselves, as in the USA, with a narrowed market. In 1956, a merger had been agreed that saw Ohlsson's Cape Brewing and Union, which had grown out of the Chandler's Brewery, incorporated under the SAB umbrella. SAB's strength was further reinforced in the 1960s when the company won the right to brew three prominent overseas beers – Amstel, Guinness and one that would later become an identifying beer for many South Africans, Carling Black Label. Other breweries attempted to enter the field, perhaps most notably the Luyt Brewery, established in 1972. Assertive marketing campaigns followed, but the start-up was no match for the long-established competitor and SAB soon bought the brewery. Founder Louis Luyt later established a microbrewery in Ballito, KwaZulu-Natal and his legacy – and brewhouse – now lives on at the Stellenbrau Brewery in Stellenbosch (see page 109).

Then in 1983, almost a century after the last beer boom in South Africa, a new player arrived on the scene – one that could not and didn't want to challenge the might of SAB, but that did challenge the palate of the South African beer drinker. Ales, once the staple pint in the country, had gradually fallen out of favour, but with the country's first microbrewery – at least since this term had been coined – came a new style of beer. Mitchell's Brewery (see also page 87) began with a lager, but quickly moved into the realm of English ales and it weathered the storm until the craft beer boom of the twenty-first century. Throughout the 1990s and early 2000s, small breweries began to crop up around the country, with an early cluster emerging in KwaZulu-Natal. During this period, SAB continued to expand overseas, with its acquisition of breweries round the world peaking with the purchase of US-based Miller Brewing Company in 2002. SABMiller was now the second largest brewing company in the world by volume, after American giant Anheuser-Busch InBev.

Back on South African shores, interesting changes were taking place, albeit on a considerably smaller scale. A decade into the twenty-first cen-tury, beer experienced a popularity explosion the like of which had not been seen in more than 100 years, with imports on the increase and a range of styles available that even went beyond the choice on offer during the gold rush era. Today there are over 40 microbreweries – so named for the smaller batches of beer that they produce – sitting in almost every province. The brewers have largely stepped forward from the country's army of home-brewers in yet another trend that mirrors happenings in the USA. Deep down, South Africans were always homebrewers – from the sorghum beer brewed by African women through the experimental brews of questionable drinkability from Jan van Riebeeck and Pieter Visagie and on to the "needs must" offerings of the twentieth-century Shebeen Queens. Today, as beer appreciation spreads, there are scores of homebrewers brewing away in their kitchens, sheds and garages – a sure sign that South Africa will be able to count on a multitude of microbreweries for many years to come.

Man – it's GOOD!

A really grand lager with the full-flavour we lager drinkers appreciate. That's Castle Lager! Pure enjoyment from the first eager sip to the last reluctant drop — that's Castle Lager! If you want to know how good a lager CAN be — try Castle Lager!

Castle LAGER

CASTLE LAGER

CASTLE ALE ADVERT C. 1950

FROM GRAIN TO GREATNESS – HOW BEER IS MADE

THE FOUR ELEMENTS

When it comes to basic ingredients, beer appears to be a simple recipe based on water, malted barley, hops and yeast. There are many variations of each of these though and changing just one variable will result in an entirely different beer. Unless you're a beer puritan and a devout follower of Germany's purity law, there are no limitations on what you can add to your beer, whether it's herbs, spices, fruit or cereal adjuncts … but let's begin with the basics.

Water

The most abundant ingredient in beer is one that many brewers consider to also be the most important – so important in fact, that in the beer world, humble H_2O is known as "brewing liquor". It's no coincidence that South Africa's first ever brew-route grew up in Cape Town's Newlands suburb. The purity of the water flowing from the Newlands Spring made for perfect brewing liquor and homebrewers today make the journey to fill up buckets and bottles with the purest water they can find. Water is so important in brewing that people have spent years – and fortunes – trying to replicate the water found in some top brewing regions. Take the UK's Burton-upon-Trent for example: the one-time brewing capital of the country churned out such clear, flavourful beers that breweries elsewhere wanted to replicate the town's ultra-hard, calcium sulphate-rich water, developing a process that is still known today as "Burtonisation". Water has so much influence on the final flavour that certain global beer styles have grown up simply because local water was better suited to a certain style, such as in Plzen, Burton, Munich and Dublin. So just what is it that makes certain water so desirable to brewers?

One of the most important factors is the "hardness" of the water, with water rich in certain minerals being considered "hard". These minerals play a scientific role in brewing and having them in high doses can help with yeast nutrition among other things. Knowing your water – and if possible, being able to choose your water – can help you to create or avoid certain flavours in the beer since different ions can have different results. Iron, for example, can impart a metallic off-flavour; sulphate offers a desirable dryness and too much magnesium can give an unpleasant, astringent bitterness. For those without a spring or rain water reservoir to utilise, there is always tap water, though removing the chlorine is essential or it will lead to an instantly recognisable off-flavour that smells and tastes like Band-Aids or TCP. Of course, it is possible to treat the water and many breweries add certain elements to improve the quality of their brewing liquor. Others will even use reverse osmosis or ion exchange, both effective but expensive ways to end up with ultra-pure water and really only practical for larger breweries.

Many South African brewers are rightly proud of the water they use, which often comes from underground springs, trickles down through the mountains or is collected straight from the sky.

Malted barley

Usually referred to simply as "malt", malted barley gives beer its colour, its body and much of its flavour. Malt can also refer to other grains, such as wheat, but for the moment let's stick to looking at barley. Barley, of course, starts its life in the field, but once the crop has been harvested, it's only halfway through the journey and will need to spend time in a maltings plant in order to fulfil its destiny as an ingredient in beer.

In South Africa, barley is largely grown in the region around Caledon in the Western Cape, as well as near Douglas in the Northern Cape. There are two major maltings plants in the country, both owned and operated by SAB. By far the largest is in Caledon, where 13 500 tonnes of barley is malted every month.

There is a lot of science in each sip of beer and this starts with the maltster, whose job is to encourage certain enzymes in the grain to expose starches that can be successfully converted into fermentable sugars, for without fermentable sugars, your beer would be little more than a cup of sweet malt tea.

Malting is a three-step process, with an optional fourth step if you're seeking to produce dark malt.

Step one: Steeping

After being sieved and sorted, with foreign matter that you wouldn't fancy in your beer being removed, the barley kernels are steeped in water. The steeping process can take up to two days, though the grain is not soaked continually for this time, instead being drained at regular intervals and allowed air rests. Once the grain begins to sprout, or *chit* as it is known in the industry, it is ready for the second phase.

Step two: Germination

Over anything from four to six days, the grain is left to germinate. It's kept at a constant and cool temperature and regularly turned to avoid too much moisture or heat and to stop each grain's individual roots from attaching themselves to their neighbours'. This is when all kinds of brewing goodies are formulated, including the starches which will later be converted to fermentable sugars during the brewing process.

Before the malted barley can be shipped to brewers large and small, the grain has to be dried, which takes us to the final step in the process for most pale malts.

Step three: Kilning

Maltsters don't want the grain to continue sprouting, so heat is used to halt the process until the malt finds its way into the brew kettle, when our first beer ingredient, water, will rekindle the process and reactivate the enzymes.

The kilns, kept at around 76 °C, have a dual use, their other purpose being to dry the now malted barley. If there's too much moisture, the grain will simply rot, while successfully malted barley can be kept for months, if not years. Kilning gives malt its characteristic sweet, biscuit-like flavour that sees it featuring in a range of chocolate bars as well as in your pint glass.

The optional step: Roasting

It hopefully hasn't escaped your notice that beers come in a variety of shades and one of the reasons for this is found in the optional malting process. Sometimes, malt is roasted after kilning, which gives it a dark brown colour that is transmitted to the beers in which it is used, along with flavours of coffee and chocolate. Other specialist malts, such as caramel or crystal malts, are stewed before roasting to give a sweeter taste to the end product.

Malts vary greatly depending on their moisture content, the kilning temperature used and, of course, the barley originally used in the malting process. These different malts all have their own names and will offer a different flavour to the beer, leaving brewers with the task of choosing the malt that will best inject the desired flavours, colours and aromas into each batch of beer.

Hops

For every brewer who insists that water is key when brewing the perfect pint, there's a drinker who will argue that hops are the crucial ingredient in beer. It took five or six millennia for anyone to work out that hops would turn a good beverage into something great, but since the discovery was made no one has looked back. Hops bring two essential elements to the brewing table. First, and the reason that they eventually muscled *gruit* out of the beer equation, they act as a natural preservative in beer – something that was crucial in a pre-fridge world. Hops' other function is to add bitterness to beer, for without them your beer would be sweet and cloying and your taste buds might never let you make it past that first pint. Hops are cones that grow on climbing vines and are generally found between 40 and 55° latitude, growing in great numbers – and great varieties – in Germany, the UK and the USA. In South Africa, hops so far only successfully grow in one region, George in the Western Cape, where Southern Promise, Southern Dawn and Southern Star hops thrive. Much like Pinotage, these strains have been bred specially, since South Africa's climate is not ideal for a happy hop.

The South African hop harvest takes place in early March – a great time to drive between hop fields watching the vines – think Tarzan not Sauvignon – sway in the wind. "Hop trainers" encourage the plants to climb virtually invisible strings, making the five-metre-high vines seem like they're defying gravity. Sadly, the days of men on stilts striding through the hop fields to cut the towering plants from the thin thread that

> ### KEEPING IT NATURAL
>
> While the vast majority of beers ferment thanks to yeast being added by the brewer, there is one beer style that sticks more closely to beer's roots. Back before yeast was understood and fermentation was often thought to be either magic or divine intervention, it was the natural yeast in the air that performed the essential conversion. In Belgium, some breweries still employ this method, leaving their beers to ferment spontaneously rather than adding yeast. Beers made in this style are called lambic, and have a sour taste, with aromas that might just evoke a walk around a barnyard.

keeps them sky-bound are gone, but in South Africa the tool used to chop the hops is still the same – machete-like knives wielded by farm workers atop a tractor. The cones are dried and for the most part turned into pellets, though some breweries use them in their natural state, known as cone hops, flower hops or leaf hops. If not dried properly, hops are likely to rot, while over-drying can sometimes lead to an altogether more dangerous result – spontaneous combustion!

Hops (in cone or pellet form) are almost always added to the boil when brewing, though the frequency and amount added depends on the style of the beer. They can also be added to the fermenter, a process known as "dry hopping". American beers are largely known for their pronounced hop-character, with native hops imparting fruity aromas to the beers. If you can smell citrus fruits, granadilla, mango or guava in your beer, that'll be the hops.

Not all hops emit the same flavours and aromas though – the well-known Saaz hop for example has soft, spicy aromas while the British Fuggles hop emits a woody smell.

Some hops are chosen specifically for their aroma while others are used for their bittering properties. Think of the different hop varieties in the same way as grape varieties – just that you're swapping Chenin or Merlot for Cascade or Citra.

The *Humulus lupulus* plant has also long been adored for its other benefits and throughout the centuries it has been hailed as a cure for all kinds of things. Their relaxing qualities – the hop is a close relative of marijuana – led the flower to be considered top treatment for anxiety and insomnia, while they're also thought to settle your stomach. All wonderful reasons to order another beer, just in case you needed an excuse.

Yeast

It wasn't until the late nineteenth century that yeast was properly understood, but today it is a crucial component that imparts flavours unique to a certain brewery. It is also the cause of the majority of brewing woes, with most off-flavours resulting from yeast issues. Of course, if any one of beer's ingredients was missing then you'd have some weird and quite probably revolting concoction, but without yeast that concoction would not contain alcohol. Yeast essentially feeds off the sugars within the malty wort and produces two things that you most likely would not want your beer to be without – carbon dioxide (bubbles) and alcohol. While floral, spicy, piney and tropically fruity aromas result from hops, and the biscuit, coffee, toffee and caramel flavours are thanks to the malt, the yeast used is also responsible for its own idiosyncratic flavours. These can range from bananas and bubblegum in Weissbier yeast to fruity flavours in some English ale yeasts. There are hundreds of yeast strains available around the world, each imparting a slightly different flavour, so you'll start to understand how there can such an abundance of beer styles, each with a different flavour profile.

SPECIALITY INGREDIENTS

Unless you're a beer purist, there's frankly nothing you can't add to a beer. There are things that you probably wouldn't want to add – garlic might not be very nice for example, and vinegar would be utterly atrocious – but aside from your taste buds, there's nothing stopping you from adding pretty much anything you want to your brew. More common additions include brown sugar, cinnamon, molasses, fruit, honey and all manner of herbs and spices. Some of these are added to allow their flavours to shine through while others help to boost the beer to a higher alcohol level – lending their taste stamp as well, of course. Speciality ingredients can either be added to the boil or to the secondary fermenter, depending on what's being added and why.

THE BREWHOUSE AND BEYOND

With the raw materials understood, it's time to move into the brewery, where one of science's most magnificent procedures converts the lowly ingredients into a beverage that for many is nothing short of godly.

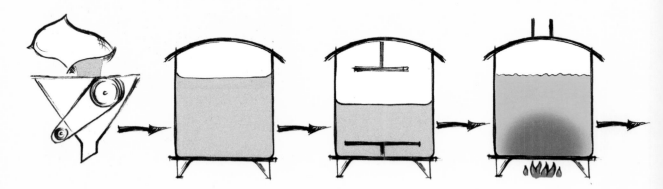

MILLING

The malted grain must be crushed before it can be introduced to the brewing process. This opens up the kernels, exposing the inside bits (the endosperm, if you want to be scientific about it), which is where the majority of the starches hang out. These are the bits that will convert to sugars and later turn malty water into beer. The result of milling – a mixture that's crushed but not powdery – is called grist. Milling can be a tricky process – if the grist is too fine, it can cause a stuck sparge (also known as a set mash or a stuck mash); if it's too coarse, extracting the sugars becomes difficult.

MASHING

Put all notions of potatoes out of your head – in brewing, mashing has nothing to do with puréeing foodstuffs (although it does create a porridge-like substance). Mashing is simply soaking the grist in warm water (usually 60–70 °C) in order to convert those starches found within the endosperm into sugars. The water used in this process is referred to as brewing liquor, or just liquor. It continues the process that was started and halted by the maltster and essentially determines the alcohol content of the end beer. Basically, in the mash, the brewer is creating a fermentable liquid.

LAUTERING

Now you have a mash tun filled with sweet malty water sitting on a bed of soggy grain. Lautering (from a German word meaning "to clarify") involves removing the liquid – now called wort – from the spent grain (the raw materials in beer get a lot of name changes throughout the process – try to keep up). The first runnings are the richest in sugar and flavour, but using these alone gives a low yield and is costly, so once the wort has been drained, brewers sparge the grains to extract further sugars. Sparging is rinsing, with the aim being to extract every morsel of fermentable sugar. If the grist is too fine, you end up with a layer of wet powder clogging your equipment and sparge water hanging around unable to pass through.

THE BOIL

This is where the wort is boiled. It is in fact a complex and essential stage in the process; the stage where you ward off nasties that could ruin your beer. The boil – which takes place in a large vat known as a kettle – lasts at least 60 minutes. In larger breweries, the kettle has a chimney, while in smaller breweries, wort will be boiled in a large lid-free container to allow the volatiles to escape. Boiling with a lid on encourages off-flavours, such as DMS (dimethyl sulphide), which gives an aroma of cooked veggies. The boil also helps to develop colour in the beer and is the stage where hops are added. Early hop additions impart more of the flower's oils, lending bitterness. Flavouring hops are added later, with aroma hopes being added last.

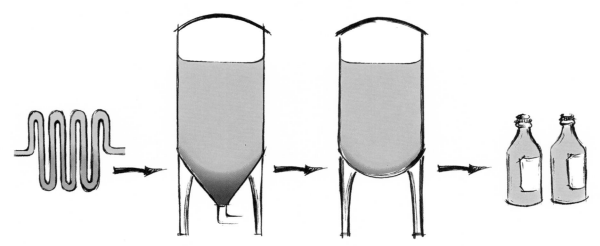

COOLING

Once the wort has been boiled, it's important to cool it as quickly as possible as an idly-dropping temperature is a probable road to bacterial infection. The wort also needs to be cooled to a suitable temperature for yeast to survive and should ideally plummet to the desired fermentation temperature, a process that is achieved quickly with the help of a counter-flow chiller, or a counter-flowing plate heat exchanger. As the wort is pumped through, cold water surrounds it to rapidly cool the wort. Homebrewers who lack fancy equipment tend to resort to more rudimentary methods, such as chilling the wort in a bath filled with iced water.

FERMENTATION

The cooled wort is transferred to a fermenter and once it is at the temperature required for fermentation (18–24 °C for ale, 6–13 °C for lager), the yeast is pitched. Some brewers use powdered yeast while others pitch yeast slurry to the wort. It's often said among brewers that, having eaten the sugars, yeast "burp out CO_2 and fart out ethanol" (don't you just love brewers and their candidness?). They continue to eat, burp and fart for a couple of weeks (the yeast, that is, not the brewers), when the beer should be fully fermented and ready to condition.

CONDITIONING

The beer is now ready for conditioning, also known as secondary fermentation, a process that can take anything from a couple of weeks to several months. The best-known and most commonly used type of conditioning is lagering, in which the freshly fermented beer needs to age at near-freezing temperatures, usually for at least a month. This creates a cleaner-tasting beer, eliminating the compounds that can cause off-flavours – or at least reducing them to levels below the human taste threshold. Other types of secondary fermentation include cask conditioning – used in English real ales – and bottle conditioning, where carbonation occurs naturally in the bottle, thanks to the presence of yeast and sugar.

FILTERING

Not all beers are filtered. Filtering removes the yeast, giving a brighter, clearer beer. Some brewers don't filter at all, wary that it also strips the beer of flavour, and they choose to serve their beer unfiltered. An unfiltered beer will be slightly cloudy, but unless it's completely hazy, this is perfectly normal and won't harm you. On the contrary, filtering beer actually removes some of the natural nutrients as well as the natural carbonation that occurs during fermentation.

BREWING AT HOME

KIT BREWING

Many hobbyist brewers get started with a kit beer, the easiest and cheapest way to brew-it-yourself and the one that requires the least amount of equipment. A kit will come with a plastic bucket with an airlock for fermenting, a long-handled spoon, brewing sugar, a tin or two of pre-hopped malt extract and a sachet of yeast. To successfully make the beer, all you need is two litres of boiling water (plus another 18 litres of cold water to top up the fermenter) and half an hour to spare. Don't expect to end up with the best beer in the world, but kit brewing is a great way to learn about the all-important sanitation involved in brewing and to see the science of fermentation in action.

Homebrewers often find that a cooler box makes a perfect mash tun.

EXTRACT BREWING

The next step up the ladder allows you a little more control over the final flavours of your beer. It will seem like you're starting with the same ingredients as a kit brew, since the extract in question closely resembles that provided with kit beer (it's essentially concentrated wort, a gloopy substance that tastes like toffee and contains all of the fermentable sugars you need to make beer). However, in the case of extract brewing, the malt extract is unhopped, allowing you to choose which hops you'd like to add. There are two ways to do an extract brew, with the simplest method largely mirroring kit brewing. If you want a little more control you can add some crushed speciality malts, first creating what is essentially a giant tea bag, then adding the grain and steeping it in the wort. These malts will affect flavour and colour, though they won't add any further fermentable sugars.

PARTIAL MASH BREWING

The "partial" part of this brewing style's moniker refers to the ingredients used in the recipes – part malt and part malt extract (either in powdered or liquid form). This is the last step before delving into the joys of all-grain brewing. The method employs a similar "beer in the bag" approach as in extract brewing, but this time you're steeping the base malts in order to convert the starch found within to fermentable sugars. You need a lot of grain to get enough sugars to make a sizeable brew though, so if you're brewing on the stovetop and have limited pot capacity, you'll need to add some malt extract to the boil to increase the fermentable sugars. Partial mash is an ideal way to brew if you don't have enough space for an all-grain setup but you want to delve deeper into the process and work a bit more for your beer. Consider it "mashing 101", where attention must be paid to temperatures.

ALL-GRAIN BREWING

Some like to spend a little time on each rung of the homebrewing ladder, others prefer to launch straight into all-grain brewing. As the name suggests, all-grain brewing uses only malted grains in the process and the shortcuts provided by using malt extract are no longer available. While you'll need to upgrade your equipment if you want to ditch the extract, hi-tech gear is not essential, with many homebrewers still boiling their wort in a giant pot on the stove. The method follows the normal brewing process (see pages 22–23) and gives you full control over the flavours, strength and body of your beer. After a week or two in the fermenter you can bottle or keg your beers, condition a while and then enjoy!

HOMEBREWING CLUBS
SouthYeasters (southyeasters.co.za)

The SouthYeasters meet once a month in a Cape Town craft beer bar to talk and taste beer. Guest speakers cover a range of technical topics and there are occasional homebrewing contests. The club also holds an annual festival in April, when members get together to share their brews with the beer-loving public.

Wort Hog Brewers (worthogbrewers.co.za)

The Gauteng-based brewing club is the country's largest, now with satellite chapters in Johannesburg and the East Rand as well as the original club, which meets in Pretoria. All chapters meet every other month, usually at a brewery, so there's plenty of beer even if the homebrew runs out. The annual Summer Beer Festival has been going for over a decade and tickets are sought after in Gauteng beer circles.

East Coast Brewers (eastcoastbrewers.za.org)

South Africa's newest homebrewing club meets every second month at the Porcupine Quill Brewery (see page 237) near Durban to talk beer, taste beer and, once the monthly technical talk is out of the way, drink beer. There's a beer tasting and a dinner at each meeting and special events held throughout the year.

BREW-IT-YOURSELF

All-grain homebrewers essentially follow recipes to make their beers, just as a home cook does with a cake. A few base ingredients can make all the difference though and three people could follow the same recipe but end up with very different beers, depending on the water available and the yeast used. To get you thinking about what goes into a beer, you'll find the grain bills for some of your favourite beers listed throughout the book. While these don't constitute a complete recipe, they'll let you into the secret of which types of malt and hops are used and form a starting point for you to try your hand at a similar brew at home. Hops are listed with a time at which they should be added, depending on whether they are for bittering, flavour or aroma. The minutes reflect a countdown during the boil, so hop additions at 0 minutes are the last thing that will go into the kettle, while additions at 60 minutes refer to the start of a 60-minute boil. Here's the basic outline of ingredients you'll need to make a Russian Imperial Stout, courtesy of Shawn Duthie from the SouthYeasters.

Russian Imperial Stout
70% Pale malt
8% Flaked barley
8% Roasted barley
8% Chocolate malt
4% Crystal malt (120 lovibond)
2% Special B malt

Hop additions:
Chinook (90g) @ 60 minutes

KNOW YOUR BEER – A BRIEF LOOK AT BEER STYLES

LAGER VS ALE

Essentially there are just two branches of the world's beer family – lager and ale. Put simply, lagers are fermented at cooler temperatures with a bottom-fermenting yeast, while ales are fermented at higher temperatures with a top-fermenting yeast (see also page 253).

Ale was the original beer and is favoured by homebrewers and craft brewers partly for the less complicated procedure entailed in producing it and partly for the range of flavours that the style can display. Ale yeast – *Saccharomyces cerevisiae* – sits on the top of the fermentation vessel and works best between temperatures of 18 and 24 °C. Too cold and the yeast won't work; too warm and the beer will potentially become prone to off-flavours. Ales are usually less fizzy than lagers and are served at slightly warmer temperatures.

Lager has also been made throughout the ages, though by chance rather than design. It wasn't until the 1800s that brewers began to understand the lagering process and to opt for these clearer, crisper beers. Lager yeast– *Saccharomyces pastorianus* – sinks to the bottom of the yet-to-ferment beer and likes temperatures of between 6 and 13 °C. Because of the cold temperatures, lager takes longer to ferment than ale and is often subject to cold maturation after fermentation. This maturation period – where the beer is kept on the yeast at very cold temperatures – is known as lagering, from the German verb meaning "to store". While most lagers are golden and relatively low in alcohol, there are a number of lager sub-types, such as Marzen, Dunkel and Bock. Light lager now accounts for around 90% of the world's beer consumption. Within these two broad categories there are over 80 sub-types – a veritable checklist for the true beer aficionado. What we've included here is a brief overview of the main styles brewed in South Africa.

AMERICAN AMBER ALE

Sometimes referred to as a red ale.
Colour: Amber to copper; can be slightly hazy if the beer has been dry-hopped.
Aroma: Balanced maltiness with likely citrus notes from American hops.
Flavour: A fairly high hop flavour, well balanced with sweet and possible caramel flavours from the malt.
Where in South Africa: Citizen, Clarens, Devil's Peak, Triggerfish

AMERICAN PALE ALE (APA)

The American version differs from the English Pale Ale due to the indigenous ingredients used, particularly the hops.
Colour: Varying shades of amber.
Aroma: Less of a malt aroma than an amber ale, but with a prominent and often citrusy hop aroma.
Flavour: A hoppy beer, usually with citrus notes. You might find some faint bready or biscuit flavours from the malt, but these should be secondary to the hop bitterness.
Where in South Africa: Chameleon, Cockpit, Triggerfish

BELGIAN DUBBEL

This beer originated in Belgian monasteries and is generally around 7% ABV.
Colour: Dark amber or copper with a dense, long-lasting head.

Aroma: A complex blend of malty sweetness with possible aromas of banana, raisins, chocolate and caramel. You might also notice a light spiciness.

Flavour: Similar to the aromas found. It's a medium- to full-bodied beer that seems sweet on the palate but leaves a fairly dry finish.

Where in South Africa: Clarens

BELGIAN TRIPPEL

A big beer, usually 8–10% ABV, though it should not taste strong in alcohol.

Colour: Deep yellow or gold.

Aroma: Often floral and perfumed, with definite spice (cloves, pepper) and possible citrus notes.

Flavour: A complex blend of citrus fruits and spice. There's a perceived sweetness but it should end on a bitter note.

Where in South Africa: Clarens

BLONDE ALE

Often viewed as "craft beer 101", the blonde ale is a stepping stone from lagers to more robust beers and a "session beer" to enjoy on sunny afternoons.

Colour: Can range from pale yellow to a vivid gold, but should be clear and with a white head.

Aroma: A subtle aroma, mainly of malt but with possible fruitiness and a touch of hops.

Flavour: An easy-drinking beer with solid but not overpowering malty notes and possibly a light hoppiness. This is a great introduction to ales.

Where in South Africa: Anvil, Chameleon, Clarens, De Garve, Irish Ale House, Porcupine Quill, Three Skulls, Triggerfish

ENGLISH BITTER

This is a traditional ale that is generally low in carbonation and as such tends not to have much head. Standard versions are low in alcohol (around 3.5% ABV) while premium bitters should be closer to 4% ABV or higher.

Colour: Can range from light yellow to copper; premium bitters should be darker in colour.

Aroma: Definite malt with possible hints of caramel and some fruitiness. Some hop aroma.

Flavour: A very drinkable beer with a medium to high bitterness. You'll often find fruitiness and caramel flavours, but the hop flavour will be low.
Where in South Africa: Birkenhead, Bridg , Mitchell's, Porcupine Quill

ENGLISH PALE ALE
This is a very easy-drinking beer that is low in alcohol (3.2–3.8% ABV) and has relatively low levels of carbonation.
Colour: Can range from gold to deep copper. The head is often slight due to low carbonation.
Aroma: Malt and hops in balanced doses, the former giving caramel and fruity aromas. A slight sulphuric smell is acceptable.
Flavour: Less bitter than an English Bitter, with well-balanced malt and hops. Possible floral notes from the hops and probably caramel flavours. You might also notice nutty and biscuit nuances.
Where in South Africa: Anvil, Cockpit, Copper Lake, Emerald Vale, Jack Black, Nottingham Road, Shongweni

INDIA PALE ALE (IPA)
The origins of India Pale Ale are a subject of much debate for beer fans, but the style essentially grew out of the English Pale Ale and gets its name from the country it was shipped to in order to feed thirsty Colonial Brits. Since hops could help preserve the beer on the long journey to India, more hops were added to the standard pale ales, with the style later becoming known as India Pale Ale. An American adaptation takes the British version to a new extreme and is one of the most popular styles among beer fans today.
Colour: Amber or copper.
Aroma: Both versions should be hop forward, though the indigenous hops offer very different aromas. English IPAs have earthy, floral notes as well as a caramel-like malt aroma. American versions have an intense hoppy aroma, displaying pine, citrus, tropical fruits and grassy aromas. Malty aromas are less prominent than in the English version.

Flavour: Flavours mimic aromas in both styles, with the English version having noticeable malt flavours (caramel, biscuit and bread) as well as medium hop flavours. The American style is low on malt and high on hops and bitterness.

Where in South Africa: Devil's Peak, Drayman's (English), Three Skulls, Triggerfish (American)

LIGHT LAGER

The world's most popular beer style needs no introduction. It's a highly carbonated, refreshing beer.

Colour: Can range from pale straw to gold.

Aroma: Generally low, though you might notice some corn-like grainy aroma or maltiness.

Flavour: A subtle, easy-drinking beer that is generally crisp, dry and refreshing. Neither malt nor hops tends to jump out as the beer should be well-balanced.

Where in South Africa: Birkenhead, Black Horse, Boston, Copper Lake, Darling, Gilroy's, Jack Black, Mitchell's, Old Main, SAB, Saggy Stone, Stellenbrau

PILSNER

The original pilsner was brewed in 1842 in what is now the Czech Republic. There is a German version of the beer, using local ingredients, as well as the original Bohemian style.

Colour: Can range from very pale straw to deep gold; German styles tend to be lighter.

Aroma: Depending on the style it can exhibit some grainy, corn-like aromas (German) or a rich maltiness (Bohemian). Both versions show spicy hoppiness.

Flavour: A bitter, refreshing beer with balanced malt and hop flavours. German versions tend to have a bitter finish while the Bohemian style exhibits equal amounts of hop and malt flavour.

Where in South Africa: Birkenhead, Brauhaus am Damm, Bridge Street, Jack Black, Little Brewery on the River, Nottingham Road, SAB

PORTER

This was a precursor to the now more popular and widely known stout. It exhibits similar flavour

profiles, but is generally lighter in body and has less of a burnt, coffee-like character than stout.

Colour: Can range from light brown to very dark brown and almost black.

Aroma: A roasty aroma with possible hints of toffee, chocolate or coffee.

Flavour: Similar to the aroma, with malt dominating and chocolate, caramel and perhaps nutty flavours emerging, as well as possible coffee and biscuit notes. Robust porters, generally higher in alcohol, exhibit a more acrid, burnt character.

Where in South Africa: Little Brewery on the River, Nottingham Road, Wild Clover

SAISON

This seasonal Belgian beer comes with added spice, including orange zest, coriander and ginger.

Colour: Pale orange to amber.

Aroma: Predominantly fruity, with orange and lemon notes common. Possible floral/peppery notes from the hops. Any added spices should be subtle, if noticeable at all.

Flavour: It's a refreshing, thirst-quenching, complex beer with fruit and spice flavours in balanced measures. Can be tart and usually has a dry finish.

Where in South Africa: Anvil, De Garve, Devil's Peak, Dog and Fig, Three Skulls

STOUT

Stouts emerged in the 1800s as a higher alcohol version of the porter. Today the two styles are similar in alcohol content but stout tends to be more bitter and acrid due to the addition of roasted unmalted barley (as opposed to dark malt). There are various styles of stout though, and In South Africa, sweet stouts prevail.

Colour: From deep brown to jet black.

Aroma: Prominent coffee and chocolate aromas, and in sweet stouts the sweetness is often evident on the nose.

Flavour: Dry stouts can exhibit a slight acidic sourness while sweet versions offer a medium to high level of creamy sweetness. Both sweet and dry stouts display coffee and chocolate flavours.

Where in South Africa: Anvil, Birkenhead, Bridge Street, Chameleon, Clarens, Cockpit, Dog and Fig, Mitchell's, Old Main, SAB, Three Skulls, Triggerfish

WEISSBIER

A summery, refreshing German beer made with at least 50% malted wheat.

Colour: Ranges from pale straw to a deep gold colour and is hazy unless it has been filtered. It should always have a prominent and long-lasting white head.

Aroma: A complex blend of spicy clove-like aromas and sweet banana and bubblegum notes.

Flavour: Similar to the aroma, with cloves and banana in varying quantities. Possible bubblegum flavours and you might notice a bread-like flavour from the wheat.

Where in South Africa: Boston, Brauhaus am Damm, Chameleon, Clarens, Cockpit, Dog and Fig, Drayman's, Triggerfish

WITBIER

A highly refreshing, delicate but complex beer originating in Belgium. Orange peel and coriander are usual additions to this wheat-based beer.

Colour: From a very pale straw/cream colour to a light gold colour. It is hazy and should have a noticeable white head.

Aroma: You will notice a complex blend of sweetness, citrus and perfume-like spice.

Flavour: As with the aroma, there's a lot going on in this beer, including coriander notes, citrus, herbal flavours and both sweetness and tartness in the same glass.

Where in South Africa: Anvil, Darling

SPECIALITY BEERS

Unless subject to the Reinheitsgebot (see page 195), brewers can and do put all sorts of spices, herbs and fruit in their beers. In South Africa, seek out beers with buchu (Dog and Fig, Triggerfish), honey (Birkenhead), pumpkin and spice (Boston), cinnamon (Mitchell's) and even brandy (Birkenhead).

HOW TO TASTE BEER

Beer has an unfortunate reputation as a drink that you order just to quench thirst or worse, just to get drunk. It's long been thought of as a non-thinker's drink – something that you order without considering what you really want to be supping. Luckily, this is rapidly changing as people realise that beer deserves just the same respect as wine. And like wine, there is a tasting ritual that the connoisseur completes each time they order a drink. Of course, no one would expect you to do it with every sip, nor even necessarily with every beer, but following is a brief look at the beer tasting process:

1. LOOK

Note the colour of the beer – is it suited to the style? Look for carbonation (but remember that some styles are designed to be a little lacking in the bubble department) and for clarity. Many craft beers are unfiltered and can be a little hazy, while wheat beers are almost always opaque. Bits (which will most likely be yeast unless the brewer has made a terrible error) floating around in your glass can be a sign of a bottle-fermented beer, but all save the most devoted beer buff will probably find this a little unappealing. Beer served on tap should never have anything floating in it! Most beer has some sort of head, which should be made up of small, densely packed bubbles rather than large, cola-like bubbles. English ales tend to have very little head, but should still have some evidence of white or cream foam.

2. SMELL

Like wine, beer's aromas might take a while to emerge, but unlike wine, swirling the glass vigorously is not usually appropriate as it can affect the carbonation and head retention, potentially having an impact on your overall enjoyment of the beer. A slight swirl, however, can release the aromas and also test head retention. Beer can emit a wide range of aromas, from bread and biscuit to toffee and caramel, from citrus and tropical fruits to pine, bananas, pepper and spice. Aromas should be appropriate for the beer style (see pages 26–30) – sometimes an aroma found in one style can be inappropriate for other beer styles. Off-aromas that are always inappropriate include Band-Aids, cider and baby vomit, though you hardly need a book to tell you that the latter is not an appealing start to a beer! For more on off-flavours and aromas, see pages 250–251.

3. TASTE

Again, swilling beer around your mouth as you would when tasting wine is not the done thing as you'll kill the carbonation. Do gently roll the beer around your mouth though, letting it cover the entire tongue. Look for both flavour – is it sweet, dry, bitter, sour? – and mouthfeel, which could be light and fizzy, velvety, heavy or creamy. Try to pick up the different flavours imparted by the hops (tropical fruits, pine, spice, citrus), the malt (toffee, coffee, biscuit or indeed, maltiness) and the yeast (a plethora of flavours, including spice, bananas and bread).

4. SAVOUR

Beer tasters do not spit, since the aftertaste, or finish, is an important part of beer tasting – at least, that's the excuse given! Hops tend to impart a palate-cleansing, bitter finish. A sweet finish could be from malt or from added sugars, as with Belgian beers.

5. REPEAT

"A fine beer may be judged with only one sip, but it's better to be thoroughly sure." So goes the oft-quoted Czech proverb. Enjoy your beer, hopefully noticing new aromas and flavours with every sip – just remember to drink responsibly!

FOOD AND BEER PAIRING

For some reason, beer is all-too-often overlooked when people are seeking a boozy accompaniment to their dinner. This might be because it's long been overshadowed by its supposedly more classy peer, wine. Or perhaps it's because people feel that a beer is too filling when you're dining out. It's also likely that people don't see beer as offering the same range and variety that wine can offer – a great fallacy indeed. In fact, since beer is made up of a range of very different core ingredients, each offering distinct flavours, beer styles offer a range of tastes and aromas that wine can only dream of. In fact, it's frankly laughable that people think beer cannot be paired with food – beer *is* food, just in liquid form.

What's the first thing that's generally brought to your table when you sit down at a restaurant, the thing that dining out experiences will never be without? Bread – and beer is essentially liquid bread; liquid bread featuring a vast array of "herbs and spices" (or malt and hops). It's also the only alcoholic beverage that is "cooked" from start to finish, suggesting closer affinities with cooked food.

Since beer rarely reaches the acidity levels of wine, its original flavours are not so heavily affected by foods. Salt and sweetness – arguably the two most commonly found flavours in all that we eat – can have a profound effect on acidity, meaning that salty and sweet foods can considerably alter the taste of your wine. That's great if you didn't care for the wine in the first place, but presuming that you were enjoying your tipple, having its flavours messed with by food might be a tad annoying. Since beer doesn't have the same acidity as wine, this taste altering phenomenon doesn't apply, meaning that, generally, beer stays true to its original flavours, regardless of what you eat it with. I think that's a point for beer in the great grape 'n' grain debate. It is true that beer, thanks to its bubbles, is more filling than wine – but beer doesn't have to be drunk out of pint glasses. With a 250 ml glass – or even a 100 ml taster glass – per course, you should still have room for dessert. And, of course, one last beer to go with that dessert.

If beer and food pairing is new territory for you, here are a few points you might want to think about before choosing the best beer for your dinner …

It's not just about the meat – play around with marinades and sauces to find the best pairing for your chosen brew.

INTENSITY

The perceived "weight" of a beer should match the delicateness or robustness of the food you're preparing, just as with wine and food. A delicate beer like a Belgian witbier or a crisp pilsner is not the best match for a hunk of steak, just as a full-bodied roasty stout would smother the subtle flavours of sushi. Don't forget to consider the sauce used in a dish as this can be the critical factor in marrying the drink with the food.

CARBONATION

While some complain that CO_2 makes beer too filling to enjoy with food, it is in fact those bubbles that offer beer an advantage over sipping wine with your lunch. Each sip is essentially a palate-cleanser, with the fizz awakening your taste buds for the next forkful. More highly carbonated beers – in particular the various wheat beers from Germany or Belgium – marry well with mouth-coating morsels such as cheese or creamy sauces.

AROMA AND FLAVOUR

Thanks to beer's varied ingredients, the range of food-friendly flavours is vast and it's not too tough to find a flavour – or aroma – that will match with something in your pantry.

Malt

Since malt is the source of sugar in beer, it can give a sweetness – perceived or real – to the end result: your pint. If your chosen beer has an underlying sweetness, consider matching it with a dish that contains sugar in some measure – perhaps a teriyaki dish or a savoury dish that features dried fruit. Malt also offers caramelised flavours – look out for them and pair with roast dinners or meat cooked on the braai.

Hops

Hops are bitter, but don't let that convince you that a hoppy beer can't be paired with food. In fact, hops provide the perfect backbone for all that malt and the sheer range of hops used in different beer styles opens up a host of pairing opportunities. If you think of hops as the spice in beer, it will help you remember that a beer heavy in hops makes a perfect partner for spicy food – think Indian curries or Mexican dishes. Hops can also help cut through the fat in a dish, particularly when it comes to a rich, creamy sauce.

A FINAL WORD

These are general guidelines, but there is no better way to find out which pairings work for you than to experiment. Buy a range of beers, cook up a few dishes and taste away, or consider hosting a beer pairing dinner, where you allocate certain beer styles to your invitees and sample a range of beers with each course you've cooked.

Above all, break the rules, for beer is supposed to be fun and following rules generally isn't. If you want to try stout and sushi or pilsner with goat meat, go for it – the worst thing that can happen is that you'll find a pairing that you won't want to repeat.

Throughout the book you'll find recipes kindly provided by beer-loving chefs around the country. Some use beer as an ingredient, others have been designed to pair with a beer; all should be cooked with a beer in hand.

AMPLIFY OR NULLIFY?

Similar flavours tend to balance each other out, so think what you're trying to achieve with your pairing. Do you want contrast or balance? For example, if you want to tone down a piece of smoked fish or meat, try pairing it with a rauchbier (a beer made with smoked malt); if your dessert is a little on the sweet side, try a sweet stout to make it appear less cloying. That said, the "spice" of a heavily hopped beer tends to accentuate the chilli in a spicy dish, so if you're a wimp when it comes to hot foods you might like to try a beer with a little less zing.

BEER AND CHEESE – A MATCH MADE IN HEAVEN

If there's one thing that sparks a debate between disciples of grape and grain, it is which of the beverages pairs better with cheese. As with any food pairing activity, your own opinion is the only one that counts in the end, but let us make the case here for pairing beer and cheese.

The two start out in much the same way – cows produce cheese, cows eat grass, barley *is* grass and barley makes beer. It just makes sense that the two are going to end up tasting great together. Many of the flavours found in cheese are echoed in certain beer styles, such as the nutty notes found in both a chunk of Cheddar and a glass of brown ale; the toffee-like flavours of a pint of porter and a piece of well-aged Gruyère. And then there is the texture issue. The fine bubbles of a good beer help to cut through the fattiness in a chunk of cheese, cleansing the palate for the next piece on your plate. And if you're not yet convinced, consider this

– beer is made up of grain, yeast, water and hops; bread is made up of grain, yeast, water and seasoning. Would you need anyone to convince you that a great match for a plate of cheese would be bread?

TIPS FOR PAIRING BEER AND CHEESE

Start off thinking about intensity – match more delicate beer styles such as witbier, Weiss and lager with more delicate cheeses like Brie, chèvre or feta. Slightly more robust beers – English Pale Ale or Bitter for example – pair well with a tastier cheese like a good, sharp Cheddar, while stronger cheeses like Parmesan or well-aged Gouda need bolder beers like bock or an Extra Special Bitter. For the big cheeses you need a big beer – try a lighter blue cheese with a well-hopped American IPA and a great pongy Stilton-like blue cheese with its long-term partner, barley wine.

WHERE TO FIND THE BREWERIES

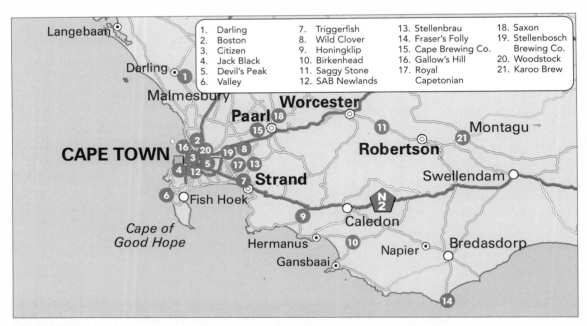

1. Darling	7. Triggerfish	13. Stellenbrau	18. Saxon
2. Boston	8. Wild Clover	14. Fraser's Folly	19. Stellenbosch
3. Citizen	9. Honingklip	15. Cape Brewing Co.	Brewing Co.
4. Jack Black	10. Birkenhead	16. Gallow's Hill	20. Woodstock
5. Devil's Peak	11. Saggy Stone	17. Royal	21. Karoo Brew
6. Valley	12. SAB Newlands	Capetonian	

Western Cape

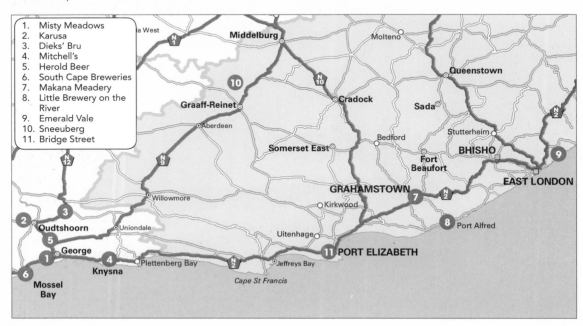

| 1. Misty Meadows |
| 2. Karusa |
| 3. Dieks' Bru |
| 4. Mitchell's |
| 5. Herold Beer |
| 6. South Cape Breweries |
| 7. Makana Meadery |
| 8. Little Brewery on the River |
| 9. Emerald Vale |
| 10. Sneeuberg |
| 11. Bridge Street |

Western Cape/Eastern Cape

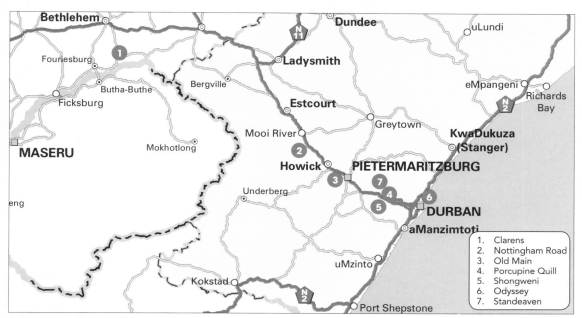

Free State/KwaZulu-Natal

1. Clarens
2. Nottingham Road
3. Old Main
4. Porcupine Quill
5. Shongweni
6. Odyssey
7. Standeaven

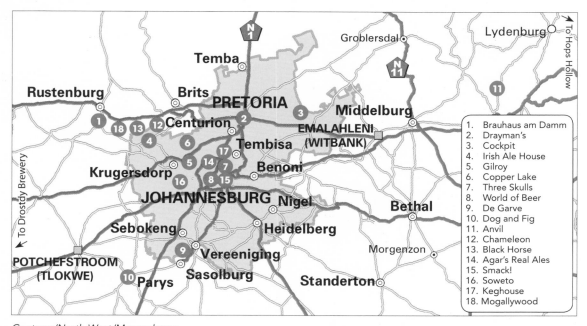

Gauteng/North West/Mpumalanga

1. Brauhaus am Damm
2. Drayman's
3. Cockpit
4. Irish Ale House
5. Gilroy
6. Copper Lake
7. Three Skulls
8. World of Beer
9. De Garve
10. Dog and Fig
11. Anvil
12. Chameleon
13. Black Horse
14. Agar's Real Ales
15. Smack!
16. Soweto
17. Keghouse
18. Mogallywood

Western Cape

BIRKENHEAD BREWERY

Need to know...
Location: R326, Stanford **Web:** birkenhead.co.za
Tel: 028 341 0013 **Amenities:** Beer tasting, restaurant, winery, accommodation, off-sales

Breweries are often seen as being aesthetically inferior to wineries – as places that are more industrial than attractive. There are, of course, breweries that are designed more for takeaways than for a lingering pint, but Birkenhead Brewery is not one of those places. Perched just outside the picture-perfect town of Stanford, the brewery – and the estate that it sits upon – boasts comfy couches, roaring fires in winter and picnic tables in summer offering majestic views of the Klein River mountains beyond. This is definitely a place that you come to sit and savour a pint of their long-established beer.

The brewery was founded in 1998 and named for the ship that sank in nearby waters 146 years earlier. The survivors sought refuge on a Stanford farm and, in launching the Western Cape's second microbrewery, the original owners hoped to provide refuge for beer drinkers seeking something different to the mainstream beers then available.

The brewery has changed hands since that time, but some staples remain. The beer catalogue is largely unchanged, the grounds are still as picturesque as ever, and Benson Mocuphe is still a solid

member of the Birkenhead staff. Benson joined Birkenhead when it first opened its doors, originally working in the storage area of the brewery. It took only a few weeks for his work ethic to be noticed, and he was soon promoted to working in the fermentation room. From there Benson became the protégé of Andy Mitchell, Birkenhead's brewmaster, who learnt the trade through a career with SAB.

Today Andy has moved to Australia, but Benson remains and is now the head brewer at Birkenhead. "I love my job," he beams, his enthusiasm instantly contagious. "I love to brew, though I'm not a big drinker." Like the general public, Benson's favourite in the range is the premium lager, though he insists that since his 2007 marriage he is a taster, not a drinker. Birkenhead's beer menu is varied, from the very popular Honey Blonde Ale to the love-it-or-loathe it Black Snake, a blended beer with a brandy kick.

Of course, for all that has stayed the same at Birkenhead, plenty has changed. There is now accommodation on the property and in 2003 vines were planted with the first harvest happening in 2007. Perhaps the biggest change though has been the renewed interest in beer since the craft revolution began.

"We were perhaps a little ahead of our time," says General Manager Chris Boshoff. "But recently beer sales have started to take off again." A new brew was being devised when we visited, but all details were being kept under wraps. Oh well – having to head back to find out what's new won't exactly be a chore, when the beer is this drinkable and the views this pretty.

TASTING NOTES

PREMIUM LAGER (4.5% ABV): A full-flavoured, malty lager whose sweet character is offset perfectly by the bitterness of the Saaz hop.

HONEY BLONDE ALE (6% ABV): There is upfront honey on the nose, but it's well harmonised when you taste. This is a deceptive beer, whose high alcohol level is not evident in the light and über-refreshing flavour.

BIRKENHEAD PRIDE OLD ENGLISH ALE (4.5% ABV): There are savoury notes on the nose of this English-style bitter, as well as hints of allspice and cinnamon. It's a medium-bodied beer with nutty flavours and a lingering, spicy finish.

CHOCOLATE MALT STOUT (4.5% ABV): Huge coffee aromas prevail with a prominent sweetness on the nose. It's surprisingly light in body for a stout, with a robust flavour that's far drier than the aroma would have you imagine.

BLACK SNAKE (10% ABV): Most definitely not a session beer, this curious concoction is a blend of the stout and the honey blonde, with a touch of brandy for an added kick. Think cold Irish coffee and you won't be far off.

Also look out for Birkenhead Pilsner, a refreshing beer that's light on alcohol but still has plenty of flavour.

With the Klein River mountains as a backdrop, Birkenhead is one of the country's prettiest breweries.

TRADITIONAL CAPE MALAY BOBOTIE

RECIPE COURTESY OF CRAIG CORMACK, EXECUTIVE CHEF AT SOFIA'S AT MORGENSTER

Pair with a honey beer, such as Birkenhead Honey Blonde Ale. Chef Craig says: "The 'almost' sweetness in the beer is a perfect companion for the spice and 'almost' sweetness in the bobotie." The recipe is based on an old Cape Malay classic and uses braised lamb rather than mince as many modern recipes do.

SERVES 5

Place the shoulder of lamb in a pot of beef or chicken stock or water and simmer for 2–3 hours until soft – 1 kg of meat will leave you with around 600 g of braised lamb due to shrinkage. Allow the meat to cool and then shred.

While the lamb is braising, prepare the salsa. Combine all of the ingredients in a bowl and set aside until ready to serve.

Preheat the oven to 180 °C.

Heat the oil and butter in a saucepan and sauté the onion and garlic with the curry powder, ground coriander, ginger, cayenne pepper, paprika, turmeric and cinnamon – this is known as tempering the spice. Add the shredded lamb along with the chopped herbs, grated apple, sugar, apricot jam, vinegar, seasoning, bay leaves, chutney, raisins, almonds and dried fruit. Lastly add the beef jus or stock.

To make the topping, beat the eggs while gradually adding the cream and yoghurt. Season.

To assemble, place the lamb mixture in a bowl. Pour over the topping mixture and sprinkle with paprika. Bake for 10–15 minutes.

Serve with traditional condiments: sambal, sliced bananas and yoghurt, Mrs Balls chutney and shredded coconut – and a glass of Honey Blonde Ale of course!

1 kg shoulder of lamb

Beef or chicken stock to cover

20 ml oil

15 ml butter

1 large onion

1 clove garlic

10 ml curry powder

10 ml ground coriander

5 ml ground ginger

5 ml cayenne pepper

5 ml paprika

5 ml turmeric

5 ml ground cinnamon

A pinch of freshly chopped mixed herbs

½ apple, grated

10 ml sugar

10 ml apricot jam

15 ml vinegar

A pinch of salt and pepper

3 bay leaves

50 ml chutney (Mrs Balls)

30 ml raisins

30 ml chopped almonds

100 g mixed dried fruit, roughly chopped

30 ml beef jus or stock – homemade is best, but the cubed variety is a viable substitute

FOR THE ONION AND TOMATO SAMBAL

⅓ onion, diced

½ tomato

10 ml vinegar

10 ml sugar

5 ml chopped fresh coriander

FOR THE TOPPING

3 eggs

100 ml fresh cream

100 ml yoghurt

Salt and pepper

Paprika

BOSTON BREWERIES

Need to know...

Location: 48 Carlisle Street, Paarden Eiland, Cape Town
Web: bostonbreweries.co.za   **Tel:** 021 511 4179
Amenities: Off-sales. Official tasting room at the Market Bar in the Cape Quarter on Somerset Road, Green Point

Chris Barnard's son, Matthew, is proud of the fact that if it wasn't for him, Boston Breweries might never have been launched. Not that Matthew had any hand in the brewing process of course – he wasn't yet in pre-school when Boston sold its first pint. But if Matthew's nappies hadn't overtaken Chris's humble plastic fermenters, he might never have made the leap from home- to craft brewer.

It all started years before when Chris and now-wife Babette took an extended trip to Europe. "We were in this tiny village in Germany and we wanted a beer so we went to the local bottle store, which was basically a cellar underneath a woman's house. Back in the eighties we didn't have much to choose from in South Africa, and here we saw all these different beers. So we said 'give us two of every beer you've got'." Chris perhaps underestimated the sheer range of beers available, for when the beers were delivered to their door he got a little more than he bargained for. "In came this guy with a crate of beer. As he was bringing it through there was another knock and in came another person with a crate. In the end we got about four crates of beer. It was an absolute eye-opener – we'd come from having about four brands to having in excess of 40 different brands in this one tiny village!"

Slowly but surely, Chris and Babette set about the not-unpleasant task of tasting all the beers and getting used to new styles. The new-found passion for beer saw them tasting the local brews throughout Europe – and discovering the staunch pride each place had in their beer. "You'd move from one village to another and ask for the beer from the previous village and they'd almost want to beat you up!" Chris laughs. "It was so enlightening as to what beer is about."

On returning to Cape Town, Chris decided that the only way he could get his beer fix was to brew for himself. Saturday mornings were spent at the only shop selling supplies, the kitchen was commandeered and the bathroom became overrun with fermenters. Once Chris and Babette married and Matthew came along, Chris felt he could no longer take over the kitchen all weekend – and when he started finding baby gear in his fermenters he decided it was time to find a new home for his brewery. It was then that he upgraded to a 100-litre system and set it up in the family factory in Paarden Eiland. He soon found himself with a problem that many people would be keen to suffer with – Chris was brewing too much beer for him and his friends to drink! He started selling his beer to some of

the factory workers and it was then that the foundations for a brewery were laid. "A shebeen owner phoned me and asked me where my rep was, saying that he needed stock. I didn't know what was going on! Then I found out that the guys from the factory were reselling it to shebeens to make some money and that they'd taken the company name – Boston Bag – and just written Boston Breweries on the beer labels." Thanks to their entrepreneurism, Chris suddenly found himself with a functioning brewery – and a name for it too.

Boston Breweries proper was launched in 2000 with the flagship beer, Boston Lager. For the next six years, the brewery's success waxed and waned with just two beers in the range – the lager and Whale Tale Ale. Chris began to import malt, allowing him to introduce new styles including the very popular Johnny Gold Weiss, which launched to much acclaim at the inaugural Cape Town Festival of Beer in 2010. It wasn't the only beer that met instant and – to Chris at least – surprising approval. In 2011 Chris added Van Hunks Pumpkin Ale to the collection following a test brew that was borne out of a dare.

Ask the brewer

My beer kind of smells like Band-Aids – someone said that this is the smell of hops, is that right?

"I have found the most common cause for a Band-Aid or 'medicine chest' flavour and aroma is either from our water or yeast. A phenolic flavour can be caused by chlorophenols in the water – the use of a carbon filter will eliminate these in your brewing water. Chlorine sanitizers that haven't been rinsed properly can be another cause. While Band-Aid aromas are always a sign that something is wrong, and definitely not the aroma of hops, phenolic flavours are not always bad. A Weiss beer yeast will impart a clove-like phenolic flavour that you would want in your Weiss beer."

TASTING NOTES

BOSTON LAGER (4% ABV): A well-balanced beer with the hop bitterness backing up the sweetness from the malt. Good body and with a perfect level of carbonation that won't leave you feeling bloated.

WHALE TALE ALE (3.5% ABV): A copper-coloured ale that is lighter in body than you might expect. Aromas of toffee and caramelised sugar leave you expecting a sweet beer, but in fact there's a pleasantly dry finish.

NAKED MEXICAN (4.5% ABV): There's a very mild malt aroma on this light lager, which is ideal for summer days. It's refreshing, with a pleasantly bitter aftertaste.

JOHNNY GOLD WEISS (5% ABV): Aromas of bubble-gum and banana emerge from this Weiss, typical of the style. You'll also pick up a hint of cloves in the aroma, thanks to the Weiss yeast. Not as heavy as some Weiss beers, but exhibiting all the flavours of the style – bananas, bread and to a lesser extent, cloves.

VAN HUNKS PUMPKIN ALE (5% ABV): "Like Christmas in a glass" is how some have described this spiced ale. Cinnamon is the predominant aroma – and flavour – with less obvious notes of nutmeg. Dark copper in colour, it's surprisingly light-bodied for a beer so full in flavour.

HAZZARD TEN ALE (10% ABV): A bold, after-dinner beer boasting flavours of caramelised sugar, boiled sweets, spice and toffee.

"After the American show *Brewmasters* had been on TV, people called me asking if I could make a pumpkin ale," Chris recounts. A friend challenged him to brew a batch, so Chris set about re-searching the style, concentrating on which spices to use and how much to add. "Six weeks later we brewed it and the very first batch we brewed, people liked," says Chris. The beer that started as a dare has become a familiar face on the Cape Town beer scene and one that really expanded beer drinkers' horizons as to what a beer can be.

Introducing new beers helped Boston to finally bloom, but it wasn't the only reason that the brewery took off after so many years. "The craft beer boom has affected business massively," says Chris. "Four years ago we were ready to shut. Then the farmers' markets started and, of course, Jack Black was launched. Ross [McCulloch, of Jack Black] did a lot of work promoting craft beer. In the last two years it has really taken off. It's great that people have really become open-minded."

These days Chris spends more time behind his desk than he does at the brew kettle, but he has two assistant brewers to keep things ticking over. He does, however, take the helm when a new beer is added to the catalogue and still prides himself on his hands-on quality control.

"I test every batch we brew," he says – no mean feat for a brewery that operates 24 hours a day, four days a week.

Chris has various beers in the pipeline as his brewery receives yet another upgrade. "I have a unique way of testing new beers," Chris says. "On Saturday my house is all about rugby – no one gets invited, people just pitch up, so I try out new beers on them. If a brand works then the next week there are loads of people!"

Whatever the future may bring for Boston, you can be sure it doesn't suffer with the supply and demand problem from the early years. These days there's never a shortage of people – friends or otherwise – lining up to drink his beer.

OXTAIL AGNOLOTTI WITH PARMESAN CHEESE SAUCE

RECIPE COURTESY OF PETER TEMPLEHOFF, GROUP EXECUTIVE CHEF FOR THE COLLECTION BY
LIZ MCGRATH & RELAIS & CHÂTEAUX GRAND CHEF

Pair with Boston Breweries Van Hunks Pumpkin Ale. Chef Peter says: "The pumpkin beer has hints of clove and coriander, which are accentuated by the salty yet neutral Parmesan sauce."

OXTAIL

Heat half the oil in a heavy-based saucepan and sear the oxtail until browned. Remove and reserve.

Add the rest of the oil to the same saucepan and colour all the vegetables. Add the tomato paste and cook for a further minute. Add the oxtail, red wine, peppercorns, bay leaves and stock and bring to a light boil. Turn the heat down and simmer for 2 hours with the lid on – the oxtail must be succulent and falling off the bone.

Strain off the liquid and reserve it for another dish. Pick the meat off the bone and shred finely with your fingers. Add the thyme, truffle oil and salt to taste.

SAFFRON PASTA

Combine all the ingredients and knead until the dough is silken. Set aside for 1 hour before using.

PARMESAN CHEESE SAUCE

Sweat the onions in the butter until soft and transparent. Add the wine and cook for 5 minutes. Add the water, cream and cheese offcuts. Cook for 20 minutes over low heat, making sure the cheese does not stick and burn on the bottom of the saucepan. Add lemon juice. Strain the sauce and check seasoning.

TO ASSEMBLE THE AGNOLOTTI

Roll out the pasta until very thin. Place a teaspoon of oxtail at the top end of the pasta and roll the pasta over it so that the pasta just overlaps. Push down on either side of the oxtail to encapsulate the filling – it should look like a small pillow. Roll the pillow 90 degrees, crimp the ends and cut it with a rippled pasta wheel to form the agnolotti shape.

Boil the agnolotti for 4 minutes in rapidly boiling water. Place on serving plates. Finish with the Parmesan cheese sauce. Serve at once with sautéed mushrooms and roasted butternut, garnished with deep-fried parsley leaves.

SERVES 6

FOR THE OXTAIL

60 ml oil
500 g oxtail
2 carrots
1 onion
1 stick celery
2 cloves garlic
15 ml tomato paste
250 ml red wine
Peppercorns
Bay leaves
500 ml beef stock or water
5 ml chopped fresh thyme
1 ml truffle oil (optional)
Salt

FOR THE SAFFRON PASTA

500 g cake flour
150 g egg yolks
30 ml saffron water
2 drops yellow food colouring
20 ml extra virgin olive oil

FOR THE PARMESAN CHEESE SAUCE

390 g onions, sliced
100 g butter
300 ml white wine
200 ml water
500 ml fresh cream
200 g Parmesan cheese offcuts
Juice of ½ lemon
2.5 ml salt

CARROT AND CITRUS SALAD
WITH JOHNNY GOLD DRESSING

RECIPE COURTESY OF TANJA KRUGER, EXECUTIVE CHEF AT MAKARON AT MAJEKA HOUSE

Chef Tanja says: "I paired this salad with the Johnny Gold because I wanted to enhance the beer's fruity notes with the citrus and also because the slight bitterness from the grapefruit is a great compliment to the beer. It's a light, fresh, summery beer and pairs well with a light fresh salad."

DRESSING

Mix the mustard, garlic, honey and vinegar together in a bowl. Slowly add the olive oil while whisking. When the dressing is emulsified, add the Johnny Gold and whisk. Set aside.

SALAD

Wash the lettuce and arrange in a bowl or on a plate.

Segment the orange and the grapefruit and scatter over the leaves.

Peel and blanch half the carrots and then cut them in half. Using a vegetable peeler, make shavings from the rest of the carrots and then scatter them and the blanched carrots over the lettuce.

Sprinkle the chèvre over the salad. Tear the fresh coriander and scatter over the salad.

Finish by pouring over the Johnny Gold dressing. Serve with Johnny Gold Weiss.

VARIATION

Toss all the ingredients togther in a bowl and then layer them on a plate, restaurant style.

SERVES 2

FOR THE DRESSING

5 ml Dijon mustard

1 clove garlic, minced

20 ml honey

50 ml white wine vinegar

150 ml olive oil

50 ml Johnny Gold Weiss

FOR THE SALAD

2 baby gem or baby cos lettuce

1 orange

1 ruby grapefruit

10 rainbow carrots (available from Woolies or Food Lover's Market)

150 g chèvre, crumbled

20 g fresh coriander

Salt and pepper to taste

HAZZARD TEN BBQ PORK BELLY

RECIPE COURTESY OF GREG CASEY, OWNER OF BANANA JAM CAFÉ

Mix all the dry rub ingredients together in a bowl. Slice into the pork skin at 1 cm intervals to make it easier to cut once cooked. Rub the pork belly with olive oil then the dry rub, making sure to get the rub in all the cuts under the skin. Refrigerate for 1–2 hours.

Preheat the oven to 150 °C and roast the belly for 3–4 hours.

While the belly is cooking, mix the sauce ingredients together, gradually adding the beer – and maybe taking a sip along the way. Once the pork is cooked, baste with the Hazzard Ten sauce, slice and serve with your favourite side dish. Alternatively, shred the meat and mix with a little of the Hazzard Ten sauce. Serve with coleslaw on beer bread for amazing pulled pork sandwiches.

Serve with a beer of your choice – naturally the Hazzard Ten works well, as does a porter or a hoppy beer such as an American Pale Ale.

SERVES 4–6

1 large pork belly – approximately 2.5 kg
Olive oil for rubbing

FOR THE RUB
100 g brown sugar
50 g Cajun spice
40 g paprika
10 g ground cumin
10 g garlic powder
5 g fine black pepper

FOR THE SAUCE
250 ml tomato sauce
100 ml Worcestershire sauce
100 ml lemon juice
15 ml paprika
15 ml Cajun spice
15 ml beef stock
150 g sugar
50 ml soya sauce
100 ml vinegar
A pinch of thyme
A pinch of white pepper
330 ml bottle Boston Breweries Hazzard Ten or 330 ml cola for the teetotallers out there

Boston Lager, the brewery's flagship beer, fresh off the bottling line.

CITIZEN BEER

Need to know...

Location: Cape Town **Web:** citizenbeer.co.za
Tel: 072 657 9851
Amenities: The beer is available at bars around Cape Town

Across the globe, people tolerate jobs they despise with only one thought in mind – the weekend and the blissful beers it might bring. Gary Pnematicatos decided that rather than making beer his weekend goal, he would bid farewell to an unfulfilling job and make beer his life.

"I started making champagne and wine with friends," says Gary, "when I overheard them discussing plans to make beer. I thought that sounded amazing and started brewing all-grain with them. About six months later I was sitting at my desk at work and I thought – I hate this. I'd been making beer every weekend and I realised that was what I wanted to be doing."

Fast-forward two years and the dream Gary conjured up at his desk has been realised. Along with local restaurant entrepreneur Hugo Berolsky, Gary launched Citizen Beer in April 2012 with their debut beer, Alliance American Amber Ale. Although currently brewed under contract at Boston Breweries (see page 45), the recipe is very much Gary's baby and it took half a dozen brews for him to perfect it. "When I initially quit my job, my intention was to build a 1 000-litre system, have lots of fermenters and brew every day, but we came up against licencing and the difficulty in getting equipment so we decided to focus instead on the brand and the logistics of selling the beer. I'd already been speaking to Chris [Barnard, of Boston Breweries] about brewing in general as he's a very affable guy, so it just made sense to ask him to brew the beer for us."

But that's not to say that the guys won't have their own brewery in the future. "We would love to have our own brewery someday, maybe three or four years from now," says Hugo. They're both keen brewers, constantly working on future recipes in their R&D lab – the 30-litre homebrewery Gary built when he left the corporate world. Hugo admits that his eyes were opened to a beer culture he had no idea about when he started brewing with Gary. "I didn't realise how much there was," Hugo admits. "Suddenly I started realising this complex and hugely interesting world of endless variety."

Their combined enthusiasm for all things beer is evident and infectious, from the eye-catching labels and logo to the beer itself, refined over time thanks to Gary's perfectionism. When he first left his job he brewed every second day until he felt he'd made enough mistakes – and good beer – to introduce his beer to a wider world.

And it seems the wider world is grateful, with demand quickly outstripping supply and exceeding the duo's every expectation. "It's been a very humbling experience," says Hugo, referring not only to the customer response to their beer, but also to the support from within the brewing community. "The first thing we noticed about this industry is just how helpful everyone in it is," he beams. "It's not about keeping secrets to stay ahead of the game. Everyone pours out their knowledge. Everyone is just so excited for more beer. I've never encountered anything like it in any other industry."

When Gary quit his job, the craft boom was very much in its infancy but his brave gamble for a fun-filled working life paid off. "I quit because I was passionate about making beer and I wanted a profession where I would love to wake up every day. Now this is all I do – and it's the best job in the world," he says.

Citizen's logo was inspired by stained-glass windows and the heraldry of the Middle Ages.

The next step is to get back to the brewery and there are plenty of plans for further beers, with an English IPA, Saboteur, on its way and "two new beers that promise to widen the South African beer landscape" in the pipeline. In the meantime, enjoy the Alliance – maybe it will inspire you to follow a dream as well.

TASTING NOTES

ALLIANCE AMERICAN AMBER ALE (5.5% ABV):
This roasty, toasty beer is full of rich toffee aromas. It starts with the expected sweetness of caramelised sugar and crème brûlée flavours, but finishes with a pleasant, bitter note.

Also look out for the Saboteur English IPA, a malty, moderately bitter beer that uses East Kent Goldings hops.

Kegs of Citizen's Alliance American Amber Ale ready to be distributed to bars throughout Cape Town.

Slow Beer R20/80
Native Ale R20/80 *

Black 11 75

*Four-Pack

Fresh Juice
Pomegranate   R25
Apple   R20

te Post
parkling Wine   R110

Semillon   R70
                     R60

DARLING BREW
SLOW BEER
www.darlingbrew.co.za

DARLING BREW

Need to know...
Location: 5 Main Road, Darling (tap room)
Web: darlingbrew.co.za **Tel:** 022 492 3798
Amenities: Tasting room, restaurant, off-sales

When Kevin and Philippa Wood set off on a nine-month trip through Africa, there was one goal in mind – to seek out spots for the new safari company they were planning to launch. They were three days into the trip when the entire plan changed and the safari company they had long discussed morphed into a microbrewery.

"We stopped in Nieu-Bethesda because I'd always wanted to see the Owl House," explains Kevin. "A friend had also told me to go to the brewery there to taste the kudu salami, so we dropped in. I wasn't a big beer drinker at all and when I got to this brewery and said I was there for the kudu salami and cheese platter, the guy looked at me like I was mad – I mean, who comes to a brewery and doesn't order a beer?" Although hesitant to sample "homemade beer", the brewer – André Cilliers of Sneeuberg Brewery (see page 151) – convinced Kevin to taste, telling him that if he didn't enjoy it, he wouldn't have to pay. "I tasted the beer and it was really nice and that's basically where it started," says Kevin of his five-year journey into beer.

Kevin could instantly see the concept working in his adopted hometown of Darling, with the then unusual anchor of microbrewed beer working in conjunction with homemade bread and cheese. Before they left the little Karoo town, Kevin had made a deal to buy equipment and recipes from André and a whole new dream was born.

"We quickly forgot all about the safari idea," he admits. "Suddenly it was all focused on how many beers there were in Africa in the countries we went

Darling's beers are each represented by a South African animal. From left to right: Verreauxs' Eagle (Black Mist), Geometric Tortoise (Slow Beer), Loggerhead Turtle (Native Ale) and Spotted Hyaena (Bone Crusher).

to. We started to notice lots of new things – from the flavour of the beer to the size of the bottle and during the trip we talked a lot about opening a microbrewery."

Nine months later they returned home and the "Romeo and Juliet" phase of planning a brewery had come to an end. "Now you've got to do what you said you were going to do and it's pretty daunting," says Kevin. "Especially when you don't know what you're doing!" But he was adamant that this was the path he wanted to walk and what followed is a story that is as entertaining – and sometimes ridiculous – as it is inspiring for anybody considering a career change. Kevin is the first to acknowledge that he had bitten off more than he could chew, describing himself as "like a rabbit in headlights, numb because I didn't know where to start".

André arrived from Nieu Bethesda with the equipment – a bakkie full of plastic vats, some hops and malt extract – that left Kevin wondering how on earth he'd ever make any money from his new brewing venture.

Problems prevailed, beginning with finding premises and continuing with tensions between the various parties involved. Meanwhile Kevin kept brewing, fastidiously churning out 100 litres of beer every day in a bid to build up considerable stock before launching his brand. Luckily he took

to the whole process, falling instantly in love with the aromas emerging from the boil. "I thought the smell of brewing was the most amazing smell from the first batch we did," he recalls.

The beer reserves were filling up – aided enormously by Kevin purchasing another 50 food vats to add to the original eight – and Kevin poured his first pint at the 2008 Voorkamerfest in Darling. Despite technical problems, the beer was well received, Kevin remembers. "We had a lot of trouble with the kegs as the pressure was wrong because of the altitude difference between Darling and Nieu Bethesda. It was like having a foam bath, and by the time we'd worked it out, we were selling flat beer!"

Although jovial about the whole experience, Kevin's frustration at taking on something he knew almost nothing about is evident. "You're doing something that no one else is doing and you're almost embarrassed because people think that you don't know what you're doing – and they're quite right!" he says, acknowledging that by that time he had ploughed so much money into the project there was no turning back. But the operation was getting too large – Kevin had close to 6 000 litres of beer that he couldn't sell and was running out of capital when someone recommended that he chat to Chris Barnard of Boston Breweries (see page 45).

"I went to meet Chris, not to see if he would brew my beer for me but to see if he could bottle and keg it," says Kevin. "Imagine the situation – I've got 6 000 litres and only five kegs!" Kevin poured out his story to Chris and, by the end of the meeting, Kevin was so impressed with Boston that he decided he would like Chris to brew the beer for him after all. Kevin brought his recipes and Chris soon started to produce the beer that Kevin had been so desperately trying to create and sell.

The first pint of Darling Brew as we know it today was poured at a Stellenbosch market in May 2010. With production fully up and running, Kevin's challenges changed totally, with the next issue being how and where to sell it all. But when he looks back you can quickly tell that Kevin doesn't regret a moment. "Craft brewing is everything one wants," he gushes. "There's adventure, there's innovation. People say I'm living the dream and in a way that's exactly what I'm doing. I'm able to take all my corporate knowledge and take my biggest passion, which is wildlife, and put it all together."

The wildlife side of things can be seen in the labels, each of which features a South African animal hand-picked to represent each beer. For Kevin, the crowning glory of the collection to date is Bone Crusher, a cloudy, Belgian-style witbier represented by the hyaena. "The beer is misunderstood and so is the animal," he says, rolling the striking 550 ml bottle in his hand.

For now it seems that Darling Brew's biggest hurdles have been left far behind, with the über-fashionable brand well established in the Cape and starting to take off elsewhere in the country. And what of those 6 000 litres of beer, you might ask? "Most of it was thrown away," reveals Kevin. "Though I did drink a lot of it at home – it was a great beer … in fact I think I've still got two 20-litre kegs of it in my store room …"

TASTING NOTES

SLOW BEER (4% ABV): Darling's flagship beer and biggest seller is a full-flavoured lager. You won't find much on the nose, but it's a crisp, dry sipper that's a perfect intro to craft beer.

NATIVE ALE (4% ABV): A clear, rust-coloured ale with mild caramel notes on the nose. It's a light yet flavourful beer with hints of candi sugar.

BONE CRUSHER (6% ABV): A bottle-conditioned witbier seasoned with coriander and orange peel. There's perfume and spice on the nose and a highly spiced flavour that hits you in the face but leaves your palate clean and refreshed.

BLACK MIST (5% ABV): This dark ale is a deep, deep brown with a light tan head. There's a definite coffee aroma and flavour, with a mild but lingering hint of molasses.

BONE CRUSHER TEMPURA PRAWNS

RECIPE COURTESY OF PHILIPPA WOOD OF DARLING BREW

Serve with a Belgian-style witbier, such as Darling's Bone Crusher.
Witbier is a delicate beer and its flavours and body make it a perfect partner for seafood.

Make a watery paste using the flour and Bone Crusher – extra flour can be added to make a thicker batter.

Make a crumb mixture from the bread and sesame seeds.

Lightly dust the prawns with flour. Dip into the batter and roll in the breadcrumb mix. Fry in olive oil until golden brown on both sides.

Serve on a bed of rocket with homemade sweet chilli sauce and a glass of chilled witbier.

If Bone Crusher is not available, you can substitute another witbier in the recipe.

SERVES 5 (AS A STARTER)

75 g flour for batter, plus extra for dusting
275 ml (½ bottle) Darling Bone Crusher
   Witbier
100 g bread
100 g sesame seeds
20 prawns, shelled and deveined, tail intact
Olive oil for frying

Kevin and Philippa Wood are to be found behind the bar at their stylish tasting room, the Slow Quarter in Darling.

SPRINGBOK, BLACK MIST AND DUMPLING STEW

RECIPE COURTESY OF PHILIPPA WOOD OF DARLING BREW

Heat the oil in a large saucepan and sauté the onions, celery and carrots in olive oil. Add the springbok and fry until brown. Add the chopped tomatoes and stir for 5 minutes. Add Black Mist until the meat is almost covered, taking a sneaky sip while you're cooking. Add the paprika and bay leaf. Cover and simmer for 2 hours, or until the meat falls off the bone. Add stock if you need to top up the liquid. Season to taste.

DUMPLINGS

Mix the flour and butter until coarse breadcrumbs are formed. Add the mustard and seasoning and enough water (about 45 ml) to form 12 small balls. Add the dumplings to the simmering stew 20 minutes before serving. Add roughly chopped chives or spring onions for colour.

Serve with a cold glass of Black Mist.

If Darling Black Mist is not available, you can substitute another dark ale in the recipe.

SERVES 4–6

15 ml olive oil
2 onions, chopped
2 sticks celery, chopped
2 carrots, chopped
750 g shoulder or leg of springbok
1 kg tomatoes, chopped
550 ml (1 bottle) Darling Black Mist
Paprika
1 bay leaf
Salt and pepper
Chives or spring onions, roughly chopped,
    for garnishing

FOR THE DUMPLINGS
240 g self-raising flour
125 g butter
5 ml prepared mustard
Salt and pepper

DEVIL'S PEAK BREWING COMPANY

Need to know...
Location: 95 Durham Road, Salt River
Web: devilspeakbrewing.co.za **Tel:** 087 230 0106
Amenities: Tastings, brewery tours, off-sales

While other breweries have tiptoed towards the bold styles that they really want to make, conscious of keeping the consumer happy, Devil's Peak has basically punched South Africa in the face with a bag of hops. Launching to a fanfare of praise at the 2011 Cape Town Festival of Beer, the brewery seemed to emerge from nowhere with its brazen American beers and teased us with a rich, chocolaty stout that is yet to be repeated. But of course this brewery did not come from nowhere – it is the product of years of planning, passion and hard work.

It all started in 2008 when consulting services company owner Russell Boltman began to sneak beer into the wine tasting group he enjoyed with friends. Having lived for two years in San Francisco and travelled extensively in the US, Russell had got hooked on hops and was a huge fan of big, bold American-style beers. Russell's varsity friend and now partner in the brewery, Dan Badenhorst, recalls Russell introducing him to the idea that beer, too, could be sipped and savoured, though Russell remembers "it taking a while to convince him that beer could be as good as wine". But convince him he did and soon the friends decided they wanted to start a craft brewery. Of course, there was one obvious hurdle to begin with – while Dan and Russell were keen beer appreciators, neither was a brewer. "We thought of approaching guys to put up a brewery but we couldn't afford it," says Dan. "And in retrospect it was good that we didn't as we wouldn't have known what to do with it!" It

was through one of Cape Town's best-known and best-loved brewers, Wolfgang Ködel, that the guys found their brewmaster – and a third partner in the business – Greg Crum.

Hailing from New Mexico, Greg was an engineer and a passionate homebrewer, churning out superlative American-style beers from his garage in Somerset West. It was a match made in heaven – hop heaven that was, although Greg was also dabbling in Belgian beers, another genre that Dan and Russell were interested in. After a few false starts, Greg built the 500-litre brewery from scratch, using

TASTING NOTES

FIRST LIGHT GOLDEN ALE (4.5% ABV): From the first whiff you can tell this is a perfectly balanced beer offering equal doses of hoppy spice and malty sweetness. On the palate, sweetness and bitterness are in perfect harmony. It's the perfect "intro to hops" beer.

WOODHEAD AMBER ALE (5% ABV): There's a hint of grapefruit on the nose here and a touch of sweetness. A faint flavour of caramelised sugar is overridden with awesome hoppiness on this bitter, balanced beer whose finish is so clean it's like a palate-cleanser.

THE KING'S BLOCKHOUSE IPA (6% ABV): If you're obsessed with the olfactory, this is your beer – you could sit and sniff the sharp, tropical fruit aromas for hours. Flavour-wise, the heavily-hopped IPA continues to wow, with granadilla notes and a slightly sweet, malty backbone.

SILVERTREE SAISON (5% ABV): Typical aromas characteristic of Belgian yeast waft from this delicate beer, as well as a welcome noseful of spice. It's a complex beer with restrained flavours of orange peel and spice.

tanks bought from wine farms, from dairy farms and there were even tanks bought from a cattery, though Dan is quick to add that they didn't end up using them! In the meantime, Greg was furiously

Brewer JC wears a mask when mashing in to avoid inhaling dust from the crushed malt.

brewing on a 90-litre system to gather together the stock for the Cape Town Festival of Beer. Although most people attending the festival had never tasted anything quite like Devil's Peak's in-your-face flavours, the beers were the hit of the festival. Then, just when it seemed that everything was working out, Greg announced his move back to the States. "Greg's wife got a job offer over there," says Dan. "We thought that might derail us a bit." But luckily Greg was around long enough to train a replacement brewer – and that brewer would be JC Steyn.

"I was a winemaker at Dornier for seven years," says JC, "and I was getting frustrated. There's so much competition and you're constantly trying to make your wine stand out and be different." That would not be a problem at Devil's Peak, whose beers were immensely different to most of what was available in South Africa. JC admits that he'd always wanted to brew and decided to take the plunge with the fledgling brewery. Dan calls it a "great leap of faith", but it's definitely one that has paid off. "I'm loving it!" JC effuses. "It's a big change but I'm stoked that I did it." And how does brewing compare with winemaking? "Well, the thing about wine that kind of frustrates me a little bit is that there are so many variables," JC explains.

"You can do your best, you can work hard every day but you might not make the best wine if, for example, your vineyard is lacking. With beer you're working with very few variables; the variables are more in control so it's all down to the brewer."

The only challenge now is to keep up with demand in a city that seems to have a new-found thirst for hops. Luckily, there are plans to upgrade the brewery and the team – including fourth partner Derek Szabo – is seeking a spot in Cape Town for their swanky new setup, using the much sought-after equipment from the former Paulaner Brewery at the V&A Waterfront. No doubt the public will be thrilled once the new equipment is installed and the beers are more widely available.

But it's not just what's within the bottle that has wowed – Devil's Peak have also been lauded for their elegant labels, each emblazoned with a tarot-card style ambigram. "For us it's important that what's outside the bottle represents the same craft and creativity as what's inside the bottle," Russell explains. The names all relate to Devil's Peak itself, with the Blockhouse a well-known feature and the Woodhead Dam sitting atop the mountain. "We make largely Belgian and US-driven beers so we wanted to localise them, to give them a sense of place in Cape Town," says Russell who, like the rest of the team, hails from the Mother City. There are also plans to use more local ingredients, though at present the ingredients are largely imported.

And along with the imported hops, it seems Devil's Peak have imported a new attitude towards beer. Some would have snubbed the idea of entering the market with a beer so far from the familiar, but the public is literally lapping it up. "Even if some South Africans are not ready for it now, they will be," Russell asserts. "We're at the start of what's basically a revolution," adds Dan. "It would be wonderful if in 10 years' time we could feel that we were partly responsible for setting it in motion."

Devil's Peak use a bottle-filler built by Glenn Adams of Valley Brewery.

ALLEPEY FISH CURRY

RECIPE COURTESY OF HARPREET KAUR, EXECUTIVE SOUS CHEF AT THE BOMBAY BRASSERIE

Pair with an American-style IPA, such as Devil's Peak The King's Blockhouse IPA. "The full-bodied structure of the beer and its intense hoppiness brings out the coconut flavours in the dish," says Chef Harpreet. "Extra spice in the dish complements the robust spiciness of the beer."

SERVES 4

30 ml coconut oil
5 ml mustard seeds
8 shallots (Madras onions), sliced
15 ml julienne of fresh ginger
4 green chillies, slit
12 curry leaves
4 ml turmeric
5 ml chilli powder
1 mango, peeled and cut into wedges
500 ml coconut milk
500 g fish fillet (kingklip recommended)
Salt

Heat the oil in a saucepan and fry the mustard seeds until they pop. Add the shallots, ginger, chillies and curry leaves. Add the turmeric and chilli powder. Add the mango, coconut milk, fish and salt. Simmer the fish in the coconut curry until it is cooked.

Serve hot with steamed basmati rice and a cold glass of American IPA.

CAPE MALAY-INSPIRED KABELJOU

RECIPE COURTESY OF PETER TEMPLEHOFF, GROUP EXECUTIVE CHEF
FOR THE COLLECTION BY LIZ MCGRATH & RELAIS & CHÂTEAUX GRAND CHEF

Pair with a lightly-hopped ale, such as Devil's Peak First Light Golden Ale. Chef Peter says:
"The First Light has hints of passion fruit and coriander which just scream Malay curry flavours.
We serve this combination in the Greenhouse to rave reviews."

ROAST KABELJOU

Heat the oil in a pan and caramelize the skin side of the fish portions. Remove from the pan, place skin side down on butter paper on an oven tray and roast in a hot oven for 3–4 minutes until just cooked. Finish with a squeeze of lemon and a crack of sea salt. Serve immediately with the sauce, cauliflower and onion rings.

CAPE MALAY SPICE SAUCE

Sweat the shallots in the butter and a pinch of salt until soft but without colour. Add the spices, mushrooms and lime leaves and sweat for a further 1–2 minutes. Add the curry powder and cook out for another 1–2 minutes, then add the garlic and cook on low for a further minute. Add the wine and reduce by a half, then add the stock and reduce by half again.

Add the coconut milk and bring to the boil for a few more minutes but not reduced past a third. Strain the sauce and add the 70 g butter while blending with a hand-held blender. Add a dash of lime juice and salt to taste. Do not let the sauce boil or cool once the butter is added.

GRILLED CAULIFLOWER

Rub the cauliflower slices with oil and blacken directly on a flat top stove until charred on the edges.

TEMPURA ONION RINGS

Mix the soda water and flour with chopsticks to a thin, lumpy crêpe batter consistency. Dredge the onion rings in the batter and deep-fry until cooked and a light golden colour. The batter must be very light and crispy.

SERVES 2

FOR THE ROAST KABELJOU
2 pieces kabeljou
10 ml olive oil
Salt

FOR THE CAPE MALAY SPICE SAUCE
80 g butter
8 shallots, thinly sliced
Salt
12 coriander seeds
8 cardamom pods
8 button mushrooms, thinly sliced
4 kaffir lime leaves
30 g Cape Malay curry powder
3 cloves garlic, sliced
250 ml white wine
500 ml lobster or fish stock
500 ml coconut milk
70 g cold unsalted butter
Limes
Salt

FOR THE GRILLED CAULIFLOWER
1 small cauliflower, florets thinly sliced (about
   3 mm thick)
Olive oil

FOR THE TEMPURA ONION RINGS
2 small onions/shallots, sliced
Tempura flour (equal parts all-purpose, corn
   and rice flours)
Ice-cold soda water

DIEKS' BRU

Need to know...
Location: 1 Church Street, De Rust
Web: dieksbru.com **Tel:** 073 232 2527
Amenities: Tasting room, off-sales

Dieks Theron's first ever brew was not exactly a rousing success. He brewed a kit beer in 1968, bottled it and then it exploded, leading his wife to understandably quash the hobby while her nerves healed. His interest in brewing lay dormant for close to four decades, when Dieks and a friend decided they fancied trying their hand at making a homemade version of Jack Daniels. "But to make whisky, you first have to make beer!" Dieks says. Luckily for the South African brew scene, Dieks hasn't quite made it to the whisky, getting hooked on brewing in the interim.

"I used kits for the first six months," says Dieks, "then said to myself – this is for the birds; I've got to have control over what I'm doing!" He went to a meeting of the Wort Hogs – a Gauteng-based homebrewing club – and soon got hooked on all-grain, but his job as a metallurgist hindered his progress somewhat. "I was working in the Congo and you couldn't get any supplies or equipment there," he says, admitting that he sneaked some malt and a mill in with him so that he could pursue his new hobby. The job required him to work six days out of seven, but it was worth it for the joy that the seventh day brought. "On Sunday I would play golf in the morning and then brew in the afternoon," he recalls fondly. He would share his homebrew with colleagues and quickly found they couldn't get enough of his beer – especially the Americans, who were well acquainted with a range of beer styles.

Soon afterwards Dieks decided that he had found the retirement job that he had been seeking as he neared his 70th birthday. He and wife Frances uprooted from their Somerset West home to join their daughter in the tiny Karoo dorp of De Rust and plans for the brewery got underway. It's a brave move to launch a range of beers in a town with a mere 300 residents, but Dieks is tapping into the region's tourism market, selling his beers in Oudtshoorn as well as in De Rust's six restaurants. The feather in his new brewery's cap though, is getting his beer into that ultimate of Route 62 institutions, Ronnie's Sex Shop, where a light beer will be on sale to passing bikers and anyone else who stops to admire the bar's impressive bra collection.

Diek's Bru was established in 2012 and he plans to do a brew a week on his 280-litre system, much of which he has built himself. His scientific background has also helped keep the brewery green. "The spent grain will be used as animal feed and the liquid residues will be going into a digester to make biogas for heating the boiler," Dieks explains. "My fermenters are designed to capture the carbon dioxide and compress it for carbonating my beers and later on I will sell what I don't need to homebrewers." Most of Diek's beer will be bottled rather than kegged and the labels are as close to his heart as the beers they represent, since they feature paintings by his daughter, well-established Karoo artist Glendine.

Throughout his almost-seven decades, Dieks has worked as a metallurgist and a minister, lived in virtually every South African province plus a handful of other southern African countries but it seems that in De Rust – and his brewery – he has finally found his true calling.

JACK BLACK

Need to know...
Web: jackblackbeer.com
Tel: 021 447 4151
Amenities: Jack Black is available in bars throughout Cape Town

It takes a lot of beer to make good wine, the old saying goes, but in the case of Ross McCulloch and Meghan MacCallum things worked the other way around. The two met in Meghan's native Canada in 2002 over a wine tasting stand, where Ross was representing the well-known Gallo brand and Meghan was embarking on a career as a wine writer and sommelier. "There's kind of an underground beer culture within the wine industry," says Meghan, and that's exactly how the two started dabbling in craft beer, a trend that was just starting to show its face in Canada.

"I was travelling for one or two weeks each month for my job," says Ross. "I'd stop in a lot of small places but I wouldn't go and hang out with the reps and drink wine in the evenings, I'd go and find the craft beer bars in whatever town I was in and try the beers. It was something I really looked forward to – I became a kind of a travelling beer taster." Meanwhile Cape Town was calling, as Meghan recollects: "We'd be sitting in dark, cold offices and getting emails with photos of people surfing in the sun." Ross made occasional trips back to his home town to visit family – and of course to start researching the craft beer industry in South Africa, or at least to see if one existed. By the middle of 2005, the seed of an idea had been sown and the couple decided to leave their corporate jobs and take a chance. "I was enjoying my job," says Ross, "but we decided that either we were going to make a break for it or we were going to just drink craft beer that other people made."

So plans were put into place and research – much of it of the rather enjoyable tasting kind – began. "It all starts with the beer," says Meghan, speaking of the pre-prohibition-style lager that they decided they wanted to make after researching and tasting different beer styles. "We wanted an amazing all-malt lager that makes something more of a lager than most people are used to," Meghan continues. But it wasn't only about the style – Ross and Meghan loved everything about the pre-prohibition idea: the story, the era and, of course, the flavour.

To get the flavour they were looking for, Ross and Meghan developed a recipe in Vancouver, brewing test batches of the beer at the Russell Brewing Company. After experimenting with various recipes using traditional hops found in the US during the pre-prohibition era, such as the cluster hop, Jack Black Premium Lager was born. The name comes from an early twentieth-century American brewer, John Jack Black, whose family had a flourishing farm in the hop-growing region of New York State.

With recipe in hand, Ross and Meghan moved to Cape Town in 2006, quickly realising that their beer would have to change a little to use locally available ingredients. "We had to make natural changes because of what was available in raw materials," says Ross. "We have also made some tweaks based on consumer preferences here, but we have remained true to a pre-prohibition style. We feel strongly about the heritage of the beer that we're doing but we're also integrating it into what's locally available."

So with a recipe, a name and enough capital to keep them afloat for a couple of years, Ross and Meghan set out to find a brewery that could help them achieve their dream. Jack Black was first brewed at Birkenhead Brewery and later moved to Boston Breweries in Cape Town. Ross and Meghan had allowed themselves two years, thinking that if it hadn't worked in that time they would return to Canada and the corporate world. It was touch and go at times, Ross admits, and they were starting to think that it wasn't going to work when suddenly things took off. "After two years we could see that it was going to be a success," says Ross, who has been instrumental in helping get South Africa's craft beer industry off the ground. "There was a real demand suddenly and the third year was very exciting."

Quenching the crowd's thirst at the 2011 Cape Town Festival of Beer.

TASTING NOTES

PREMIUM LAGER (5% ABV): A good dose of malt on the nose and a malty fruitiness on the palate. It's a very refreshing brew, with richer mouthfeel than most lagers provide, and a clean, dry finish.

PALE ALE (4.5% ABV): An amber-coloured brew with subtle flavours of toffee and biscuit. Like all of Jack Black's beers, the Pale Ale leaves your glass with superb lacing.

PILSNER (5.2% ABV): There's almost no aroma on this light straw-coloured beer. A slightly fruity entry is followed up with mild spice from the hops. Hugely refreshing on a summer's day.

Look out also for Lumberjack Amber Ale and the seasonal Great White Weiss.

Early on, Ross and Meghan realised that draught beer was where it was at, installing their first tap into a most illustrious location – the Mount Nelson Hotel. Since then, well over 100 Jack Black taps have been fitted in Cape Town and around the Western Cape, with Ross overseeing or installing a great number of them himself. "I call myself the sales guy," he says, "but I can install a tap like nobody's business!"

With the first taps recently installed in Johannesburg, things are looking rosy for Jack Black, though Ross still refuses to look at a spreadsheet he penned back before the company had launched. "After about three months I never looked at it again because according to that we became millionaires within six months!" he laughs. "We're

QUICK AND EASY PAIRING: PILSNER AND POSH SNACKS

While caviar can often leave your wine tasting fishy, pilsner is a perfect partner for a blini smothered in fish roe. The beer's delicate flavours also make it a fine accompaniment to fish, so add some smoked salmon to your platter and sip on a well-chilled pilsner.

still smaller now than after three months on that spreadsheet. It's been harder than we thought, but if I was working in a normal job, I wouldn't be having as much fun."

You can expect plenty from Jack Black in the not-too-distant future, with speciality brews to take place at other breweries and Ross's desire to "come out with a bloody great IPA at some point". Whatever the team comes up with, you can be sure that it will stay in line with the company's mantra – to make craft beer accessible to the average guy on the street. We'll all drink to that!

"All I ever wanted to do was to open a surf shop!" says Ross, admitting that beer and surf are perfect partners.

KARUSA

Need to know...

Location: Off the R328, Schoemanshoek, just outside Oudtshoorn
Web: karusa.co.za **Tel:** 044 272 8717
Amenities: Restaurant, tasting room, wine tasting

Brewing was a natural leap for Jacques Conradie. Having already produced wine, port and MCC at some point in his career, it was only a matter of time before he added beer to his repertoire. Jacques is a trained winemaker and after years working at Graham Beck and Boplaas among others, he took the reins at his family vineyard just outside Oudtshoorn. "We pretty much reached our maximum wine volume, so the beer just seems to make sense," says Jacques, himself a keen beer drinker.

Indeed it makes sense in more ways than one. Karusa sits just off the road to the Cango Caves, giving Jacques a steady stream of thirsty tourists passing by. Add to that the Klein Karoo summer heat – perfect beer-drinking weather – and it seems he's onto a winner. In fact, the biggest problem has been keeping up with local demand – well, that and mastering the finer points that set brewing aside from winemaking.

"I've struggled with my mash temperatures and fermentation temperatures," says Jacques, whose first foray into brewing was in June 2011. "But it's coming together now! I understand winemaking holistically and it's important that I do the same with brewing so I've been doing a lot of reading and a lot of practising."

Self-taught from brewing books, his background in booze production has surely been a great help, though Jacques is well aware of the differences between wine and beer – not least the resilience of the former and the absence of preservatives in the latter, something that Jacques admits he finds challenging, especially with Oudtshoorn's elevated summer temperatures.

Jacques is brewing just one beer – a pale ale – but there are plans to add an amber ale and a stout to the list once the brewery is fully up and running. His ales are available on tap at Karusa and a couple of venues in Oudtshoorn, as well as in bottles to sip at home. Other plans will fuse together his winemaking background with his new-found love in a beer matured in red muscadel barrels. And of course, having mastered champagne, wine, port and beer, Jacques intends to dabble in one of beer's by-products, whisky, giving visitors a tour of the entire alcohol spectrum in just one stop.

TASTING NOTES

KAROO DRAUGHT (4% ABV): A good dose of malt and fruitiness on the nose belies the bitter finish of this gold-hued pale ale.

MISTY MEADOWS MICROBREWERY

Need to know...
Location: Off the R102, George **Web:** mistymeadows.co.za
Tel: 072 714 2292 **Amenities:** Restaurant, accommodation, craft shops, artisanal foods, brewing weekends, off-sales

Sometimes, when you're enjoying a pint, you want hustle and bustle, music and banter. And sometimes you just want to sit quietly and sip – to be at one with your beer, if you will. Misty Meadows is definitely a spot to head to if you're seeking the latter. Situated on a former dairy farm just out-

side George, it's a tranquil place where both the weather and landscape often live up to the brewery's name. Established in 2008, it is the brainchild of Jo'burg-based property developer Howard Rawlings. "I looked all over the country for a spot to set up," Howard explains. "One day I was driving

Misty Meadows' barn-like restaurant and tasting room is one of the country's more rustic brewpubs.

Johann Steenberg is one of the many former SAB brewers who has come out of retirement to join the craft beer revolution.

from Groot-Brakrivier and suddenly I was hit by all this green. It was amazing and I knew I'd found the right spot."

It turned out to be the right spot for more than just its view. Close to the country's hop-growing region, Howard was sourcing ingredients when one of the hop farmers mentioned a retired SAB brewer living in George. Howard now had property, a recipe designed by Moritz Kallmeyer of Drayman's in Pretoria (see page 179), a brewery and the missing piece of the puzzle – a brewer, Johann Steenberg.

"I didn't say yes straightaway," says Johann, who had retired in 2005 after 34 years with SAB. "But it of course raised some interest. Once a brewer, always a brewer!" It didn't take too long for Johann to relent and the first batch of Buzzard Country Ale was brewed at the end of 2009, a process that for Johannes was like going back to his early brewing years. "The equipment here is of course totally different to what I was used to at SAB. You're doing

things manually and nowadays in large breweries it's all computerised – I refer to them as TV screen brewers. But when I started it was very much a manual process and this is like stepping back to my roots. It's much more hands-on and you get much more of a feel for what you're doing."

That's largely the ethos of Misty Meadows, where Howard has plans to create a self-sustaining village filled with hands-on artisanal foodies. The

TASTING NOTES

BUZZARD COUNTRY ALE (4% ABV): Easy-drinking and uncomplicated yet expertly made, this ale has malt aromas and a mild sweetness that lends itself well as a partner for pizza.

beer is already in place and there's a butcher on site. "I'd like to start making cheese on the property as well and would like to produce honey, leather, muesli, ice cream and bread. Eventually all the waste products will go back into the cycle – like we feed our spent grain to the chickens and any extra beer now gets distilled into whisky." Misty Meadows is all about staying local, with all of the ingredients for the sole beer, Buzzard, coming from within South Africa. Whenever demand dictates, Johann brews an 800-litre batch along with Artsheal Oktober, who lives and works on the farm.

Along with the beer itself, perhaps the farm's biggest draw card is its brewing weekends, where beer fans can follow the process from mash to fermentation while nipping out for the occasional round of golf on George's renowned courses. The rest of the time the brewery is open to casual visitors who want to sample wood-fired pizza, buy a braai pack to throw on the coals or to just sit and sip while enjoying the meadows beyond.

The restaurant at Misty Meadows has a chalkboard menu reflecting whatever is locally in season.

Ask the brewer

Are there any chemicals in beer?

"Many brewers use what we call processing aids. These can vary from specific enzymes to materials that assist with breaking down of troublesome compounds such as proteins. Calcium salt is also a common addition that brewers use to balance the minerals in brewing. Some brewers will add it straight into the mash tun with the base volume of brewing water or liquor, others will mix it into the brewing water tank prior to pumping it to the mash tun. Food-grade acid is also common for pH control."

MITCHELL'S BREWERY

Need to know...

Location: Arend Street, Knysna
Web: mitchellsbrewery.com **Tel:** 044 382 4685
Amenities: Tasting room, light lunches, brewery tours, off-sales

You know a beer is good when it stops someone in their tracks and it alters their whole career path; their entire life plan. This is just what happened to Dave McRae in 1985. Fresh from university and with the smell of Cape Town in his nostrils, Dave left his native Port Elizabeth, travelling the coast en route to a Mother City job hunt. On the way, he stopped off in Knysna to host his 21st birthday bash at his parents' holiday home on the lagoon. When he popped in to the newly opened Mitchell's Brewery, he couldn't have known that opting to put on draft beer for his party guests would have changed the course of his whole life, for Dave never quite made it to Cape Town. Dave walked into Mitchell's to buy a birthday keg and essentially never left.

"The brewery had just started and I went in to get a keg of Forester's," says Dave. "I remember

South Africa's oldest microbrewery is in an industrial area just east of Knysna's town centre.

helping Lex carry it up the 39 steps to my parents' place. Jokingly I said: 'If you ever need anyone to sell your product, I'm your man.' Two weeks later I'd fallen in love with Knysna and I found a job with CNA Gallo." A month down the line the brewery's founder and then owner, Lex Mitchell, offered Dave a sales position and Dave has never looked back.

You could say that Lex Mitchell is the godfather of craft brewing in South Africa. University dabblings in the likes of pineapple beer escalated into a career with SAB in 1977. "They put you through all departments very thoroughly, so you get an incredibly good grounding," says Lex, though four years later the urge to brew his own way took hold. "When I joined SAB it was the first time I'd been exposed to a brewing magazine and in the very first magazine I looked in there was an article about small breweries in Britain." A year later Lex and his beer-loving wife Sue toured British breweries for six weeks "stealing with their eyes" on a fact-finding mission that would result in South Africa's first and longest-standing microbrewery.

Mitchell's was established in 1983, originally at Thesen House in Knysna's town centre, but two years later, when sales demanded a bigger brewery, it moved to the industrial area. The brewery has changed hands a few times over the years, including a stint with British brewing giant Scottish and Newcastle in the 1990s and forays into breweries based in Johannesburg and Cape Town. But today all of the beer is once more brewed in Knysna and Mitchell's is again a locally owned company,

QUICK AND EASY PAIRING – OYSTERS AND STOUT

There is perhaps no more polarising pairing than that of oysters with stout. But whether you love the combination of slimy sea creatures with the full-bodied roastiness of a stout or you find the combination gruesome, you can't dispute its history. The pairing of oysters with stout dates back to the eighteenth century, when stout (then referred to as porter) was all the rage and oysters were abundant and affordable. It might have been borne from circumstance rather than flavour profiles, but this once-humble union is now a prestigious pairing and experts insist that the burnt barley flavours offset an oyster's saltiness, while the velvety texture makes it an excellent partner for something a little gooey. Although dry stout was traditionally used, sweeter stouts also work and there's no better spot to sip on stout and enjoy oysters than in a town known for the latter – Knysna. Mitchell's offer a stout and oyster pairing at the brewery – bookings are essential so that the freshest oysters can be brought in.

with Dave McRae as a director and shareholder. Lex no longer has a stake in Mitchell's but has recently made a welcome and long-awaited return to the craft in a new Port Elizabeth brewpub. He fondly recalls his early encounters with Dave. "In 1985 I realised I needed somebody else at the brewery," says Lex. "I'm not very happy being the frontman and I decided that I needed a buffer and that David was going to be it." But demand soon outstripped supply and Dave quickly moved from sales to brewing. "I cleaned tanks and scrubbed floors and learned the ropes from Lex," Dave laughs. "It's the last thing I thought I'd land up doing and it's become my life. It *is* my life – here I am 27 years later."

Despite its obvious staying power and success, Mitchell's remains a surprisingly modest brewery. The atmosphere is familial and you get the idea that one of the factors behind its prosperity is Dave's cheery demeanour. He's particularly effusive about the craft beer boom in South Africa – a boom that Mitchell's had been awaiting for almost three decades. "The interest in craft these past three or four years has been phenomenal. Of course there's a little bit of competition, but I think that the

Ask the brewer

Does darker beer have more alcohol than lighter coloured beers?

"I have found that there is no hard rule when it comes to darker beer being stronger. Some of the lagers that are very light in colour are high in alcohol. I think that the conception by many is that colour denotes higher alcohol, but a lot of dark ales are relatively low in alcohol."

positives far outweigh that. At the end of the day we're all in the same game – to promote beer."

The beers have remained largely unchanged since the eighties and nineties. The original beer, Forester's Lager, is still the most popular, with the moreish and very drinkable Bosun's Bitter coming a close second. "Bosun's was launched in the mid-1980s and it shot to 80% of our sales immediately," says Dave. "People were crying out for something different – we'd had lager, lager, lager until then." Next on the brew sheet were Raven Stout and 90 Shilling Ale, the latter designed as a carbo-loader for the Knysna Forest Marathon but whose unusual cinnamon notes made it a perennial favourite. Milk & Honey Ale and Old Wobbly Lager completed the family in the early 1990s. Sadly there are no current plans to expand the range. "Space is a huge issue," explains Dave. "We'd love to add more beers but we would need to expand first."

But Mitchell's isn't stuck in the past and there are changes afoot, including a long-awaited move to glass bottles, stout pairings with Knysna's famous oysters and a new deck where you can enjoy a pint of your favourite after a tasting session in the brewery. Here's to another three decades of British-style ales, hopefully with Dave at the helm.

Brewer Lionel Harker has been an integral part of the Mitchell's team for over two decades.

TASTING NOTES

FORESTER'S LAGER (3.6% ABV): Not as heavily carbonated as lagers you might be used to, Forester's is a light-bodied brew with malty undertones and a finish less dry than commonly found in lager.

MILK & HONEY ALE (5% ABV): A delightful copper colour draws you into this speciality pint that is sweet but not cloying. Lactose and honey add both body and flavour, including hints of caramelised sugar.

90 SHILLING ALE (5% ABV): A festive-smelling pint, thanks to the addition of cinnamon in the boil. Although caramelised sugar and cinnamon flavours jump out, it's a well-balanced pint whose nose belies its not-too-sweet taste.

RAVEN STOUT (5% ABV): There's an underlying sweetness beneath the savoury notes and coffee aromas of this stout, a lighter-bodied beer than you might be expecting.

BOSUN'S BITTER (3.6% ABV): SA's first "real ale" was modelled on a Yorkshire Bitter. English in flavour, body and appearance, it has a barely-there hop aroma and toffee notes that don't follow through to the palate. It's a subtle and perfectly balanced blend of malt and hops with a finish that is bitter but not overly so.

Also look out for Old Wobbly, a strong lager brewed in two batches, with a stronger version served at Mitchell's pub at the V&A Waterfront in Cape Town.

SALDANHA BAY MUSSELS
COOKED IN OLD WOBBLY LAGER

RECIPE COURTESY OF LEON COETZEE, EXECUTIVE CHEF AT KURLAND HOTEL, MEMBER OF RELAIS & CHÂTEAUX

"I chose Old Wobbly Lager to go with the mussels due to its strong, robust flavour. For me it was a perfect marriage of the mussels and the seasoning, which when combined create a hearty, full-bodied flavour."

MUSSELS

Wash the mussels thoroughly and remove the outer "beard". Heat the oil in large pot and sauté the onions, garlic, carrots, leek and parsley until soft and fragrant. Add the beer and water and deglaze the pot, then add the bay leaves, peppercorns and mussels. Place a lid on the pot to steam the mussels for 8–10 minutes. Carefully stir the pot every 5 minutes until all the mussels are open (remove the unopened mussels should there be any).

Strain the stock from the mussel pot, place in a smaller pot and bring to the boil. Reduce the stock by half. Reserve this stock for the mussel cream.

Carefully remove the entire "beard" from the opened mussels and wash off all sand and shells.

MUSSEL CREAM

Place the cream in a saucepan and bring to the boil. Simmer until the cream has reduced by half, then add the mussel stock and remove from the heat. Place the cream and stock mixture in a large saucepan, add the garlic and mussels and bring to the boil. Add the basil pesto and mix through thoroughly. Add the shredded basil and seasoning, heat the mussels through and serve in a bowl. Drizzle with the sauce and garnish with a sprig of basil.

* To roast the garlic, place a bulb of garlic in a preheated oven at 200 °C until soft. Squeeze out all the garlic purée.

SERVES 5

FOR THE MUSSELS

1 kg fresh Saldanha mussels

A touch of oil to coat the base of the pot for frying

2 onions, peeled and chopped

5 cloves garlic

5 carrots, chopped

1 leek, washed and chopped

1 bunch parsley, washed

400 ml Old Wobbly Lager

250 ml water

2 bay leaves

10 black peppercorns

FOR THE MUSSEL CREAM

2 litres fresh cream

350 ml mussel stock (from cooking the mussels)

5 ml roasted garlic*

30 ml basil pesto

10 basil leaves, shredded

Salt and fresh ground black pepper

SAGGY STONE BREWING COMPANY

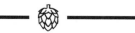

Need to know...

Location: Off the R60, Nuy Valley, near Robertson
Web: saggystone.co.za **Tel:** 072 550 7602 **Amenities:** Restaurant and pub, children's play area, brewery tours by appointment

A butcher, a baker, a candlestick-maker – you might know it as a nonsensical nursery rhyme, but it also sounds a little bit like Adrian Robinson's CV. OK, so he never worked as a butcher and doubtless hasn't got the most impressive homemade candlestick collection – but he did use to be a baker. He was also a geography teacher, a warehouse worker packing peanut butter and a soldier, and it seems he still can't quite decide on one job, now working simultaneously as a production manager for a peat moss plant, a fruit farmer and, of course, the reason he belongs in this book – a brewer.

Adrian had his equipment custom-built; it sits in the former farm church.

"I'm constantly reading and learning," says Adrian.
"I make lots of mistakes – it's the best way to learn."

Of all the earlier jobs, it was his 12-year stint baking bread in his own Cape Town bakery that was most helpful in learning to brew, for beer is really just liquid bread after all. But there would be a few steps that Adrian would take to get from bread to beer, starting with a life-changing motorbike accident in 2002. "I almost died. I had an epiphany and decided I wanted a change. I was making lots of money but just chasing my tail – I was working insane hours and never saw my wife," Adrian explains. "Then one day I was sitting in a Jacuzzi with my brother, Phillip, drinking red wine and we decided to buy a wine farm!" Adrian's farm sits in the Nuy Valley, just west of Robertson. There he grows grapes and other fruit; the former to sell to local wineries, the latter for export. He decided not to try and enter the highly competitive wine market but then, in 2007, he and Phillip began to experiment with homebrewing.

After a couple of kit beers, Adrian decided it was all-grain or nothing and for the next three years the brothers brewed for themselves and their

buddies before deciding to make a business out of it. Phillip had spent time travelling in Australia and noticed a healthy smattering of breweries woven in among the vineyards there, yet among Robertson's wineries there wasn't a sole beer being brewed. And so the idea was born. "We didn't originally want a brewpub," admits Adrian. "We were just going to distribute our beer to other pubs, but then we decided we wanted to see how the customers reacted rather than just delivering and not knowing what they were saying about our beers."

Adrian is a humble guy, happy to talk about early teething troubles and competing with other craft beers in the market. "You get a bit intimidated, but then you get out there and realise that people are really friendly and sharing. Some of the guys will even share recipes because, at the end of the day, everyone's water is different, so even if I gave you my recipe you couldn't make it the same."

The story behind the brewery's unusual name is a cute one, since the moniker was thought up by Adrian's daughter, then 10 years old. "I had built a stone lapa out on the farm. I was trying to make it look really natural and it looked great until the baboons came and jumped on it, then it sagged in the middle," Adrian explains. "Then my daughter called it a saggy stone lapa and it just came off the tongue nicely. We Googled it to see if anyone else had the name and all it came up with was saggy boobs, so we thought it was a sign from God!"

Work then began on the brewery building, a striking stone structure that is one of the country's cutest brewpubs. Adrian built the pub himself, giving up his weekends for a year to create the dry stone walling effect and the wooden deck. He was aiming for a building that would blend with the environment and he's rightfully thrilled with the result. "I love it!" says Adrian, a rare burst of pride from one of the country's most modest brewers. "It came out even better than the original concept. What's amazing is how it blends into the environment, which is what we wanted. We live on our own in the middle of nowhere and it's not that we didn't want to share it, but that we didn't want to spoil it." Adrian's other stipulation was that the brewpub must be family friendly and a playground and plenty of outdoor space certainly fulfils that goal.

The brewpub opened in November 2010 with Adrian and Phillip's flagship beer, the very well-received steam ale. The big launch though, came a year later at the first Cape Town Festival of Beer. "The festival was an eye-opener," says Adrian. "It's quite hard to put yourself out there, competing with 30 other guys. We got a lot of feedback – some good and some bad, so we tweaked some of the recipes afterwards." Phillip is largely responsible for the recipes, while Adrian brews on the 200-litre system along with his father who he claims "is getting old and needed something to do!" At the moment Adrian admits that the setup is tiny but hopes that it will expand. "The future of farming is rough, so I see the brewery as my cash cow for later," he says. "I hope that when you come back in two or three years' time I'll have six or eight beers and they'll all be different."

Future projects include some "edgier" beers to add to the current easy-drinking range, as well as a plan to host an Oktoberfest event where revellers could camp on the farm afterwards. "Our philosophy is very basic," adds Adrian. "We want it to be really accessible; we want people to come and drink the beer that they like. You might not like all of them but hopefully you'll like one of them." And you'll certainly love the setting and the laidback, family-friendly vibe that the Saggy Stone team is successfully striving for.

Labour of love – Adrian built the quaint Saggy Stone pub from scratch.

TASTING NOTES

CALIFORNIA STEAM (6.5% ABV): Tropical fruit aromas on the nose lead you into this beer that is dangerously sippable considering its high alcohol content. Tropical fruit and a hint of toffee give a somewhat sweet taste, but it's nicely balanced with the bitterness lent by the cascade hops.

DESERT LAGER (4.5% ABV): A lightly carbonated lager with a pleasant, slightly fruity aroma. An understated bitterness makes this a moreish pint, perfect for summer drinking.

Also look for Big Red, a dark Irish ale with nutty flavours.

CHEESE 'N BEER BREAD

RECIPE COURTESY OF ADRIAN ROBINSON OF SAGGY STONE BREWING COMPANY

Mix all the ingredients together, adding more liquid if it is too dry. Knead for 10 minutes until the dough is smooth and elastic. Put the dough into a greased bowl, cover it and leave in a warm place to rise. Open a second bottle of beer and enjoy while waiting for the dough to rise.

After 40 minutes (or when the dough has doubled in size), knock it back and shape into 1 large loaf or 2 medium-sized loaves (or place the dough in 1 or 2 loaf pans, seam side down).

Prove (leave to rise) for another 20 minutes or so while preheating the oven to 180 °C. Bake for 30–40 minutes. The bread is done when it sounds hollow when tapped underneath.

Best eaten warm out the oven with butter and a California Steam, Big Red Ale or Desert Lager!

If you can't get your hands on any Saggy Stone, you can substitute a beer of your choice.

**MAKES 1 LARGE LOAF OR
2 MEDIUM LOAVES**

600 g cake flour

15 ml salt

2 sachets (10 g each) dry yeast

15 ml honey

15 ml mustard powder

100 g grated Cheddar (the stronger the better)

340 ml Saggy Stone beer

SOUTH AFRICAN BREWERIES – NEWLANDS BREWERY

Need to know...

Location: 3 Main Road, Newlands, Cape Town
Web: newlandsbrewery.co.za **Tel:** 021 658 7440
Amenities: Brewery tours with tasting, history museum

It was 1820 when Swedish businessman Jacob Letterstedt decided to build a brewery in the shadow of Table Mountain. It was clear that the man knew what he was doing, since an important brewery still stands on that same site – undoubtedly SAB's prettiest premises, Newlands Brewery.

Jacob's reason for building his brewery here is the same reason that a spate of nineteenth-century breweries popped up in the area; the same reason that SAB still brews here today – its proximity to a pristine source of what many brewers consider to be beer's most important ingredient – water. The Newlands Spring and the lesser-known Kommetjie Spring both feed the brewery, which has owned the rights to the water for more than 150 years. Alcohol production here predates Letterstedt though, with the original farm being used for wine production back in the 1670s. The farm, known as Questenburg, eventually made its way into the hands of the recently widowed Maria Barendina Dreyer. After jumping ship en route to Settler Country, Letterstedt ended up working as Maria's gardener and he didn't waste too much time before marrying her. The brewery he set up soon afterwards was named for his wife, while the adjacent mill took its name from Sweden's then-queen, Josephine.

As rival breweries popped up and in some cases popped off again, the Mariendahl brewery continued to trade until 1889, more than two decades after Letterstedt's death. The brewery and mill, along with the rights to the Newlands Spring, were then leased to Anders Ohlsson, who was rapidly establishing himself as a brewing mogul in Cape Town. He later bought the brewery and it remained a part of the Ohlsson's Cape Brewing until 1956, when South African Breweries took over the historic site. Although Newlands is not SAB's largest brewery, it quickly expanded and today the historic brewing buildings have been retired in favour of a larger, more modern plant. The malt house, oast house (where hops and barley were once dried) and nineteenth-century tower brewery still stand though and form an essential part of Newlands Brewery's

One of Newlands Brewery's old kettles now sits in the courtyard.

tour, showcasing the Cape's brewing history and giving insight into how beer-making practices have changed throughout the ages.

Naturally, more than one brewer heads up Newlands Brewery but who better to talk beer with than a man who boasts almost as much beer history as the time-honoured brewery in which he spent most of his career. Reto Jaeger is a brewing legend in Cape Town, a Swiss beer maker representing the fourth generation of brewers in his family. Actually, to be accurate, Reto was not born in Switzerland, though he was born to Swiss parents. In fact, his father was heading up a Cairo-based brewery when he came into the world and it seems only fitting that he should be born in a spot also boasting a lengthy history with beer. His own beer education though,

began in Switzerland. "I never felt pressured to continue the tradition," Reto says, "but I was very interested in beer and brewing and started a technical traineeship as a brewer when I was 17."

Reto worked for seven years in various Swiss breweries, brewing to the strict statutes of the Reinheitsgebot (see page 195). In 1975 he moved to South Africa, though it was not his first trip to the country. Reto had completed much of his schooling here, while his father headed up Johannesburg's Chandler's Brewery, later bought by SAB. Reto returned to South Africa for a "brief stint" to widen his brewing knowledge – a stint that would turn into a career spanning close to four decades. "I came to South Africa to understand a different way of brewing, to learn about different brewing

Newlands' current brewhouse is one of the stops on the brewery tour.

TASTING NOTES

CASTLE LITE (4% ABV): There's a mild maltiness on the nose and a good balance between malt and hops when you taste, with a lingering finish. Light and refreshing, it's a great beer for summer afternoon imbibition.

PERONI NASTRO AZZURRO (5.1% ABV): An uncomplicated, sweet aroma with malt and hops in equal doses if you sniff hard enough! There's a faint hoppiness in this dry, easy-drinking lager.

CASTLE LAGER (5% ABV): There's virtually no aroma – a characteristic of the style. There's both a hint of sweetness and a mild dose of bitterness, with a dry finish.

CARLING BLACK LABEL (5.5% ABV): Of all SAB's lagers, Black Label perhaps has the most recognisable aroma and flavour, with its characteristic fruitiness making it instantly identifiable. Some smell banana, others get pears, but there's definitely fruit and a sweetness when you sip.

HANSA PILSNER (4.5% ABV): Like all of SAB's beers, Hansa is well balanced, with malt and hops both evident but with neither overpowering the other.

PILSNER URQUELL (4.4% ABV): Look for the distinctive hop aroma of this thoroughbred beer. It's not the tropical fruit aroma characteristic of American hops, but a more subtle, spicy character that carries through to the palate. Perfectly balanced and endlessly refreshing.

CASTLE MILK STOUT (6% ABV): A definite whiff of coffee, with a distinctly sweet, toffee-like aroma. Flavour-wise, look for coffee and molasses, though the beer is not as sweet as it smells. In bottles, it is quite light-bodied, though the draught version has a luscious mouthfeel.

Also look out for Grolsch and Miller Genuine Draft, as well as the limited edition beers brewed for various beer festivals throughout the year.

---

processes and culture," says Reto. "Here they use maize in the brewing process. If I had been brewing in China or Korea it would have been rice that I'd have been using," he explains.

Reto might well have had plans to move to the Far East to learn about brewing with rice, but he fell in love with Cape Town. "I'll never forget telling the production manager at the time that I planned on staying for five to eight years – 10 as an absolute maximum, then I wanted to move on and gain more brewing experience." Instead, Reto ended up working at Newlands Brewery for almost 37 years, retiring in the winter of 2012.

Whether it was the beer, the beauty of Cape Town or more likely meeting his wife Nina while working at Newlands that kept Reto here, one

thing is for sure – he will be missed at the brewery. But as seems the trend with retired SAB brewers, Reto isn't likely to stay away from the beer scene for long. He's planning to help out at local beer festivals and with training sessions – and there are a few independent plans bubbling away. "I would like to take tourists on a beer route instead of the usual wine route – once I've had a bit of a breather that is!" he says. Of course, the question that everyone asks is not just about Reto's future, but the future of the Jaeger family – will there be a fifth generation brewer? Reto smiles as he shakes his head and talks about his son, a passionate musician and 3D animator, and his daughter, who works in catering. "They both enjoy the product," he laughs, "but there isn't much interest in brewing."

Ask the brewer

What's the difference between a bottle of Castle Lager and a bottle of Castle Draught?

The word "draught" is derived from an Old English word *dragen*, meaning "to carry", with the original word evolving over time to drag, draw and eventually draught. Over time draught became associated with both a beer type and serving style. Draught was traditionally described as an unpasteurised beer supplied in kegs or casks and as this beer was not pasteurised or aseptically filled, the shelf life of the product was limited. Due to the short turnaround in trade of draught beer, it was the freshest beer and as such draught has come to reflect beer that is served in a glass or tankard from a keg that is "brewery fresh".

In modern brewing, this is translated as beer that is differentiated on taste from bottled or canned beer as having a "fresher" flavour, achieved by being sterile filtered, unpasteurised and unfiltered or flash pasteurised. In all of these beer treatments, no or very low heat is used to stabilise the beer, enhancing the shelf life but maintaining the "draught fresh taste". Draught beers are also carbonated at a slightly lower level to help with product differentiation and palate smoothness.

In the late nineteenth century, delivering beer by dray was the norm. Today, Newlands Brewery has revived this tradition, transporting fresh kegs of Castle Lager to three pubs near the brewery on the first Friday of each month.

But Reto has a plan that he hopes will appeal to his son so that the Jaeger tradition might continue. "Maybe the two of us will start a microbrewery," he says. "So there may still be a fifth generation ..."

The craft brewing industry has long been close to Reto's heart. "The brewery I did my traineeship at was purchased by Heineken and closed five years later," he says. "They decided it wasn't a viable brewery. In that town now four or five microbreweries have opened, making me think about 'my' brewery. My great grandfather, Franz Jäger, had his own brewery, the Jäger Brewery, in Switzerland so it's definitely something I have a connection with and something I've given a lot of thought to."

Reto talks effusively about South Africa's craft beer boom as he sips a pint from one of the Western Cape's craft breweries. You can tell he's spent years appreciating beer – he served on one of SAB's rigorous tasting panels – as he looks and sniffs before each savoured sip. "Now there's more interest in beer, which is absolutely great. I will support it in any way I can," he says. "All these new styles really interest me – I've never been exposed to this range of beers."

Back at Newlands Reto is sorely missed, though business must continue as usual. The brewery can put out two million quarts in 24 hours and operates 365 days a year. Despite this, Newlands is only the fourth largest of SAB's seven South African breweries. The largest, Alrode, sits near Johannesburg, while other breweries operate in Polokwane, Port Elizabeth, Durban, Pretoria and Krugersdorp. There is no doubt that the beer industry is changing in South Africa, but SAB is not being left behind. Their speciality beers have appeared at beer festivals across the country and have covered everything from a blueberry Weiss to the chocolaty goodness of the Newlands Extra Special Stout, lovingly known as Nessy.

Norman Adami, SAB's chairman and managing director, is in no doubt as to who holds the key to the future of South Africa's beer scene. "I think consumers are being more adventurous and including more types within their repertoire," he says. "I think they're exploring and experimenting more and we are listening and experimenting too."

Former Newlands brewer Reto Jaeger worked in the beer world for 45 years before he retired.

Norman maintains that competition is good for the category of beer, an opinion that is echoed by others in the brewing community who believe that as long as people are drinking beer, they're not drinking wine or coolers or spirits. "Competition has lifted the quality of all the players involved," says Norman. "It has stimulated creativity, and if we ensure that the beer category remains exciting then that's going to be good for all of us."

Although SAB is still the giant of the South African beer world and there are differences in style, equipment and quantity when you compare them to the craft brewers, there is an obvious thread that ties all of the breweries together – a shared passion for beer. Norman perfectly sums up all that the brewers, large and small, have in common. "We don't only believe in beer," he says, "we believe in South African beer. There is something special about it and while we may not have the heritage that the Europeans have, we certainly don't have to stand back when it comes to brewing credentials, imagination or producing a beer that is just right for the palate of South Africans, for the climate of South Africa, for South Africa itself."

VEAL AND BACON MEAT LOAF
WITH MARINATED CABBAGE

RECIPE COURTESY OF PETE GOFFE-WOOD, FOOD ALCHEMIST

Pair with a pilsner, such as Pilsner Urquell. Chef Pete says: "This full-bodied pilsner is the ideal accompaniment for this meat loaf, which can be served hot or cold. The bitterness of the beer works very well with the smokiness of the bacon. In addition, the veal and sage work wonderfully with the lovely 'hoppiness' of the pilsner and the astringency and crispness of the cabbage brings out a sweetness in the beer."

Combine the chopped onion and red wine in a small saucepan over medium heat and reduce until all of the liquid has evaporated. Remove from the heat and leave to cool.

Preheat the oven to 160 °C.

Cut the bacon into small dice and add to the mince. Add the cooled cooked onions to the mince, along with the rest of the ingredients. Fry a small piece of the mixture and taste it to make sure the seasoning is correct, as you cannot change the seasoning once the meat loaf has been cooked.

Pack the mixture into a terrine mould or a loaf pan. Cover with a piece of foil and cook in a *bain-marie* in the oven for 1½ hours.

Best served the following day, hot or cold. To reheat the meat loaf, slice and fry in a hot frying pan.

MARINATED CABBAGE

Slice the cabbage, onion and celery and combine in a large stainless steel bowl. Place the rest of the ingredients together in saucepan and bring to the boil. Remove from the heat and pour over the cabbage. Make sure the vinegar is evenly mixed throughout the cabbage. Leave the cabbage to macerate for 20 minutes before serving. Will keep for weeks in the fridge and it keeps getting tastier and tastier.

SERVES 4–6

1 onion, finely diced

250 ml red wine

200 g smoked streaky bacon

750 g veal mince

3 cloves garlic, finely chopped

10 g sage, roughly chopped

2 eggs

30 ml sugar

Salt and pepper

**FOR LANNICE SNYMAN'S
MARINATED CABBAGE**

½ head white cabbage

1 onion

½ head celery

250 ml white wine or rice wine vinegar

250 g sugar

10 ml caraway seeds

30 ml mustard powder

15 ml salt

STICKY TOFFEE PUDDING

RECIPE COURTESY OF PETE GOFFE-WOOD, FOOD ALCHEMIST

Pair with a sweet stout, such as Castle Milk Stout. Chef Pete says: "The richness of the pudding brings out wonderful caramel flavours in the stout. You can also pick up a hint of liquorice on the beer that was not evident before combining it with the pudding. There is also a beautiful clean finish on the stout that is a perfect counterbalance to the very sweet dessert."

Preheat the oven to 150 °C. Grease an ovenproof mould or pan.

Place the dates and water in a saucepan and cook until the dates are completely soft and puréed. Remove from the heat. Cream the butter and sugar in a mixing bowl until light and fluffy. Add the eggs, one at a time, beating well after each addition. Add vanilla, followed by the flour and bicarbonate of soda. Fold in the date purée. Pour the mixture into the prepared mould and bake for 30 minutes, or until a skewer inserted in the centre comes out clean. While the pudding is in the oven, make the caramel sauce.

CARAMEL SAUCE

Heat the sugar and water until the sugar caramelises and turns golden brown. Remove from the heat and whisk in the butter and cream. Remove the pudding from the oven and immediately pour over the warm caramel sauce.

SERVES 4–6

340 g pitted dates
500 ml water
60 g butter
340 g sugar
4 eggs
1 capful vanilla essence
340 g self-raising flour
10 ml bicarbonate of soda

FOR THE CARAMEL SAUCE

600 g sugar
250 ml water
500 g butter
500 g fresh cream

The bottling line is the most mesmerising part of the Newlands Brewery tour.

STELLENBRAU

Need to know...
Location: Woodmill Lifestyle Market, Vredenburg Road, Stellenbosch
Web: stellenbrau.co.za **Tel:** 021 883 3622
Amenities: Tasting room

It's no exaggeration to say that when Deon Engel-brecht first tasted Luyt Lager, he enjoyed it so much he bought the brewery. The brewery wasn't even for sale at the time, yet just 18 months after he first chatted with the brewery boss, the equipment and recipes were enjoying a new home in Stellenbosch.

It was in 2010 that Deon had that first fateful sip, when a colleague brought a bottle to Deon's hometown of Potchefstroom. Tasting it gave Deon a kind of epiphany as he explains: "I had stopped drinking beer because I always felt bloated and I got headaches. But I drank one Luyt beer and then another one and instantly loved it. I said next time I go to Ballito I want to meet Louis Luyt." Deon's wife, Margriet, must already have been trembling then, as Deon admits that "when I say I have a plan

Stephen (left) and Deon both seem like they were born to be in the brewing trade.

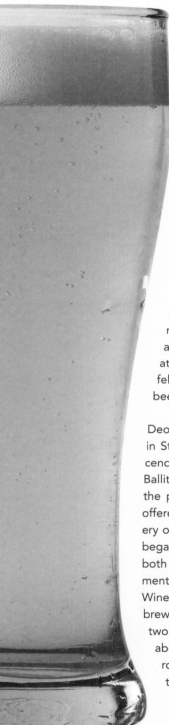

she gets very worried". True to form, Deon stuck to his plan and in January 2011 he met up with Louis Luyt, founder of the KZN-based brewery. After chatting beer the two started to drink some and Deon's epiphany continued. "I can't remember how much beer I drank," he admits, grinning. "But it was a lot! Yet I didn't feel bloated and I really enjoyed the taste, the aroma. I knew straightaway that there was something special there. Then the next morning I went for a run – I always take my running shoes wherever I go – and I felt nothing, no headache at all. This beer tasted good, it felt good and I started liking the beer environment again."

Negotiations soon began for Deon to set up a sister brewery in Stellenbosch, brewing under licence from the long-established Ballito branch, but within months the plans changed and Deon was offered the chance to buy the brewery outright. He snapped it up and began the preparations to move both the extensive brewing equipment and his entire life to the Cape Winelands. By February 2012 the brewery was installed, along with two staff members so passionate about their jobs that they uprooted to continue brewing in the Cape. "There's a Zulu in my brewery," Deon jokes, in reference to the 1993 Hofmeyr movie. In fact there are two –

Keeping tabs – recording every step of every brew is an essential part of the process.

assistant brewer Nosh Cingo and draught machine specialist Vincent Magwaza – and it's evident that Deon is thrilled to have them on board.

The head brewer though, is a new addition to the team. After interviewing a number of established commercial brewers, Deon and his interview panel met Stephen de Jager. Stephen had been homebrewing for 15 years, but it wasn't just his

TASTING NOTES

CRAVEN CRAFT LAGER (4.5% ABV): A sparklingly clear beer that's completely true to style. Refreshing, crisp and dry with an obvious but not overpowering malt aroma and flavour.

Also look out for Alumni Ale and Hausbrau, the first beer recipe to be devised in-house at Stellenbrau.

obvious passion for beer that wowed his prospective employer – there wasn't a single technical question that they threw at him that Stephen couldn't answer. "I was basically waiting 12 years for this job," Stephen says. He started making beer when he was at Cape Technikon, where he admits he did more brewing than studying. A career in the electronic engineering field followed, but it was brewing that he always wanted to do. "The whole thing started way back when I was in Standard 6," he remembers, his eyes lighting up at the chance to discuss his passion. "I walked past a chemist and saw a 'make your own beer' kit. I told my dad I wanted it and he said 'there is no chance in hell, your mother would kill me!'" But at the first opportunity Stephen started to brew, shunning commercial kits in favour of a 200-litre stainless steel setup that he made himself. From the first brew he knew it was what he wanted to be doing with his life. His sheer enthusiasm is utterly contagious as he raves about Stellenbrau's equipment – a brewery that most craft brewers would indeed envy deeply.

Stellenbrau completed its first brew in June 2012 and the Craven Craft Lager – named for rugby guru Danie Craven – was released to an influential and rather daunting audience. Dozens of fellow brewers and others from the beer industry met at Pete Goffe-Wood's Kitchen Cowboys Canteen in Cape Town and Deon served his beer alongside other Cape craft brewers. The reception was good – so good in fact that the temporary tap system he set up became a permanent one, with the celebrity chef's restaurant inadvertently becoming Stellenbrau's first outlet. The lager – based heavily upon the recipe that caused Deon to change his whole life – has been well-received wherever it has been served, leaving Deon admitting: "I'm having fun – that's the best thing. I'm very happy."

If just a fraction of the passion and joy that is shared by every member of the Stellenbrau team can find its way into the beer, you'll be in for something special. And the self-proclaimed "beer drinker that stopped drinking beer" has been returned to his rightful state as a lover of malt and hops.

Stellenbrau's conical fermenters used to be a part of the Luyt Brewery in Ballito, KwaZulu-Natal.

Triggerfish
BREWING
BLONDE ALE
SWEET
LIPS
A light refreshing
golden ale

TRIGGERFISH BREWING

Need to know...

Location: Paardevlei, De Beers Avenue, Somerset West
Web: triggerfishbrewing.co.za **Tel:** 021 851 5861
Amenities: Tasting room, light meals, off-sales

There was definitely something in the water in Eric van Heerden's year at varsity. No fewer than four of South Africa's craft breweries were set up by graduates of the same year at TUKS – one of which is Triggerfish in Somerset West. In fact, it was a couple of Eric's university pals who introduced him to the idea of homebrewing – André de Beer of The Cockpit Brewhouse (see page 159) and Stephan Meyer of Clarens Brewery (see page 215).

"I had travelled widely so I had tasted a lot of different beers, but five years ago there was pretty much no other way to try different beers than to brew them yourself," Eric explains. "Stephan and André were already brewing but I never got a chance to get up there and see their systems, so I spent five or six months on the telephone to them to learn all about homebrewing!"

Eric brewed his first batch in 2007 – a blonde ale from an André de Beer recipe – and was instantly impressed with the results. Lucky, since he had already sunk a fair amount of money into setting up his equipment. "When I started homebrewing I had it in the back of my mind that I'd like to turn it into a small business at some point," he says. "So I built a single-tier, all-grain brewery from the word go and started kegging from day one." Soon, Eric realised that his 40-litre system was too large, meaning he couldn't brew as often as he'd like since he and his friends couldn't drink the beer fast enough. Then a year later, a work opportunity in the USA arose and Eric's homebrewing hobby really took off.

With a new 20-litre system in place, Eric could brew every couple of weeks, offering up his beers for critique at meetings of the local homebrew club, Charlotte Brewmasters. "It was a very active, very competitive homebrewing club," says Eric. "The average brewer had between 10 and 15 years of experience behind them and the range of equipment and supplies available was amazing." When

Assistant brewer James Beyile is Eric's right-hand man.

Eric returned to the Western Cape in July 2010, he had a year of intensive brewing behind him and the decision to start up a microbrewery didn't take long to reach, thanks in part to a nudge from his old friend Stephan. "He is the ultimate optimist and remembers only the good," Eric smiles. "He was the one who convinced me to go into it commercially." The decision was sealed when Eric took some of his American-brewed beers for tasting at the local homebrewers' club, the SouthYeasters, and they met with instant approval.

Equipment was upgraded and in late 2010 Eric launched his beers at a Stellenbosch market to instant acclaim. Premises were sought, though costs prohibited Eric from finding what he considered the perfect location, instead setting up the brewery at an old dynamite factory outside Somerset West. "I was still actively looking for premises for a tap room," says Eric, "because I was behind a security gate in the middle of nowhere and nobody knew where it was!" But then a bustling eatery in Stellenbosch asked to stock his beers and, with an outlet in town secured, Eric decided to keep his offbeat location for brewing. A small tasting room – sitting in the old anthracite store room – followed, then in 2012 Eric had to expand to house the ever-growing number of beer drinkers descending on the brewery each weekend to taste his eclectic range. Now, with the well-known cheetah outreach project around the corner, visitor numbers are set to rise even higher. "I grew into this brewpub in this funny location by accident and it just worked," beams Eric.

Something else that really works is the theme that Eric chose for his brewery and beer names. A keen scuba diver, Eric always knew that his brewery would be named for something oceanic, but pinning down a specific sea creature ended up being a very last-minute decision. "I'd been trying to think of a name for six months," he recollects, "but in the end we came up with it the night before I handed in my licensing application! They needed a name on the form so we had to make the decision." It was in part a homage to Eric's brewing hero, Sam

Calagione of Dogfish Head Brewery in the USA, but the final choice came from something that Eric's wife, scuba instructor Wilna, commented on. "She said that when she took students on a dive, the one fish they always asked about was the clown triggerfish," says Eric, and so the striking and instantly memorable fish became the name of the brewery and its gold-and-black markings the company logo. After that the beer names – some of the most memorable in the country – just flowed. "I have a backlog of cool-sounding fish names for future beers!" says Eric.

Since Triggerfish opened its doors in April 2011 business has been booming, with volumes doubling in a year. Eric juggles the brewing with his IT job, but luckily there is help very much on hand when the brewery gets really busy. "It's very much a family operation," Eric says, "and when it comes

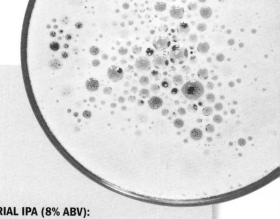

TASTING NOTES

SWEET LIPS BLONDE ALE (4.2% ABV): A clear, golden beer that's light-bodied and easy to drink. The light malt aroma is followed up with plenty of malt on the palate.

OCEAN POTION APA (5.4% ABV): A punch of passion fruit, lychee and other tropical fruits hits when you inhale this beer. Velvety mouthfeel brings with it fruit flavours associated with American hops; finishes dry.

HAMMERHEAD IPA (6.2% ABV): A somewhat sweet aroma leaning a little more towards malt than hops. From the first sip you can tell this is a big beer, full of flavour yet well balanced.

ROMAN RED AMERICAN AMBER ALE (5.2% ABV): A dark copper-coloured beer with a creamy off-white head. The overriding aroma is of toffee, though there are subtle undertones of tropical fruit. Although the initial perception is of sweetness, the beer has a dry finish.

BONITO BOMBSHELL BUCHU BLONDE (4.2% ABV): The buchu aroma is evident but not overpowering and you can smell the malt beneath. It's a summer sipper, with smoky notes and a subtle buchu flavour.

TITAN IMPERIAL IPA (8% ABV): The heady grapefruit aromas might make you expect a fruity, refreshing beer, but in fact this IPA is full of toffee flavours. It's a big, boozy beer that should be sipped in small doses.

EMPOWERED STOUT (5.2% ABV): Light on aroma but bold on flavour, this is a warming pint with rich coffee notes and plenty of body.

BLACK MARLIN RUSSIAN IMPERIAL STOUT (9.9% ABV): If you're not afraid of flavour, this could well be the beer for you. Rich coffee and chocolate aromas and flavours and a velvety mouthfeel make it the perfect end-of-the-night beer.

Also look out for Triggerfish's occasional beers, including Great Weiss, Black Bass Oatmeal Stout, Englishman Mild Brown Ale and Four Legs Altbier.

down to the wire I call in the kids and they'll be labelling bottles. Just before Christmas people were coming into the brewery and buying beers as fast as the kids could label them!"

Eric's oldest son, Francois, is a keen brewer himself, with a penchant for unusual ingredients and experimentation that he must surely have picked up from his father. Eric's ever-expanding beer collection is as varied as it is bold, featuring an imperial IPA, a blonde ale infused with buchu and a not insignificant sprinkling of American hops to be found throughout the range. The most recent addition to the family was Black Marlin, a Russian

imperial stout. Like many of Eric's beers, it started as a one-off brew but he admits it's likely to become a fixture. "I'm a sucker for imperial stout so the Marlin might well become a staple because I want to drink it!" he acknowledges.

There are no plans to expand at present and to explain why Eric refers to Dogfish Head in Delaware. "I saw their system and realised that until you brew six batches a day, six days a week, you haven't outgrown your brewery – you just haven't got your process right." One thing you can expect though is a continued range of cutting-edge beers, each with their own carefully thought out fishy nametag.

HOT-SMOKED YELLOWTAIL, FENNEL AND ASPARAGUS SALAD WITH AÏOLI

RECIPE COURTESY OF PETE GOFFE-WOOD, FOOD ALCHEMIST

Pair with Triggerfish Bonito Bombshell Buchu Blonde. Chef Pete says: "This fragrant beer has summer written all over it. The clean palate from the buchu works perfectly with the smoky fish and the rich aïoli. The fennel and asparagus will give a lovely textural element to the dish, as well as complement the earthy flavours that are evident in the beer."

Place the yellowtail in the brine and leave in the fridge for 3 hours. Remove the fish from the brine and arrange in a smoker. Season with salt and pepper and smoke over a gentle heat for approximately 20 minutes. Remove from the heat and leave to cool in the smoker.

Blanch the asparagus, followed by the peas, in boiling salted water. Refresh them both in ice-cold water after cooking. When they have cooled, remove from the water.

Thinly slice the fennel bulbs and dress with the lemon juice and olive oil. Season the fennel with a good pinch of salt, pepper and sugar.

To assemble the salad, combine the rocket, peas, asparagus and marinated fennel together in a bowl. Toss so that the ingredients are evenly distributed throughout.

Flake the smoked fish using two forks; try and keep the flakes quite large. Arrange the fish pieces in the centre of a plate. Drizzle the smoked fish with liberal amounts of the aïoli. Place a handful of the tossed salad on top of the fish and serve.

BRINE

Combine all the ingredients in a stainless steel bowl and whisk until the sugar and salt dissolve.

AÏOLI

Crush the garlic to a paste. Add the egg yolks and the mustard. Whisk in the vinegar. Slowly whisk in the oils, and season to taste.

SERVES 6

1.2 kg yellowtail fillet
1 litre brine (see below)
300 g asparagus
100 g fresh peas
6 bulbs baby fennel
Juice of 2 lemons
50 ml extra virgin olive oil
Salt, pepper and sugar
20 g wild rocket
200 ml aïoli (see below)

FOR THE BRINE

500 ml Triggerfish Bonito
60 g salt
60 g brown sugar
5 ml juniper berries
5 ml black peppercorns
4 whole cloves

FOR THE AÏOLI
MAKES ABOUT 450 ML

8 cloves garlic, roasted or smoked
2 egg yolks
5 ml Dijon mustard
15 ml white wine vinegar
200 ml extra virgin olive oil
200 ml vegetable oil
Sea salt and pepper

CHINESE BRAISED PORK BELLY, EGG NOODLES AND PAK CHOI

RECIPE COURTESY OF PETE GOFFE-WOOD, FOOD ALCHEMIST

Pair with an Imperial IPA, such as Triggerfish Titan. Chef Pete says: "The rich maltiness of the fragrant ale is the perfect accompaniment for this unctuous dish. The bitterness of the ale cuts through the fattiness of the belly and the aromatic broth stands up perfectly to the high alcohol content."

Remove the skin from the pork belly and cut away the layer of fat underneath. Cut the pork into 8 large pieces. Place all the ingredients together in a large saucepan and simmer slowly for about 3 hours, or until the pork is very soft. Remove the pork pieces from the broth and then strain it. Place the belly pieces back into the broth.

Reheat the broth. Steam the pak choi and blanch the noodles and divide them among eight bowls. Place a piece of pork belly on top of the pak choi. Pour over the broth and garnish with the sliced chillies, spring onions and coriander.

Eric and his family live so close to the brewery they can cycle there in minutes.

SERVES 8

2 kg pork belly, bones removed

1 large onion

2 carrots

1 head celery

6 cm-piece fresh ginger

1 bulb garlic

5 whole star anise

1 stick cinnamon

600 ml Chinese cooking wine or a dry sherry

250 ml Kikkoman soy sauce

5 litres water

FOR THE GARNISH

8 small head pak choi

400 g egg noodles, blanched

3 red chillies, very thinly sliced

1 bunch spring onions, finely sliced

10 g fresh coriander

CARAMEL AND DARK CHOCOLATE FONDANT SERVED WITH WHIPPED CREAM

RECIPE COURTESY OF STÉFAN MARAIS, EXECUTIVE CHEF AT SOCIETI BISTRO AND SOCIETI BRASSERIE

Pair with a sweet stout, such as Triggerfish Empowered Stout. Chef Stefan says: "The Empowered Stout's bitterness is well balanced, with a detectable sweetness that works very well with the caramel and dark chocolate flavours in this dessert. I find that this complex and full-bodied sweet stout pairs very well with braised meat dishes as well as desserts."

CHOCOLATE TRUFFLE MIXTURE

In a saucepan, bring the cream to the boil, then remove from the heat. Add the chocolate and stir until melted. Add the butter and stir until melted. Spoon into a small, shallow tray to 1 cm deep and refrigerate for 45 minutes. Once set, use a warm knife to cut into 2 cm rectangles. Set aside.

FONDANT MIXTURE

Preheat the oven to 180 °C. Butter 8 ramekins and dust with flour.

First make a caramel sauce by placing the sugar and water in a large saucepan over medium heat. In a separate pot, bring the cream to the boil, then remove from the heat. As soon as the sugar starts to turn to a caramel colour, switch off the heat and carefully whisk in the boiled cream. This will bubble up vigorously, so be careful. Whisk in the butter.

Sift the flour and add the salt. (The salt will prevent that sickly sweetness often found in caramel desserts.) Weigh off 800 g of the sauce and place in a large mixing bowl to cool (reserve the leftovers for plating up). While the sauce is cooling, place the flour in a roasting pan in the oven for 5 minutes, giving it a stir after 2 minutes (this will prevent a raw floury taste from the liquid centre of the baked fondants). Sift the flour into the caramel sauce and whisk in the eggs until smooth.

Spoon the mixture into the prepared ramekins until half-full. Push a truffle rectangle into the centre and cover with more of the fondant mixture. Leave the ramekins in the fridge for at least 3 hours before baking and serving.

TO SERVE

Preheat the oven to 200 °C and bake for 8 minutes, straight from the fridge. Turn out onto a plate and serve with left-over caramel sauce and unsweetened whipped cream.

SERVES 8

FOR THE CHOCOLATE TRUFFLE MIXTURE

75 ml fresh cream

200 g dark chocolate (preferably 70% cocoa), chopped into small pieces

30 ml unsalted butter

FOR THE FONDANT MIXTURE

800 g white sugar

80 ml water

800 ml fresh cream

80 g butter

240 g cake flour

2 pinches of Maldon sea salt

8 eggs (preferably free-range and organic if you can)

Extra flour and butter for lining the ramekins

VALLEY BREWERY

Need to know...

Location: 20 Fish Eagle Park, Kommetjie, Cape Town
Web: facebook.com/valleybrewery **Tel:** 083 709 6759
Amenities: Brewery tours, tasting, off-sales

What do you do when your lifestyle means you could go for weeks without seeing a bottle store, and even when you finally find one, a cold beer costs almost as much as you'd pay for Champagne at home? It's simple – you dock your yacht, invest in some plastic buckets, pots and yeast and brew your own beer on board. That's exactly what Glenn Adams did when he and his wife, Margie, took four years out to sail around the globe.

"I drank some great beers in Central and South America," says Glenn, "but when we got to the South Sea Islands we hadn't had a beer for a while and it was just so expensive – I had to go without until we got to Australia!"

Not an ideal situation for a beer lover who was following a lifelong dream to quit the rat race and sail around the world. So on arrival in Australia, Glenn decided to take his thirst into his own hands and stock up on homebrewing equipment so there would never be an on-board drought again.

Whenever they docked, Glenn brewed kit beer in the 28-foot yacht's lazarette and later bottled it in the cabin. "I had 90 quart bottles on board, so it was enough to get us across the Indian Ocean as we headed home!" says Glenn. The bottles had to be well-packed in case of stormy weather, but all in all it was a perfect place to start homebrewing. "When you're cruising, you have nothing to do and all day to do it in, so there couldn't be a nicer place for kit brewing," Glenn reminisces.

On returning to Cape Town, Glenn started all-grain brewing, aided by members of the South-Yeasters Home Brewers Club. Soon, homebrew-sized batches weren't enough and Glenn put his steel manufacturing knowledge to use, building a 300-litre brewery at his Kommetjie workshop. "I built the brewery on weekends over about eight months," he says. "Then I decided to try and sell my beers. I wanted to see if I could turn my hobby into a business." Thanks to his passion for beer and the superlative equipment he's built from scratch, Glenn is now proudly at the helm of Valley Brewery, producing flawless beers to a loyal local audience.

Glenn's enthusiasm for his duo of trades is infectious and the brewery is a jovial place where locals drop in to chat, taste and buy beer. And it's not just beer that Glenn sells – his much-admired self-made brewery brings in brewers from around the Cape seeking bottle washers and other equipment for their own breweries. "There's been a lot of interest in the equipment," says Glenn. "And luckily a lot of interest in the beers as well!"

TASTING NOTES

LONDON ALE (4.5% ABV): A beautiful, golden beer topped with creamy foam. London Ale is an understated brew, with a subtle, fruity nose and perfectly balanced fruitiness and bitterness.

Also look for Dublin Dark Ale and Valley Weiss.

CREAMY SALT HAKE WITH GRILLED POLENTA AND SLOW-ROASTED TOMATOES

RECIPE COURTESY OF STÉFAN MARAIS, EXECUTIVE CHEF AT SOCIETI BISTRO AND SOCIETI BRASSERIE

Pair with a blonde ale, such as Valley's London Ale. Chef Stéfan says: "I find that the salty, creamy texture of the hake works very well with this blonde ale's subtle but complex flavours. The smoky flavour of the grilled polenta also contrasts well with the beer."

CREAMY SALT HAKE

Day 1: Place one-third of the salt on a tray and lay the hake on top of it. Cover the hake completely with the remaining salt and refrigerate for 24 hours.

Day 2: Remove and discard all the salt. Wash the hake in cold water and soak in clean water in the fridge for 24 hours.

Day 3: Add the garlic, thyme, bay leaf and ground cloves to the milk in a saucepan and simmer for 5 minutes. Remove the bay leaf and blend the mixture until smooth. Remove the hake from the water and place in the milk. Bring to a gentle simmer – do not boil the hake as this will make it tough. Once the hake is soft, remove from the liquid and flake the flesh into a bowl. Using a spatula, beat in the mashed potato, half of the milk mixture and the olive oil. Season with the white pepper, and salt if needed. Set aside until ready to serve (reserve the remaining milk mixture).

POLENTA

Bring the water and salt to the boil in a large saucepan. Lower the heat to a simmer and slowly "rain" in the polenta. Stir constantly with a whisk. Reduce the heat to its lowest setting and cook the polenta for about 40 minutes – stir with a wooden spoon every few minutes. The polenta is cooked when it thickens and starts to pull away from the sides of the saucepan. Transfer to a tray and spread out to form a cake about 2 cm thick. Leave to cool completely.

Cut the cooled polenta into wedges. Preheat your grill to very hot, brush the polenta with the olive oil and grill for about 3 minutes on each side.

TO SERVE

Gently warm the hake mixture with a dash of the remaining milk mixture. Place two slices of grilled polenta on a warm plate, spoon the creamy hake mixture on top and garnish with the sweet tomatoes and dressed rocket.

SERVES 8

FOR THE SALT HAKE

1 side of hake, all bones removed

1 kg coarse sea salt

5 cloves garlic, thinly sliced

3 sprigs thyme, leaves stripped from the stalks

1 bay leaf

1 ml ground cloves

1 litre milk

2 large baking potatoes, peeled, boiled and mashed

60 ml extra virgin olive oil

1 ml white pepper

Salt to taste

Dressed rocket for serving

FOR THE POLENTA

1 litre water

2.5 ml salt

175 g polenta

50 ml olive oil

Black pepper

SLOW-ROASTED TOMATOES

Cut 4 large tomatoes into wedges and place on a tray. Drizzle with olive oil, and sprinkle with sugar, salt and pepper. Place sliced garlic on each tomato and sprinkle with the thyme leaves. Place in your oven on its lowest setting and leave overnight.

WILD CLOVER BREWERY

Need to know...
Location: R304, Stellenbosch
Web: cloverfarm.co.za **Tel:** 021 865 2219
Amenities: Restaurant, tasting room, wine tasting, accommodation

Beer before wine makes you feel fine, they say, but for Ampie Kruger, opting for wine first has also worked out pretty well – making it that is. An accomplished garagiste winemaker, Ampie's winery Notre Rêve put out its first vintage in 2007 – the year he was also introduced to the hobby of homebrewing. It had been a long time coming for Ampie, who experimented with kit beers while at university. "I was drinking beer like hell as a student," he says, "but after a while I just couldn't drink it any more. Then whenever I went to England, the beer was fantastic and I could pub-crawl from one bar to the next."

In 2007, Ampie hosted a braai to which a friend brought a batch of homebrew. "I tasted it and said 'yes, this is the beer that I remember from the UK; this is what I can drink' and I asked how to make it." Ampie soon fell in love with the process, deciding to make both wine and beer. "It's the same sort of equipment, the same idea – except that wine is easier since you've already got the sugar in the grapes," he explains. "With beer you first need to convert the starches to sugar."

In the interests of "paying it forward" Ampie introduced his friend Karel Coetzee to the world of homebrewing and so Ampie's fate was sealed. "I had my reservations about homebrewing," admits Karel, who became a discerning beer drinker during a six-year stint living in Chicago, "but I realised that this was good stuff and in 2009 I told him the beer was good enough to put onto the market." The two decided to embark on a commercial microbrewery together. Ampie was already looking for a spot for

his winery, feeling the time was right to move out of his garage. That's when he happened upon Wild Clover Farm in the northern reaches of Stellenbosch.

Plans to upgrade from the 30-litre homebrew system were put into place, though all did not run smoothly with the first 300-litre brew. "It was farcical," Karel laughs. First there was the gas accident that nearly saw them burning the brewery's new-found home to the ground; the hole in Karel's hand; the "blood all over the place". And then there was the issue of a 300-litre batch of undrinkable beer. "You think it will be easy to scale things up 10 times," says Ampie. "Wow, what a wakeup call that was!" Fluctuating mash temperatures meant the starch converted to the wrong type of sugar so although it fermented, Ampie admits he didn't finish a single glass. Unfortunately, some other people did.

"I wanted to test out all the equipment, so I put the beer through every process regardless and had kegged some of it," Ampie explains, shaking his head. "While I was on leave, the restaurant ran out of beer so they sold a keg of ours. I say to this day that they have damaged our name for life – those people will never come back!"

Wild Clover currently produces a porter, a much-lauded brown ale and a "summer beer" brewed with wine yeast, and plans to add a pilsner and a weiss are on the cards. Eventually, the dream is that one or both of the brewers can quit their IT day jobs, but for the moment, Ampie is happy that he made the first leap from homebrew to a setup he likes to call "farm brew".

Eastern Cape

BRIDGE STREET BREWERY

Need to know...

Location: Bridge Street, Brickmaker's Kloof, Port Elizabeth
Web: bridgestreet.co.za **Tel:** 041 581 0361
Amenities: Restaurant, beer tasting, coffee shop

People have been waiting years for the Bridge Street Brewery to open. They might not have realised they were waiting for it to open, but they were, for the brewer at the helm of this stylish brewpub is a man who could be called the godfather of South African craft brewing – Lex Mitchell. The founder of the country's first microbrewery, Mitchell's in Knysna (see page 87), has been conspicuously absent from the brewing scene for too long and his return seems like a sign that craft brewing has finally come of age in South Africa. And it seems no one has been waiting for Bridge Street to open more than Lex himself. Since selling Mitchell's in 1998, Lex looked at starting breweries in some unlikely locations – the remote islands of Mayotte and St Helena among them. Then, after several setbacks, an opportunity arose a little closer to home – in fact, in the very city he calls home: Port Elizabeth.

"I was quietly sitting at home looking at other ventures when I was approached by Gary [Erasmus – the landlord of the building and a partner in the brewery] in April 2011," Lex explains. "My involvement was simple – he asked if I'd be interested

TASTING NOTES

BOAR'S HEAD BEST BITTER (4.5% ABV): Modelled on the British beer that first inspired Lex to launch a microbrewery, this is an understated ale with only the vaguest of aromas. Malt and hops are in perfect balance, giving a beer that has hints of fruit and bitterness in equal doses.

CELTIC CROSS PREMIUM PILSNER (5% ABV): Light fruit on the nose and with a pleasant but subtle sweetness, Bridge Street's most popular brew is dangerously easy to drink and infinitely moreish.

BLACK DRAGON DOUBLE CHOCOLATE STOUT (4% ABV): A medium-bodied stout that is rich in coffee and dark chocolate both on the nose and the palate. There's a luscious, long finish with lingering flavours of espresso.

and I said yes!" Lex had already been brewing up some business plans of his own and while his vision to open an English-style pub didn't transpire, some of the ideas live on in the names of the beers. The restaurant side of things – something Lex admits he didn't know anything about – was left to Donovan Noyle, a familiar face on the Port Elizabeth food and beverage scene. The brewing was left to Lex. "I had an idea of what I wanted to brew," he says and had been practising his recipes on an adorable wood-panelled homebrew system over the years. Bridge Street's trio of beers are reminiscent of the long-established Mitchell's brands in that they're not overly fizzy and are faultless in every way, but the styles are all new, as are their names. "The names of our beers perhaps have an unusual provenance," Lex explains. "I had the idea to start a medieval village, an idea that stemmed from the medieval fair that I've put on in PE for the past 11 years. That never came to pass but I had a page full of beer names, and that's where these came from." While the pub is named for the street on which it sits, the brewery's moniker – Boar's Head – is taken from the Mitchell's family crest and the beer names from Lex's passion for all things medieval.

Between talk of Lex's hobby of "Robin Hooding", which he describes as "shooting foam animals with a longbow", and of the research he's done into the family name, it is evident that he still also has an immense passion for brewing.

For the first few months of Bridge Street's existence, Lex was rising at 5 a.m. and brewing up to five times a day on the 50-litre system he'd brought from home while the 300-litre system was waiting to be installed. The pressing need for a larger brewery was also the reason that a change-over was proving difficult – the huge and constant demand for beer, especially the flagship Celtic Pilsner, meant Lex was frantically stockpiling enough to get him through the days when the new system would be set up and tested. Luckily though, and rather unusually for a brewpub, Bridge Street stocks a wide range of South African craft beers – something that helps out when demand gets to be too much. Alas, you're unlikely to ever find Lex's beers on tap anywhere else – he's adamant that they'll only ever supply Bridge Street. This is in no small part because the constant brewing takes up so many hours, there is no time left to experiment. "I do feel that the creative side has been stifled because of the hours that I've had to put in. I have done some unusual brews at home that I would like to do again," he says, but is tight-lipped on what those future brews might be. There are firm plans to add a cider to the range, a perfect pint for sipping on the terrace overlooking the Baaken River.

Bridge Street manages to marry classic beers and modern décor, creating an instantly popular hang-out – one which launched quietly and gained popularity without any real marketing. The building started out as a fibreglass factory and Donovan laughs when he thinks back to the day he first saw it. "Two years ago if you'd looked at this building people would have said you're absolutely mad – it was totally derelict," he says. But the revamping of the building has led to a rejuvenation of the valley, making the area a popular spot for weekend family outings as well as boozy midweek nights out. "The public response has more than exceeded our expectations," says Donovan, "and they were high to begin with."

Lex is coy when it comes to acknowledging his position as founder of craft beer in South Africa, but he will admit that he finds the recent beer boom exciting. "I loved the idea in Britain that you could go to a village and each place would have its own brewery. I don't think it's spread far enough in South Africa yet, but it seems that it's finally getting there."

Donovan sums up the boom perfectly with his final words before rushing back to the heaving restaurant. "Craft beer has become the best thing since wine," he says. I couldn't have put it better myself.

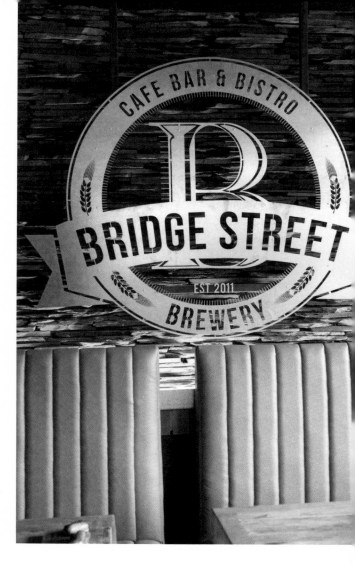

Ask the brewer

Should all beer be served ice cold or should different beers be served at different temperatures?

"My firm conviction is that to get the best out of a beer it should be served at a temperature which is not so cold as to 'lock' in the aromas waiting to be released and which contribute immeasurably to the enjoyment of a well-crafted beer. Ales and stouts have a real smorgasbord of nasal and palate exciters which are lost when poured too cold. By the same token, however, on a really hot day, an ice-cold beer goes down wonderfully well and when one is thirsty, this is about all that is necessary."

EMERALD VALE BREWING CO.

Need to know...
Location: Emerald Vale Farm, Off Cintsa East Road, Cintsa
Web: emeraldvalebrewery.co.za **Tel:** 078 614 0150 **Amenities:** Tours
by appointment, off-sales available after tours or by appointment

Chris Heaton's dreams of launching South Africa's first "estate brewery" might have hit some huge hurdles early on, but his beer has been met with such gusto in its Wild Coast home that he just can't keep up with demand and for the moment at least has put his barley field on the back burner.

It was never going to be an easy feat – estate breweries, ones where all the barley and hops are grown on site, are as scarce worldwide as breweries in any form are along the Wild Coast, though Chris certainly gave it a brave shot. "At one stage I even wanted to build my own malting plant though I think the project was a bit ambitious!" Chris laughs, shaking his head. "But I grew the barley and got to know the ingredients, which was a great exercise. And I did learn how to plough!" Chris's attempts at growing hops have been a little more successful, with his first vines producing cones after just three months. "I'd like to use 100% of my own hops for the bittering hops," says Chris, though if local demand keeps up, he'll have to look at adding a few more hop vines to his land.

It's a project that deserves to pay off. Chris is a humble guy with a hankering to learn everything about his newly chosen craft. The idea started in 2010 when Chris started making kit beers. Once he moved to all-grain brewing, Chris began to toy with the idea of opening a brewery on his family farm, just outside Cintsa. "I wanted to do something on the farm that's related to tourism," Chris explains. "There's a lot of potential in this area but it's very under-advertised. It's growing though and I'd like to be a part of it." With the land available and a

Chris Heaton is one of few brewers who grows his own hops.

background in the construction industry, Chris had the perfect launch pad and set about investigating the industry – and the competition.

"I went around to a lot of different breweries in South Africa and did a 10-day stint working at The Little Brewery on the River [see page 139] as well as the Misty Meadows weekend brewing experience [see page 83]," says Chris. "One of the breweries I

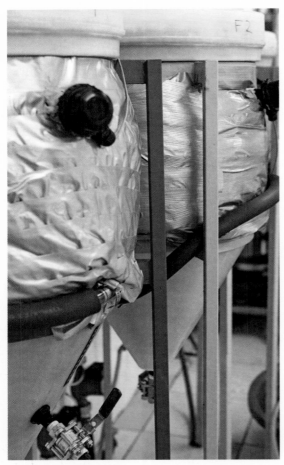

The equipment might be rudimentary, but the beers are superb.

visited was Mitchell's. I looked at their system and realised that I should keep to the basics."

Chris's system is indeed in keeping with the surrounds in its rusticity, but he has proved that good beer is as much about the brewer as the equipment. There's no doubt that his humility and self-criticism have served him well along the way. "I don't know everything about it," he admits. "I feel like I'll need at least 10 years' experience to call myself anything like a brewmaster!" Of the first seven brews, Chris ditched two, though he has no regrets about the failed batches. "I love tasting different kinds of beer, but I also love tasting things that are wrong with beer and identifying what went wrong in the process" – a philosophy that promises to take him a long way on the craft beer scene.

Solar-powered Emerald Vale – named for the farm it sits on – is one of the country's newest breweries, established in April 2012. Once Chris can keep up with demand from local restaurants and the thirsty backpackers that flock to the Wild Coast, he plans to start tours of his brewery as well as a couple of restaurants in the region. In the meantime you can count on a range of beers made only with rainwater and featuring some measure of home-grown hops. And will there be any Wild Coast malt featuring in Emerald Vale's beers in the near future? "Unlikely," laughs Chris. "But I do think the barley adds a certain ambience to the brewery!"

Ask the brewer

Why does my beer smell like a tin of sweet corn?

"The cause of this off-aroma is dimethyl sulphide (DMS). If you smell this in your beer, somewhere in the chain there is something that has not been done correctly. It could be from using poor malt, or from certain brewing procedures. Ensuring a good 70–90-minute boil with the lid off the boiler and then making sure that the wort is cooled quickly should ensure that the cause of this kind of smell is eradicated. Remember that DMS is acceptable – in small amounts – in lagers."

TASTING NOTES

GOLD ALE (5.6% ABV): This pale gold-coloured ale is mild on aroma but if you sniff deeply enough you'll find evidence of malt. It's a very well-executed entry-level ale with a perfect balance of bitter and sweet flavours and a pleasing finish that leaves you wanting more. A great first leap for lager lovers.

AMBER ALE (5.6% ABV): A little darker in colour, this highly drinkable ale also offers a hint of sweetness on the nose. There's a hint of roasted malt when you sip and a touch more bitterness than the Gold Ale delivers.

Also look out for Emerald Vale's Pale Ale, a slightly hoppier beer.

BREW-IT-YOURSELF
Emerald Vale Amber Ale
98.5% Pale lager malt
1.5% Black malt

Hop additions:
Southern Cross @ 70 minutes
Cascade @ 30 minutes

BEER AND BACON RISOTTO

RECIPE COURTESY OF GREG CASEY, OWNER OF BANANA JAM CAFÉ

Heat the chicken stock in a saucepan over medium heat. Keep it at a gentle simmer.

Heat the oil in a large pot and fry the bacon until browned. Add the onion, celery and garlic and keep stirring until just soft – about 3 minutes. Add the rice and a pinch of pepper, stirring constantly so that the rice toasts but doesn't brown. Once the rice has absorbed the flavour of the bacon and onion, add the beer, ensuring that it evaporates before you add any stock. Do not worry about the beer's bitterness as it will diminish as the dish cooks.

Once the beer has evaporated, start to add the stock. Keep stirring and adding stock 1 cup at a time, each time letting the stock be absorbed by the rice before adding more. You know it's time to add more when you can run a spoon through the rice and see the bottom of the pan for a few seconds before the rice covers it again. Do this until the rice is *al dente*.

Once the rice is ready, add the butter, stir in the Parmesan, garnish with a crispy piece of bacon and a celery leaf and enjoy with a glass of beer.

SERVES 4–6

1.75 litres chicken stock

15 ml olive oil

150 g streaky bacon, diced (keep one rasher for garnishing)

1 large onion, diced

2 large sticks celery, sliced and diced (keep leaves for garnish)

15 ml finely minced garlic

500 ml Arborio rice

200 ml of a hop-forward beer, such as Emerald Vale's Amber Ale

50 g butter

60 ml grated Parmesan cheese

Salt and pepper

THE LITTLE BREWERY ON THE RIVER

Need to know...

Location: 20 Wharf Street, Port Alfred
Web: littlebrewery.co.za **Tel:** 046 624 5705
Amenities: Restaurant, tasting room, brewery tours, shop, off-sales

The eminently affable Ian Cook doesn't mind admitting that he "bumbled into the whole brewery thing", though it might seem more like fate guided him to take over Port Alfred's long-standing but somewhat beleaguered brewery. After a brief but successful search for a semi-retirement business in small-town South Africa, Ian moved from Johannesburg to the Eastern Cape coast.

"I was initially interested in the Pig and Whistle, South Africa's oldest pub," Ian explains. "I was trying to work out how to make money and I thought we could stick a brewery in it!" With the new idea in mind, Ian started scouting around for second-hand brewing equipment and found out about the vacant brewery in Port Alfred. Although established in 1998 as the somewhat successful Coelacanth Brewery, the setup had changed hands several times and hadn't been functioning for six years when Ian clapped eyes on it. "In my naivety I honestly believed I could reverse up in a bakkie, take out two spanners and move all this kit to Bathurst," laughs Ian. A weekend at the brewery followed, which is when Ian fell in love and all the plans changed. The love in question was the mid-nineteenth century building housing the brewery. "I could really see us doing things with it," says Ian, "and by the end of the weekend I called the owner and said I don't want the equipment – I want the whole shooting match!"

Thanks to Ian, the building had finally found its goal in life. After a sombre start as the harbourmaster's offices and warehouse during Port Alfred's heyday years during the Frontier Wars, it tried a spell as the town hall, but deep down it always knew it was destined for a career in entertainment. After stints as a bottle store, cinema, restaurant and nightclub, it finally decided it wanted to be a brewery when it grew up, but it took a few brewers

The Kowie Gold Pilsner is The Little Brewery's flagship beer.

TASTING NOTES

KOWIE GOLD (4.5% ABV): This crisp, clean pilsner is crystal clear and the colour of pale straw. Although mildly fruity on the nose, it has a dry, refreshing finish – a definite session beer.

SQUIRES PORTER (6.5% ABV): Mild coffee aromas give way to a roasty pint that is dangerously drinkable considering its alcohol content. It is lighter in body than your average porter.

Also look out for the copper-coloured Coin Ale.

to help the old building achieve its potential. "It's a nice old girl!" says Ian, looking around at the high ceilings and thick stone walls, clearly glad that he opted to stick around when first spent a weekend here in 2008. That weekend was fateful in more than one way. Not only did Ian find a home for his new business, he also found a brewer. Thanks to

Bethwell (left) and Alert are probably South Africa's only teetotal brewers.

a tip-off from the SAB brewer who had given the OK to the brewing equipment, Ian tracked down Colin Coetzee, a retired SAB brewer living in nearby Kenton-on-Sea, and The Little Brewery on the River began its first brew in 2009. Colin says his foray into brewing was simple – he flunked university and applied! But it was obviously the right path since he stayed with SAB for a further 34 years, working at breweries throughout Africa. You can quickly tell that Ian and Colin enjoy a friendship rare to people who have only known each other a few years. "I haven't played one game of golf since I started here," Colin mock-complains, referring to his retirement being cut short by Ian's venture. But it seemed that Colin was just waiting for someone to urge him back to the brewing scene. "I didn't take much convincing," Colin confesses. "I got on an ego trip – I wanted to know that I could still do it." "Just as well," adds Ian. "Because we couldn't do it without him."

The camaraderie of the team is a delight to behold, and it's not just Ian and Colin who are having a ball at the brewery. The two assistant brewers, brothers from Zimbabwe, are also filled with an enthusiasm that bubbles over into the beers they brew. Bethwell Dube had been working as Ian's gardener for years when Ian made the move from Joburg to the Eastern Cape and it didn't take long for him to decide to also opt for a new home and a new career. The move involved a lot of firsts for Bethwell – his first plane ride ("I was a bit shaky"), his first sight of the ocean ("amazing") and, of course, his first time in a brewery ("a great challenge!"). His brother, Alert, followed two years later and gives off the aura of a man who has been brewing his entire life. "Colin taught us nicely," he says modestly, but Colin and Ian both acknowledge that Bethwell and Alert were perfect students. "One of the biggest satisfactions I have is seeing Bethwell running the brew house," says Colin. "I made a man out of him!" Bethwell and Alert often take care of the brewing if Colin is not around and their eyes light up as they talk about their new profession with a rare and enviable passion – no mean feat for two people who neither drink nor even taste the beers they produce.

Colin and Ian have been known to partake of the occasional pint though and the two devised the recipes for the three beers along with a little help from the SAB plant in Port Elizabeth. The range began with a crisp and clear pilsner, following a year later with an ale, then a porter another year after that. Their beers use local ingredients, save for the Saaz hop featured in the pilsner. "We have a water problem in Port Alfred," admits Colin, "but I don't." He refers to the sub-par tap water in the town and the rainwater collected on the brewery roof, the only water used in the trio of beers.

Since opening, the brewery has witnessed the kind of success it had been waiting for since it was first installed. The beers are found on tap throughout the town, as well as in neighbouring Kenton, Bathurst and in a few select spots in Grahamstown. For takeaways, you'll have to visit the brewery shop, which also stocks glasses and a range of light-hearted beer T-shirts that epitomise the cheery, amiable nature of this coastal brewpub.

Ask the brewer

What is "lacing"?

"Lacing" is the foam that is left over after you have taken a drink of beer. In general, the foamier the beer, the more lacing left over after drinking (beer is foamier, or the foam is denser, when it has smaller bubbles, as opposed to large ones). The foam is generally a function of the beer's ingredients. The proteins in the beer link together, becoming sticky, and cling onto the side of the beer glass. This foam also helps to keep the carbon dioxide in the beer, thus keeping it bubbly and creamy while it is being drunk. The higher the protein level, the denser the foam, as the CO_2 has more to adhere to. For comparison, carbonated soft drinks are low in protein, and thus have little foam. Lacing is always more evident when a clean beer glass is used; a dirty or oily glass results in less foam and lacing."

BEER-BATTERED FISH AND CHIPS

RECIPE COURTESY OF THE WHARF STREET BREWPUB

Pair with a pilsner, such as The Little Brewery's Kowie Gold. Pilsner is a clean, delicate beer that pairs well with an array of dishes. Consider it a palate-cleanser here, allowing you to savour the more delicate flavours of the fish.

SERVES 6

300 g flour
Salt (to taste)
3 eggs, beaten
500 ml Kowie Gold Pilsner (or other pilsner)
250 ml water
6 hake fillets
Oil for frying

Sift the flour and salt together in a large bowl. Add the beaten eggs to the flour, mixing constantly. Gradually add the beer and water to the mixture.

Dip the hake fillets into the batter, then fry in hot oil until golden. Serve with chunky homemade chips and salad or vegetables – and a glass of your favourite pilsner of course!

The one-time reservoir now serves as the Wharf Street Brewpub's wine cellar.

MAKANA MEADERY

Need to know...

Location: Old Power Station, Reynolds Street, Highlands Industrial Area, Grahamstown **Web:** iqhilika.co.za **Tel:** 046 636 1227
Amenities: Off-sales, tastings by appointment

People get into booze production for all manner of reasons, but none is quite so cryptic and bizarre as the reason Dr Garth Cambray gives for his induction into the world of mead-making: "somebody stole my bicycle."

To elaborate, on the day his bike was taken, Garth bumped into a university friend he might not have otherwise seen. The friend was off to India and mentioned he was giving up his job working with a professor at Rhodes University. The job in question involved honeybee research, so Garth filled the vacancy left by his student pal and from there an interest in bees developed. "As soon as I started keeping bees, my parents' gardener began pinching honey to make *iQhilika*. It was him who explained *iQhilika* to me," recalls Garth. *iQhilika* is the Xhosa word for mead and has been made in South Africa for millennia. The encounter with his parents' gardener would launch a lifelong passion for mead that stretches far beyond a passing interest.

"In my third year I did a microbiology project on *iQhilika*," says Garth, in which he learned to make it and started looking at the yeast in greater detail. From there an honours degree and PhD on the subject followed, the latter looking both at inventing new brewing technology for this ancient beverage and also at how making mead might benefit the local community. "One of the problems with university research in South Africa is that it doesn't actually create jobs to economically empower local, rural communities," Garth explains. "We're very proud to say that this does."

The research paid off in every way. Not only did Garth invent a revolutionary way to make mead that is as baffling as it is brilliant, he also succeeded in creating jobs within the local community. Sindiswa Teyise, Director of Operations at Makana, heads up the beekeeper training project and has trained close to 500 beekeepers in the Transkei area. She came to Makana to work as a receptionist, but her

Dr Cambray's mead-making invention (seen here on the right) looks simple, but the processes happening within are baffling.

oft-quoted mantra of "I can do that" now sees her training beekeepers, keeping accounts and taking care of the mead-making process.

The process is simple, though the science behind it is not – honey and water are first blended together and heated to 75 °C in a process that takes about 3 minutes. From here, Garth's invention enters the proceedings. It is a basic-looking contraption, a narrow pipe reaching from floor to ceiling in the atmospheric old building – a disused power station on the outskirts of Grahamstown. It takes a mere 90 minutes for the honey and water solution to be pumped up the pipe, en route passing through a yeast colony that has been designed to speed up the fermentation process.

Dr Garth explains the process, which is mystifying in its simplicity: "At the bottom there's a whole lot of yeast that is adapted for a high sugar, low alcohol environment; in the middle you've got the yeast that are adapted for moderate sugar, moderate alcohol and at the top you've got yeast that are adapted for low sugar, high alcohol." He likens the process to a car manufacturer's assembly line, where each worker has a set job to do. "It's essentially a colony of yeast with a number of different skills." Remarkably, the yeast used was inoculated in 2000 and hasn't needed changing since. "We have not opened or taken out the yeast since 2001 on the main fermenter, but it is derived from an earlier culture developed in 1998–2000," Garth explains, calling his colony "an immortal consortium of yeast". To put this into perspective, a lot of breweries use new yeast for every brew, while others generally limit their re-use to five or six brews.

Once the honey and water solution reaches the top of the pipe, it is fully fermented into a tangy, sweet, wine-like beverage with an alcohol content of 12% ABV. It's another remarkable process and one that's difficult to get your head around after spending time in breweries, where fermentation generally takes between three and ten days. Fermentation strips away much of the honey's sweetness and some of the flavour so each batch is re-sweetened with another honey dose. Makana can make 300 litres of mead over the course of one working day and, theoretically, it could be bottled the same day. Generally though, Garth likes to let it sit in oak barrels for a few months before exporting it, as he does with the majority of his mead, to the USA. However, plans are afoot to distribute more widely in South Africa. "We're finding that with the microbrewery boom we're getting a lot more interest in the product here," says Garth. It would be a pattern that mimics that of the States, who began with a craft beer revolution and followed it up with ever-deepening interest in cider and mead.

The finished product is perhaps an acquired taste, though Makana's range of meads means there should be something for all palates. Plus, as it keeps for up to four months after opening (assuming it's refrigerated) you should have time to develop a taste for this ancient and yet rare beverage. Garth tells of mead's antioxidant properties and insists the beverage gives little hangover – perhaps a theory to test out once you've visited this extraordinary establishment in the Eastern Cape.

MEAD

It is mentioned in legend and lore, referred to in classical literature and is widely acknowledged as the world's oldest way to get drunk, but for all of mead's distinctions it is still one of the most humble boozy beverages there is.

Although many mead makers add various herbs or flavourings to give their versions character, at heart the drink has only three ingredients – water, honey and yeast. In fact, the advent of mead actually predates the man-made stuff, created by chance when beehives received the brunt of a deluge and the wild yeasts within the honey began to ferment.

Mead is often associated with medieval wenches and European kings, though its story dates just as far back in Africa as it does in Europe. In fact, the Khoisan were making what they called *!karri* long before Chaucer had worked out which end of a quill to use. They doubtless stumbled across it by accident, but quickly took a liking to its seemingly magical powers. Indeed mead, like honey, has long been linked to the gods, be they Roman, Greek or Druid, and is thought by many to be the oft-quoted "nectar of the Gods".

Today mead is making a resurgence in some parts of the globe, often hot on the heels of a craft beer boom. Mead is not beer; its production is less complex than brewing and the end product more similar to wine, at least in alcohol strength and appearance. But mead is an integral part of South Africa's millennia-old love affair with a good tipple and a beverage that is likely to gain popularity in the not-so-distant future. Its aromas and flavours are both complex and subtle, owing to the vast number of varied flowers each bee involved in the honey-making process has visited.

Mead can be sparkling but is usually still and is best served chilled in a red-wine glass. Enjoy sweeter versions with spicy food or strong cheese, while dry styles pair well with fish, chicken and seafood dishes.

TASTING NOTES

AFRICAN TRANSKEI GOLD COFFEE (12% ABV): With aromas of Grandma's homemade gooseberry jam, you might expect something a little more bitter than that which awaits on the palate. This, like all Makana's meads, has a velvety mouthfeel akin to dessert wine and is recommended with rich meats such as duck.

AFRICAN DRY (12% ABV): There is a solid acid structure to this mead, and a flavour that is like buttered toast. Of Makana's meads, this is perhaps the best companion to food.

CAPE FIG (12% ABV): Best served cold and ideal with a cheese course, this mead displays both sweet and savoury flavours. Floral aromas prevail and there's a long-lasting aftertaste of dried fruit.

AFRICAN HERBAL BLOSSOM (12% ABV): A powerful aroma that is herbal, fresh and almost medicinal gives way to complex flavours that conjure up images of an Indian market – think chai and incense sticks.

AFRICAN BIRD'S EYE CHILLI MEAD (12% ABV): An instantly noticeable but not overpowering chilli bite is the first thing that hits here, though an underlying sweetness offers a nice balance.

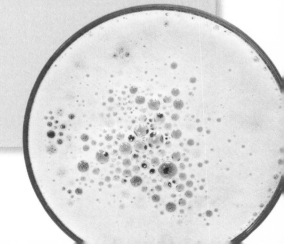

PRAWNS IN A MEAD REDUCTION

RECIPE COURTESY OF MIRABELLE SEETHA CAMBRAY OF MAKANA MEADERY

Heat the oil in a pan and brown the garlic. Add the chilli powder, turmeric, ground ginger, salt, ground cumin and mixed herbs. Mix thoroughly and then add the prawns and cook until the mixture is nearly dry.

Add the mead and cook until the mead has evaporated.

Serve with rice and a spicy beverage such as African Bird's Eye Chilli Mead, or a chilli beer.

SERVES 4–6

15 ml olive oil
10 ml crushed garlic
5 ml chilli powder
2.5 ml turmeric
2.5 ml ground ginger
2.5 ml salt
1 ml ground cumin
5 ml mixed dried herbs
1 kg prawns, shelled and deveined
250 ml sweet mead

The old power station just outside Grahamstown makes an atmospheric home for the Makana Meadery.

SNEEUBERG BREWERY

Need to know...

Location: Pienaar Street, Nieu-Bethesda
Web: nieubethesda.co.za/brewery.htm **Tel:** 049 841 1602
Amenities: Light meals, tasting room, coffee roaster, off-sales

Sometimes when you get to a brewery you just want to ditch the car and settle in for the afternoon, and where better to chill out for a day than the dusty Karoo dorp of Nieu-Bethesda. This mountain-fringed town is best known for its community of artists – in particular Helen Martins of Owl House fame – but at the Sneeuberg Brewery and Two Goats Deli you can also sample a little something I like to think of as "edible art". André Cilliers is not only a brewer – in fact if the only paved road out of town got washed away, he'd be able to survive for some time on his homemade bread, cheese, pickles and, of course, a beer or two to wash it down.

The sandy goat farm is a far cry from André's former life as an economics lecturer in Cape Town, but there is no longing for the city here. When asked if he ever yearns for Cape Town he looks around and smiles – "Would you?" he enquires. He's often asked if he gets lonely living out in the sticks, but André laughs at the idea. "I wish I could get lonely!" he says, referring to the near-constant stream of visitors who come to taste his produce.

After moving here in 2001, André quickly realised he would need an extra source of income to support his family and he instantly turned to brewing. "I had brewed kit beers for my friends while I was at Rhodes," says André. "I'd always enjoyed it so I thought a little brewery would be a nice project." Sneeuberg – named for the nearby mountain range – was established two years later, first using malt extract and later changing to partial mash

brewing (using some malt extract syrup and some malted barley). André has no plans to switch to all-grain brewing in future, largely due to the elevated transport costs involved in getting sacks of grain to this offbeat spot. And if it ain't broke, they say, don't fix it – the brewery's popularity has steadily grown through the years and André is finding that

he needs to brew his modest 100-litre batches with increasing frequency. "People come to visit the town but they've already seen the Owl House," he explains. "We're finding that more people are coming here specifically for us, which is great." Initially, local people were a little hesitant about the brewery, perhaps envisioning a factory billowing smoke over their untouched town, but now André counts on support from locals as well as tourists.

His beers are found on tap only at the brewery, where you can also buy bottles – recycled Windhoek bottles to be precise – featuring a rustic label whose logo was designed by a local artist. But it's not just the beer that keeps people coming back – it's the marriage of beer with two of its most compatible partners: bread and cheese. The eye-catching platters are as tasty as they are pretty, featuring a range of goats' and cows' milk cheeses, freshly baked bread and plenty of preserves and pickles, all made on site. Only the smoked Kudu salami comes from out of town, but despite André's pleas for the recipe, the Graaff-Reinet butcher who produces it won't spill his secret.

In fact, this salami was what brought Kevin Wood of Darling Brew (see page 59) here in 2007. He arrived with a recommendation to taste the cured meat and left with the intention to set up a brewery of his own, inspired largely by André's Roasted Ale. André has also helped another brew-

TASTING NOTES

KAROO ALE (3.5% ABV): An amber-coloured ale with a powerful hit of granadilla on the nose. The sweet aromas might leave you expecting a sweet beer, but it's dry and refreshing.

HONEY ALE (3.5% ABV): Like the Karoo Ale, this has fruity aromas, but dryness on the palate is interrupted by a dose of locally-made honey.

ROASTED ALE (3.5% ABV): Surprisingly fruity for a dark beer. Expect smoke and roasted flavours in this chocolate-brown-coloured ale, lighter in body than most dark beers.

ery to get off the ground – Karoo Brew in Montagu (see page 247).

André's laidback brewing philosophy perfectly suits the surrounds. "I don't get too bogged down with details," he says, referring to both his brewing style and the way he makes the cheese. I've got lots of goats and cows to be fed and to milk and lots of other things to do so I'm not too worried about a degree or two of temperature here or an extra few minutes there."

This ethos clashes with the way many brewers produce their beers, but with each sip of homemade ale and each mouthful of homemade cheese, you adapt to Nieu-Bethesda's sleepy pace of life, following André's lead to not sweat the small stuff – at least while you're in town.

The brewery takes its name from the nearby Sneeuberg range.

Gauteng

BLACK HORSE BREWERY

Need to know...
Location: Bekker School Road, Magaliesburg
Web: blackhorse.co.za **Tel:** 082 561 3246
Amenities: Restaurant

Nuschka Botha is instantly memorable as a brewer. Not only is she one of just two female craft brewers in the country, she is also the youngest commercial craft brewer nationwide. It wasn't exactly in Nuschka's plans to have a career in beer. Fresh out of university with a marketing degree in hand, her entrepreneur father, Bernard, launched a brewery and asked her to swot up on beer-making. In truth, the brewery wasn't entirely in his plans either – "it just kind of happened," says Nuschka.

In fact, the plan had been to build a small-scale brewery for Bernard to enjoy with friends, but fate took control, eventually giving South Africa another craft brewery to enjoy. "In 2010 my dad decided he wanted to build a small brewery, so he told the builders what he wanted and then he went on holiday. When he came back they had built this massive building!" Nuschka says, looking wide-eyed around the rustic brewpub. The building that houses Black Horse is indeed huge – three storeys to fill with diners and drinkers on weekend trips to the Magaliesberg region. But rather than getting angry with the maverick builders, Bernard opted to

Although the stud farm is no more, a handful of horses remain.

It might not have been planned, but the Black Horse brewpub is a formidable place for a pint.

roll with the punches, expanding his plans to utilise the expanded structure. A larger brewery was ordered from China – in itself a bit of a headache since it arrived with assembly instructions only in Chinese – and Nuschka suddenly found herself having a career change.

"My dad said 'Hey Nuschka – learn how to make beer!' So I started reading up on it a lot," says Nuschka. She travelled to Cape Town in late 2011 to explore the local microbreweries and pick the brains of a few brewers – a group she found that were very willing to help. After some hands-on training at a small brewery in the Cape Winelands, she completed a short apprenticeship at Heineken in Johannesburg and kept reading until March 2012, when she completed her first solo brew – the brewery's signature Red Ale. She knew her beers would then have to pass the first quality control test before she could hope to serve them to paying customers. "My dad's a big beer drinker so if

there's something wrong he's going to tell me," she laughs, rolling her eyes.

The beer met Bernard's approval and Black Horse – named for the Friesian stud farm that the Botha family used to operate here – opened its doors a month later, serving a duo of beers in a region that's rapidly establishing itself as a getaway for beer fans. The building might have been a mistake, but it's a charming place for lunch and drinks, whether you opt for the rambling, tree-studded garden or the glass-fringed main building. Once the brewery is fully up and running, a bottling plant will follow and Nuschka plans to brew at least twice a week, though in the long term she hopes to move out of the brew house and into the office. "If someone had told me five years ago that I was going to be a brewer I would have thought they were crazy," she says. "I'm really enjoying what I'm doing now though and am certainly going to keep brewing for a while, but hopefully once it's properly established I will be able to concentrate on the marketing."

In the meantime, Nuschka is enjoying her pseudo-celebrity status as a young, female brewer.

"I think everything has turned out quite well," says Nuschka of the accidental brewery.

"The other brewers are mostly men and generally quite a bit older – some of them think I can't do it, but that's okay. I like proving them wrong," she smiles as she sips a pint of her lager before heading back to the experimental brew bubbling away behind the giant windows, allowing all who pass to see that she really can produce beer.

TASTING NOTES

BLACK HORSE RED ALE (4% ABV): A light copper beer, unfiltered and slightly hazy. A fruity nose gives way to nicely balanced flavours of roasted malt, toffee and coffee, with a hint of fruit.

Also look out for the Black Horse Golden Lager, Nuschka's personal favourite.

THE COCKPIT BREWHOUSE

Need to know...
Location: 80 Oak Avenue, Cullinan
Web: thecockpitbrewhouse.co.za **Tel:** 012 734 0656
Amenities: Restaurant, beer garden, food pairing events, off-sales

If there is one man that sums up the craft beer industry in South Africa, then André de Beer is it. The aptly named brewer is humble, welcoming and always willing to share his expertise with fellow "beer nerds". He also brews some pretty awesome beers.

Cockpit is a charming brewpub sitting in an equally charming town. Cullinan has managed to fuse diamond mining with tourism – a feat helped in no small part by the opening of the brewery in 2010. Cockpit sits in one of the old mine-owned cottages on Oak Street, though it was touch-and-go whether André would secure the property for a while. "At first they thought I wanted to do a beer hall for the mine workers," André tells. "But I persisted and the GM – a teetotaller – saw the potential in the idea since they wanted to bring more tourism to Cullinan." At first the brewpub relied on overflow from nearby restaurants, but in less than two years the roles have been reversed, with other establishments now getting referrals from Cockpit on busy days. "Every business manual says that nine out of 10 restaurants fail within the first year and 80% of those left fold in the second year. We were breaking even from the very first month," André beams.

It's not too tough to see why, with a range of superb beers, a well-thought-out menu and a delightful building and gardens in which to enjoy it all. André's beers taste like he's been brewing his entire life, but in fact it's a relatively recent passion, albeit one that has long-standing roots. "My dad used to home-brew. He'd always give me the dregs out of the bottle so I guess that's where my love for it started," André reveals. "I really got into beer because I thought there must be more to it than what was available, but I was naive to think then that I could quickly brew something better."

He brewed his first beers in 2002 – a trio of kits that culminated in a stout that André called Black Widow – a name that survives to this day in the all-grain version, available on tap at Cockpit. "I guess I'm a beer nerd and a typical male – I won't follow instructions,"

TASTING NOTES

HELLES BELLES BLONDE ALE (4% ABV): Mild biscuit aromas promise and deliver a light and easy-drinking beer. Ideal as a first leap from lager to craft ale.

FOKKER WEISS (4% ABV): Bubblegum and bananas on the nose – signature aromas of the style. The Weiss yeast gives subtle banana flavours, but with a finish that is dry and refreshing.

SPITFIRE ENGLISH PALE ALE (3.8% ABV): Cockpit's "session beer" is a light and slightly sweet English-inspired ale designed to see you through a long, sunny afternoon. Caramel notes on the nose follow through on the palate, though it's far less sweet that you might imagine from the first whiff.

MUSTANG AMERICAN PALE ALE (5.5% ABV): André's signature brew is a delectable pint ideal for those seeking a bigger beer packed with flavour. A strong dose of tropical fruits on the nose with light fruits and fragrant hops on the palate. The clean, mildly bitter finish leaves you wanting more.

BLACK WIDOW STOUT (5% ABV): Chocolate and coffee aromas draw you into this medium-bodied stout, ideal as a winter warmer. If you're sipping in summer, the rich, coffee flavours make it the perfect after-dinner pint.

Look out for André's seasonal ales and "extreme beers", with something new on tap each month.

Cockpit offers free tasters for all.

admits André. "So I did my own thing with the kits and I thought that stout was a stunning beer." His peers agreed, with some of the Wort Hog Brewers club members believing the stout to be an all-grain brew. "Without the Wort Hogs I wouldn't have reached the point of brewing decent beer as quickly as I did," André is happy to admit. "The guys are very forthcoming with information and in some cases brutally honest about the taste of your beers!" In André's case, brutal honesty wasn't often a bad thing since the beers were undeniably good – he won the national homebrew championships a few years in a row, as well as a homebrewer of the year award. André is still a dedicated member of the club, serving on the committee in a role that is very dear to his heart – new brewer support. "I see it as getting people going in the movement; getting this ball rolling," he says. "I've always been very passionate about sharing my information."

About five years after he first dabbled in homebrewing, André started exploring the idea of setting up a brewpub, inspired in part by American homebrewer-turned-craft brewer Sam Calagione of Dogfish Head. After a nationwide search for the right spot, André returned to the region where he grew up and provided Cullinan with a brand new gem. The name came from André's other passion, aviation. "When we opened we wanted a theme," he says, "and I love aviation." He used to co-own a plane with Triggerfish brewer Eric van Heerden and Stephan Meyer from Clarens Brewery, but decided to sell when he started brewing. "The whole '12 hours bottle to throttle' rule didn't work for me when I was brewing!" he laughs, though his love of flying lives on in the beer names and the pub's décor.

While Cockpit took off from the beginning, it was in late 2011 and early 2012 that things really started to fly, thanks to a RASA (Restaurant Association of South Africa) nomination for best family restaurant and his flagship Mustang APA winning the best in show at the 2012 Clarens Craft Beer Festival – an award voted on by BJCP-accredited judges (the Beer Judge Certification Program is an internationally recognised body that governs over beer competitions).

Now that the brewery is showing serious signs of success, André is contemplating expanding his equipment, though only by a maximum of 50%, mindful of the framed note from wife Wendy that sits in the bar, reading "no less than this, and no more than this either".

One thing that you can be sure of in the future is more of André's "extreme beers" – seasonal ales, often packing a serious flavour punch. André is certainly not afraid of flavour, a fact confirmed by the five-year-old keg of 14.5% barley wine sitting in the brewery's cold room.

Alas, this particular beer is not for public consumption, though its story will put as much of a smile on your face as its flavour would. André brewed the barley wine three months before the birth of his first daughter and, each year on her birthday, he allows himself one glass of the beer. The last glass – well, glasses actually – will be drunk on her 18th birthday when Gerda can join her father in a celebratory toast. This is one example of André's love for and dedication to beer. He brews it, regularly holds gourmet dinners paired with it, and encourages others to make it. All you have to do is go there and drink it.

Ask the brewer

What's the difference between a lager and a pilsner?

"Both are brewed using bottom-fermenting yeasts. Pilsner is a sub-style of a lager, usually a crisp, clean, refreshing beer that prominently features noble German or Bohemian hop character. A pilsner will almost always be without any adjuncts, i.e. made only from barley malt, whereas, what is generally known as a lager, would use a high percentage of adjunct, like maize or rice, to lighten the body of the beer. This style of lager would also have very little hop character, unlike the pilsner."

CURED LOCAL TROUT ON A SALT BLOCK

RECIPE COURTESY OF CRAIG CORMACK, EXECUTIVE CHEF AT SOFIA'S AT MORGENSTER

Pair with an American Pale Ale, such as Cockpit's Mustang APA. "The tropical fruit flavours combined with hop bitterness marry well with the subtle flavours of the trout," says Chef Craig. "The Himalayan salt brings out the flavours in the beer."

TROUT BALLOTTINE

Dissolve the gelatine in the water. Lay plastic wrap on the counter and place the filleted side of trout on top. Season with salt. Brush the gelatine solution over the trout, scatter with dill and roll up tightly in the plastic wrap. Tie the ends and refrigerate until set. When ready to serve, cut into slices through the plastic to keep its shape.

CURED TROUT

Make a brine solution with the salt and water. Place the side of trout into the salt solution. Soak for 3 hours in the fridge, then remove, rinse and slice.

EMULSION

Place the milk and garlic in a blender and blend for 1 minute. Start adding the oil slowly, until the mixture emulsifies. Season with salt to taste.

TO SERVE

Deep-fry the capers until crispy, then place onto paper towel to drain most of oil. Thinly slice the onion.

Smear the emulsion on the salt block. Place the ballottine on the one end with the lemon wedge and crisp slice of bread, then add the sliced cured trout. Garnish with the greens, onions, cream cheese quenelle and capers. Drizzle with olive oil.

SERVES 6

FOR THE TROUT BALLOTTINE

10 ml gelatine powder
100 ml water
1 side of trout, skinned and deboned
Salt
Finely chopped fresh dill

FOR THE CURED TROUT

200 g salt
200 ml water
1 side of trout, deboned (skin on)

FOR THE EMULSION

125 ml milk
1 small clove garlic
130 ml vegetable oil
Salt

FOR SERVING

24 capers
¼ onion
Himalayan salt block
4 lemon wedges
Thinly sliced bread, baked in the oven until crispy
50 g baby greens
20 ml cream cheese (per serving), shaped into quenelles
15 ml olive oil for drizzling

BREW-IT-YOURSELF

Mustang American Pale Ale

86% 2-row lager malt
7% Melanoidin malt
7% Caramunich III

Hop additions:

T90 @ 60 minutes
Amarillo @ 20 minutes
Cascade @ 20 minutes
Columbus @ 10 minutes
Amarillo @ 10 minutes
Columbus @ 0 minutes
Cascade @ 0 minutes

BEEF AND STOUT PIE

RECIPE COURTESY OF THE COCKPIT BREWHOUSE

Pair with an English Pale Ale, such as Cockpit's Spitfire English Pale Ale. It's a classic pairing and a perennial winner in wintry weather.

Place the diced beef into a large bowl, add the flour and toss until the meat is coated.

Heat a drizzle of oil in a pan, add the beef in batches and brown. Remove and set aside.

Fry the onion, carrots and celery in the same pan until soft. Add half the stout, bring to the boil and then add the beef. Cook over a low heat for 2½ hours.

Preheat the oven to 220 °C.

Add the remaining stout – reserving a sip for yourself – and button mushrooms, and simmer until the mushrooms are cooked. Season to taste. Leave to cool slightly, then ladle the mixture into individual pie dishes. Cover with puff pastry and brush with egg wash. Bake until the pastry is golden brown.

Serve with chips and salad or veg, and a pint or half of your favourite English Pale Ale.

SERVES 4–6

1 kg bolo, diced into 2 cm cubes
About 80 g flour
Vegetable oil for frying
1 onion, sliced
6 carrots, roughly chopped
1 stick celery, finely sliced
500 ml Black Widow Stout (or another stout if Black Widow is not available)
250 g button mushrooms
Salt and pepper
Ready-made puff pastry
Egg wash

COPPER LAKE BREWERIES

Need to know...

Location: 17 Main Road, Sunrella, Lanseria
Web: copperlake.co.za **Tel:** 071 195 3497
Amenities: Tasting room, off-sales

The equipment at Copper Lake might look a little unorthodox, but there's a good reason for that. Pretty much the entire brewery – mash tun, fermenters, keg washers and all – was fabricated by hand; brewer Brendan Watcham's hands specifically.

"I built this brewery twice basically," he laughs. "Well, maybe that's a bit of an exaggeration, but I was learning as I was going along and a lot of things didn't quite work out so I would change it and do it again."

A metalworker and engineer by trade, Brendan was lucky enough to have the skills to build his own brewery once he decided to launch his beers commercially. His equipment has been gathered from a range of sources, including tanks from the Cullinan diamond mine, which he thinks were used to dispense beer to the workers. "Each brewery gives the beer its own character and makes it unique," says Brendan, making you eager to taste the beers originating in his idiosyncratic brew house.

"I actually first brewed beer in 1989," says Brendan, seeming surprised at the realisation that his first brew was over 20 years ago. It was kit beer that he brewed back then though, working from a homebrew recipe book of his father's that he'd found lying around the house. A lack of available ingredients led Brendan to bow out of brewing soon afterwards, though his interest in fermentation had obviously been captured.

His next venture was homemade wines, including vintages made from rosehip, mint and in an unlikely twist, beetroot – an experiment that Brendan perhaps under exaggerates as "not so good".

The interest in hobbyist alcohol production then lay dormant until 2009, when Brendan stumbled across the Wort Hog Brewers club online. "I decided to join as it had always been an interest in the back of my mind," says Brendan. "Then after a couple of meetings, I started brewing all-grain beer on a small system." He soon graduated from an urn and a bucket to his homemade three-tier system, which he later started manufacturing for the homebrewer with more than a passing interest in beer. But it was a freak occurrence that convinced Brendan to bow out of steelwork and turn his hobby into a career. "I had a motorbike accident and spent six months in bed," he explains. "I did a lot of thinking and realised I was tired of what I was doing and wanted to change my life. Brewing was what I enjoyed so I decided to start brewing commercially."

It was while Brendan was bedridden that he began studying for the Institute of Brewing and Distilling (IBD) diploma in brewing, later becoming the first independent brewer in Africa to be awarded the

Brendan previously had his own business engineering billboards and security gates. The welding and metalwork experience was invaluable, giving him the skills to build the entire Copper Lake Brewery from scratch.

diploma – something he urges other brewers to do. "Studying forces you to learn things that you might normally skip, like pH, minerals in the water and such. It gives you a great footing and background." He is now sponsoring another up-and-coming brewer to do the IBD, while he himself is studying for the IBD Master Brewer course.

Copper Lake was established in 2011, based in a workshop on Brendan's cattle farm a short hop from Lanseria Airport. He also owns a property in the Cradle of Humankind, a property that features a copper-coloured lake. "I liked it as a name because of the connotations towards beer," he says. "Copper

kettles, copper-coloured beer, and the idea of using lake water to brew." Brendan is keen to keep his business as green as possible, with about 30% of the brewery's power being solar and all spent grain being used as cattle feed. It's his hope that he can harness the methane produced by his 76 cows to become South Africa's first poo-powered brewery!

So far his trio of flagship beers have largely been available at festivals and special events, though there are plans to get into bottle stores and pubs in the region. Brendan also wants to start up a brewery bus tour, stopping at Copper Lake and taking in a number of the other breweries in the

TASTING NOTES

COPPER LAKE LAGER (4.5% ABV): A supremely drinkable lager, with enough malt and fruity flavours to offset the style's characteristic dry finish. A higher fermentation temperature than usual gives the beer its fruity edge.

COPPER LAKE ALE (5% ABV): A light, grassy hop aroma emerges from this copper-coloured beer. Cloves and fruit prevail on the palate, though Brendan plans to dry-hop in future for more of a flavour punch.

COPPER LAKE DARK LAGER (5% ABV): Using malt that Brendan roasts in his pizza oven (self-built of course), the Dark Lager smacks of coffee, both in aroma and taste. A subtle, underlying fruitiness offsets the bitterness.

area. He's also expanding his already vast brewery, joking that "he who dies with the biggest capacity wins". There are also more seasonal beers on the cards, which will come as a relief to those who tasted and adored Brendan's Double Chocolate Stout that won acclaim at the Clarens Craft Beer Festival. As well as the barley wine he makes for himself from the first runnings of every batch he brews, Brendan plans to make a Weissbier and what he calls a "queer beer", aimed at a gay audience. He's even contemplating getting back to his beetroots – using the veg to colour a beer. Considering the brewing knowledge and experience Brendan has gained since that early winemaking episode, there is little doubt that his beetroot booze will be a whole lot more successful this time around!

Ask the brewer

Is it true that "baby vomit" is a recognised off-flavour in beer?

"As unlikely as it sounds, yes it is true! Butyric is a yoghurty, baby puke aroma on a beer that has been contaminated with bacteria. It can also be caused by an unhappy yeast population. Apart from the unpleasant aroma and flavour, it won't make you ill."

DE GARVE BREWERY

Need to know...
Location: Olga Kirsch Street, Vanderbijlpark
Web: degarve.co.za **Tel:** 016 987 14 27/ 083 304 0197
Amenities: Tasting room, food pairing by appointment, off-sales

If homesickness can be defined as missing your home, then Patrick and Goedele van den Bon were almost definitely suffering from "beersickness" when they arrived in South Africa in 1980. You see, the Van den Bons hail from Belgium, so leaving a country with a cornucopia of beers to live in what was then a land of lagers was not an easy leap. It was 1982 when Patrick took up brewing – a year before the country's first microbrewery was launched and two Trappist-less years away from his beer-filled homeland.

"The early beers were … drinkable," laughs Patrick, not willing to give much more detail on the subject. "But in time the quality of the beer improved dramatically." Well, there was plenty of time for them to get better, for it would be more than two decades before Patrick would decide to turn his "hobby that got out of hand" into a small business. In 2005, reorganisation at work allowed Patrick to take a severance package – a deal that allowed him to introduce his out-of-control hobby to a wider audience.

Once the decision was made, Patrick decided that a little training in a commercial environment would be a good way to prepare for producing beer on a larger scale and he sought out the expertise of a fellow Gauteng brewer, Moritz Kallmeyer of Drayman's Brewery (see page 179) in Pretoria. "I spent a week with Moritz and learned quite a lot about brewing commercially," says Patrick. "Then in September 2007 we were ready." De Garve Brewery was born in an unlikely location on a farm outside of Vandebijlpark, its name from the Flemish for "sheave", referring to the bundles of barley harvested to make malt for brewing.

The brewery is a modest setup, made almost entirely from plastic (even the brew kettle) and remarkable in its strict spotlessness. The tap room sits

TASTING NOTES

GOLDEN BLONDE (4.5% ABV): Honey aromas suggest an overly sweet beer, but there's a perfect balance of sweet and bitter in this clear, golden ale.

MALT AND WALTZ (5% ABV): Upfront malt dominates as you inhale, though a mild spiciness lingers after sipping this Austrian-style ale. Try it with a dish that can match the spice.

JOLLY NUN (6.5% ABV): Spice and citrus aromas emerge from this Belgian-style blonde ale infused with lemon herbs. Caramelised sugar flavours offer a sweetness that is perceptible but not overpowering.

HAPPY MONK (6.5% ABV): Toffee and bubblegum aromas make this an unmistakeably Belgian brew, a complex collection of roasted, toffee-like flavours that pair well with rich desserts or blue cheese.

Look out also for De Garve's spicy Saison beer and the Premium Bitter, an English-style ale that's a great companion to a pie.

in Patrick's house, a cosy space where empty bottles from around the world bear testament to the couple's shared love of beer. The De Garve range covers styles from a quartet of countries, but their flagship ales, including award-winning Jolly Nun, are unashamedly Belgian in style – a brave first for a South African craft brewery. But it's not all about the beer for Patrick and Goedele. Food also plays a pivotal role in the De Garve experience, with pairings offered to small groups with advance bookings.

"I always tell people that when it comes to beer pairing the rules are that there actually are no rules," Patrick says. "Having said that, we tend to pair a lighter beer with lighter food and a more full-bodied beer with something more flavourful." You can quickly sense Goedele's shared passion for pairings as she shows off her collection of cookbooks featuring the kind of elaborate pairings you might normally expect with wine. But many of the Van den Bons' pairings come from experimentation rather than books, like the time a lactose-intolerant friend almost quashed Patrick's craving for pancakes. "Then we thought maybe we could swap the milk for beer and a new De Garve dish was born."

Stirring with a mash paddle helps keep the temperature even.

BELGIAN FLAVOURS – ANYTHING GOES

While German beer styles have long been stifled by the Reinheitsgebot, Belgian beers have never been subject to limitations, giving a range of ingredients found in no other beer culture. Expect herbs and spices, fruit and the liberal use of candi sugar. But the one thing that gives Belgian beer its unique aromas and flavours is the yeast used, driven by higher fermentation temperatures than are the norm. As well as imported Belgian beers, you can find Belgian-style beers at Clarens Brewery (see page 215), Devil's Peak (see page 67), the upcoming Honingklip Brewery (see page 246) and, of course, De Garve.

As the craft beer scene starts to explode in South Africa, Patrick is preparing to expand his brewery in order to distribute his brews to nearby bottle stores. For the most part though, the brews are available at festivals, markets and, of course, at the tap room, where you'll find "beers waiting for a change of ownership – against a suitable contribution."

Patrick fills the fermenter after a hard day's brewing.

Ask the brewer

Should different styles of beer be poured into different glasses?

"Yes. A light-bodied beer such as a pilsner or a blonde ale is best served in a flute type of glass. That way one can enjoy the delicate colour of the beer and the CO_2 bubbles rising. A full-bodied beer, such as an abbey beer, should be served in a chalice type of glass. This allows the aroma and bouquet of the beer to come out to the fullest."

HAPPY MONK BEEF STEW

RECIPE COURTESY OF GOEDELE VAN DEN BON OF DE GARVE BREWERY

For the best result, make this one or two days beforehand.

Heat the butter in a large saucepan and sauté the onions until translucent. Add the goulash and brown on all sides. Add the herbs, salt and pepper. Cover with a lid and simmer slowly.

After a short while, cover the meat with the Happy Monk ale. Add the bread and mustard, put the lid on and simmer for 4–5 hours or until soft. For extra thickness and meaty flavour, thicken with Bisto.

Enjoy with fried chips and a Happy Monk.

SERVES 4

50 g butter
2 onions, roughly chopped
1 kg cubed beef (goulash)
2–3 sprigs of thyme
1 bay leaf
Salt and pepper
500 ml Happy Monk
1 slice of bread
10 ml mustard of choice

BREW-IT-YOURSELF

De Garve Happy Monk

86.5% Pale malt
4% Abbey malt
3% Wheat malt
3% Carabelge
3% Caramunich
0.5% Dark malt

Hop additions:
PIH and T90 @ 20 minutes
EKG @ 10 minutes

BEER PANCAKES

RECIPE COURTESY OF GOEDELE VAN DEN BON OF DE GARVE BREWERY

Serve with a Belgian ale, such as De Garve's Jolly Nun. The sweetness of the beer makes it an ideal accompaniment to dessert, but the lemon herbs give this beer a light flavour that doesn't overpower the delicateness of the pancakes.

Beat the eggs and then add some of the beer. Slowly mix in the flour, constantly adding beer until you get the desired consistency. Let the mixture rest for at least 5 minutes, while you heat the pan.

Add a touch of oil to the pan and add just enough batter to coat the pan. Cook the pancake on a high heat, flipping after a couple of minutes.

Sprinkle the pancakes with cinnamon-sugar and enjoy with a Jolly Nun or another available Belgian beer.

SERVES 4–6

3 eggs
340 ml De Garve's Jolly Nun
175 g cake flour
Dash of sunflower oil
Cinnamon-sugar for serving

De Garve's flagship brew has won numerous local awards.

ALTSTADT

Hefe - Weissbier

DRAYMAN'S BREWERY

Hopfen und Malz Gott erhalts!

Drayman's Brewe
222 Dykor Rd
Silverton
Pretoria

Tel: 012 804-88
www.draymans.

Best before:
Mindestens haltbar bis

11.09.12

Alc 4% Vol

DRAYMAN'S BREWERY

Need to know...

Location: 222 Dykor Road, Silverton, Pretoria
Web: draymans.com **Tel:** 012 804 8800
Amenities: Off-sales, whisky tasting

Some things are just meant to be. Charles was meant to end up with Camilla, Juliet was destined to be without Romeo, and Moritz Kallmeyer was born to make booze. While most people trace their fermentation fascination back to their university days, Moritz's history with creating alcohol goes back much, much further. "When I used to go fishing with my father I collected the spent grains from the sorghum breweries which a lot of fishermen use to attract fish. I had some left over in a bucket and it started fermenting. That's when Philemon, one of the farm workers who was like my second father, explained how they made the beer and told me if I added some sugar it would start fermenting again. That was my exposure to fermentation as a young boy – I must have been in grade seven or eight."

From there Moritz's passion boomeranged, aided by a gift from his mother – a book on how to make your own wine. "I first made wine, fruit wine, at home long before I made beer," says Moritz. "I fermented it in the sock drawer of my cupboard! It was great exposure to the chemistry side and the hygiene side of fermentation." From there it was a quick leap into spirits – furtively distilling his first schnapps in a camping kettle when he was 15 and sneaking it into a biology class at school where his classmates passed it around, each one taking a swig. "I suppose that was laying the groundwork for my distilling career as well. Even though life took me in a different direction at first, I was going to come back to it in the end. It was meant to be. The passion was going to override everything else."

A career as a biokineticist beckoned, but the urge to ferment stuff was always there and when winemaking fell away at varsity, it was beer that would take over, thanks to some university housemates with a brew-it-yourself kit. "When I was working as a biokineticist, my hobby was in my garage – a fully fledged brewery. And what better audience than a gym full of people?" he grins. "If

As in many breweries, Drayman's labelling is often done by hand.

I had brought beer on any given morning I would advertise in the lifts that there would be a 'malt tea' at lunchtime in the gym. I couldn't call it a beer tasting, but people who knew my hobby put two and two together." This is where Moritz asked for criticism and fine-tuned his recipes – it's also where he met and converted Theo de Beer, now the brewmaster at Anvil Ale House (see page 209).

Eventually, the need to ferment won out and Moritz took a job at one of the country's earliest brewpubs, The Firkin in Pretoria. "Unfortunately it died a quick death," says Moritz. "It was way before its time." But graduating from his garage brewery had given him the push he needed and, in 1997, Moritz founded his own brewery, Drayman's. The brewery soon outgrew its original thatched home in Koedoespoort and moved to the Pretoria suburb of Silverton in 2000, where it remains to this day. Although successful now, the brewery didn't always flourish and Moritz turned to other types of fermentation to help make ends meet – and, of course, to indulge his passion for creating alcohol. Seven years ago he started a small-scale whisky operation and four years later added mampoer to the catalogue of mostly German-style beers.

Today the malty aromas from the mash tun mingle in the air with the sweet smell of distillation in this brewery that's a constant hive of activity. The recent additions of honey liqueur and Tej – Ethiopian mead – are as much about Moritz's passion to ferment as anything else, since he admits that the brewing side of things has finally taken off. "At last!" he enthuses. "It took 15 years but I'm so pleased that it's changing – we fought for a culture of beer and created a culture of flavour."

Moritz certainly had a hand in aiding that culture take off, offering honest opinions of other brewers' beers, training people that would later become his competition and even helping to set up a brewery, Misty Meadows (see page 83), along the Garden Route. Now this normally understated, pragmatic man effuses about South Africa's beer revolution even more than most. "Suddenly what I've been dreaming about is upon us," he gushes. "We live in very exciting times".

And for his part in the revolution, Moritz credits his mum, though the seeds were perhaps planted long before that DIY wine guide made it into Moritz's teenage hands. "Years after I started brewing I looked into the family history and discovered a huge amount of Kallmeyers in Munich and around Germany, many of whom were involved in the brewing industry. It just goes to show that if it's in the genes it's going to catch you!" As I said – it was meant to be.

Ask the brewer

What gives beer its head?

At least 40% of the protein in barley must be broken down to soluble compounds during the malting process to improve the colloidal stability of the final beer – basically to stop it from being too hazy. A smaller portion of the protein complement is also degraded during mashing. Some of the storage proteins in barley that are less easily dissolved are carried over into the final beer and are the origin of the components that make up beer foam, or head. Carry over too much protein and the beer foam will be good but the beer may also suffer from chill haze. Carry over too little and the beer foam will dissipate quickly, like when pouring a cider.

Moritz and his two true loves – sipping ale among whisky barrels.

MANNING THE DRAY

Traditionally, beer was transported from the brewery to its neighbouring pubs on a dray – a flat-bedded cart pulled by a horse. Moritz got the idea for his brewery's name from a varsity brewing buddy whose father had worked as a drayman in the United Kingdom. In South Africa, as in most places, horse-drawn deliveries have died out, but on the first Friday of each month you can listen out for hooves on tarmac as three kegs of Castle Lager are delivered from Newlands Brewery (see page 99) in Cape Town to a trio of nearby pubs.

TASTING NOTES

MORITZ'S LETZTER WUNCH HELLES (2.5% ABV): Although your "last wish" might be a more potent brew, this light beer is surprisingly full-flavoured, with tropical fruits and malty undertones on the nose that continue on the palate. It's a light, refreshing beer with a clean, dry finish – perfect for summer braais or sipping at the cricket.

BERGHOF (4% ABV): Drayman's most popular beer is a lager-like brew but fermented at higher temperatures, giving it a hint of the fruity flavours associated with an ale. Light-bodied and subtle in its flavour, expect toast aromas and a bitter finish.

ALTSTADT HEFE WEISSBIER (4% ABV): Cloudy and straw-coloured, this has the perfect appearance of a German Weissbier, though it's far lighter in body. Fennel aromas and flavours leave a fresh, minty and almost buchu-like aftertaste.

GOBLIN'S BITTER (4% ABV): A beautifully clear, copper-coloured ale with smoky nose with undertones of malt. Layers of flavour first offer hops, then follow up with roasted malt. Like all of Drayman's beers, this is a lighter-bodied version of the British original.

JOLLY MONK RAUCHBIER (4% ABV): A dark brown beer with copper tones, almost too dark to see through. Flavours are not as smoky as you might expect (rauchbier is German for "smoke beer"), but it's a very drinkable brew with a smack of crème brûlée and an aftertaste reminiscent of coffee beans.

Look out also for the Düssel Altbier and the seasonal Emperor India Pale Ale, an English IPA available only in summer.

GILROY

120 years behind the times

Create Your Own Basket

Choose your favourite items from the selection below to make your perfect basket.

GILROY BREWERY

Need to know...
Location: Off the R114, Muldersdrift
Web: gilroybeers.co.za **Tel:** 011 796 3020
Amenities: Restaurant, beer tasting, live entertainment, brewery tours

Steve Gilroy has been on the South African brewing scene, one way or another, for over 40 years and describes himself as "like the granddad … well, a cross between a granddad and a naughty Father Christmas". Never has a more appropriate description been tendered for this white-haired, long-bearded brewer who seems as innocent as a greeting card Santa … until he opens his mouth. Steve is known for his outspoken nature, his no-holds-barred opinions and, of course, for giving the finger to anyone who gets in his way – a challenge, he says, to other brewers to brew better beers than Gilroy's.

Locals and tourists alike flock to his Muldersdrift brewpub on weekends to soak up the jaunty vibe, listen to live music, hear one of Steve's renowned poems and to join in his cheery toast of "up yours".

"We're not in the beer business," Steve muses. "A lot of brewers don't realise what business they're in – it's the entertainment business. Entertainment is inherently the backbone of any successful pub." Of course, he is also in the beer business and has been brewing one way or another since he "recently" moved to South Africa. By recently, Steve means 1970 – "well, it was after the Boer War," he adds. Hailing first from Ireland, but with a Liverpool and London upbringing, Steve was used to a certain style of beer when he came to South Africa and will tell you in no uncertain terms that he was, let's say, underwhelmed by the beer available. "It doesn't take me long to get pissed off," he says. "And it took three months before desperation became the

mother of inspiration." Back in those post-Boer War days, equipment and supplies were almost impossible to come by so Steve sourced malt extract wherever he could, often from relatives with a little extra suitcase space visiting from Europe.

Steve's working history is as chequered and colourful as his conversation – starting as a rock musician for controversial and oft-banned seventies rock band Suck, then moving from playing the guitar to "playing the pornograph". A stint in the "nudey photo business" followed, before Steve settled down to a more staid career running a pharmaceutical printing company. It was then that his beers started to reach a wider audience. The brewery was moved from home to the printing shop, where brokers would regularly request a new batch of beer. Then after years offering tastings in bottle stores, it was time to take the leap. "This wasn't a business decision," says Steve. "If it had been a business decision I probably wouldn't have done it! But I didn't want to be in the rat race anymore – I wanted to have fun."

When you look around the English-style pub sporting the occasional nudey photo, a range of newspaper cuttings showing Steve in his bow tie and waistcoat regalia and the Gilroy coat of arms, featuring the famous outstretched finger, you sense that he definitely achieved this goal. The brewery and pub opened in 2008 and quickly developed a cult following of people keen to try the traditional English-style ales with a little English-style humour on the side. Steve seems like a natural publican, but he'd never worked behind bars before. "I'd never been in hospitality, never run a pub or a restaurant, but shit you learn fast when you're losing money!" he reminisces.

The brewery was an almost instant hit though, and Steve has since trained two other brewers to assist with the daily brews. After years with the beers available only at the pub and one or two selected outlets, Steve is now looking to expand. "We have plans to go into bottle stores around the province," he says. "But I've got to cut down on my drinking a bit first so that we can meet demand." There's also talk of a second pub opening east of Johannesburg, though plans are in the pre-infancy stage.

In the meantime, Gilroy's has become a mini Mecca for homebrewers, who meet here for monthly Wort Hogs get-togethers or drop in to

TASTING NOTES

GILROY LAGER (3.5% ABV): Low on carbonation and hazy in appearance, this light lager is a leap for the staunch lager drinker, but a good intro to craft beer. The lack of aftertaste leaves you wanting more, making this a true session beer.

GILROY FAVOURITE (4% ABV): Copper in colour and, like all of Gilroy's beers, low in head retention. There's a mildly malty aroma to this pale ale and fuller flavours of caramel and toffee.

GILROY TRADITIONAL (5% ABV): You'll struggle to find aroma in this ruby ale, but there's a definite flavour of molasses when you sip.

GILROY SERIOUS (7.5% ABV): A more potent version of the Traditional, with more prominent flavours of roasted malt and caramelised sugar.

buy supplies from the on-site shop. For those who prefer to keep to the theory of brewing, Steve offers weekly beer experience tours, laced with his particular brand of wit, or if you like to keep your drinking sessions insult-free, drop in for a taster tray or a pint and don't sit near the stage when Steve takes to the floor.

Steve performs his cutting poems on weekends, often covering politics and current affairs. Whatever the subject matter, every performance ends with the official Gilroy's mantra of "up yours!".

THREE SKULLS BREW WORKS

Need to know...
Location: 70, 5th Street, Wynberg, Johannesburg
Web: threeskulls.co.za **Tel:** 083 403 6661 **Amenities:** Three Skulls
beers are available at selected bars and bottle stores around the country

"Conventional thinking in an unconventional way" – that's how Jonathan Nel, the driving force behind Three Skulls, describes the brewery's ethos. Actually, it might be just as fair to say that it is Jonathan's wife, Michelle, who is the driving force behind the brewery. "I was no longer enjoying my job," explains Jonathan, "and she basically said 'You're not doing what you love anymore. Why don't you leave and set up your own brewery? Do what makes you happy because at the moment you suck!' So I did – I left and registered my company a week later."

The job that Jonathan refers to was also the thing that got him interested in brewing. He worked at SAB for six years, first in brand activations and later in innovations – both branches of the marketing department. Through work he got to attend the inaugural Cape Town Festival of Beer, which is where he was first introduced to craft beer. "I suddenly realised that I had very little idea of how you actually make beer, so I asked my wife for a homebrew kit for Christmas."

That was in 2010 and Jonathan didn't wait long to get moving, making his first batch after lunch on Christmas Day. "At the beginning I did two Cooper's kits – one was a spectacular failure and one was good," Jonathan laughs, more than willing to explain the failure. "It was because I didn't quite grasp that you have to ferment at a certain temperature and I left it by a large window. I came home one day and saw that the temperature was 29 degrees. I tasted it and it was basically nail polish remover!"

After tipping it down the drain and perfecting the next batch, he moved on to "beer in a bag" – a way to brew an all-grain beer without a lot of equipment. "I made a Belgian witbier for the Wort Hogs summer festival and the judges scored it a 40 (out of 50). I think that's what really set it off. It made me realise that either they're completely taste blind or I can actually make good beer!" So when his birthday came around in June, an all-grain system was at the top of the gift list. "I was still working at SAB then, so I used to take my beers to the SAB tasters – they really helped me to improve my beers." Not long afterwards Jonathan had that fateful conversation with his wife and decided to leave the company. "I wasn't happy at SAB anymore. I learnt a lot there and I'm thankful for that, but I had to go and do it, to try it."

Three Skulls was born soon afterwards, a concept that Jonathan came up with by "taking everything I learnt at SAB and

then doing the complete opposite". He's quick to explain what he means by that: "The rules of beer say that if you're going to release a beer in South Africa then the South African consumer wants a green bottle, a gold cap, gold foil, German heritage and hops they've maybe heard of or are at least easy to pronounce. So I looked at all of those rules and wanted to make something that you look at say 'there's no way that's a beer brand and if it is, that's really rad'."

For Jonathan, a veteran of corporate marketing, Three Skulls is all about the brand and not about him. "I'm just the guy who makes the beer!" he says. "And washes the kegs and cleans the floor of course!" He is currently running a one-man show at his modest brewery in Johannesburg's northern suburbs. There are no plans for a tap room at this stage, but Jonathan promises his beer will be appearing in some pretty weird and funky places soon.

So far it seems that the plan to create an über-cool brand is working. After a promotion campaign played out solely on Twitter and Facebook, the brewery everyone was looking for at the 2011 Clarens Craft Beer Festival was Three Skulls. It was as much about the beers as the fresh and funky logo though, with people seeking out the duo of brews – a well-hopped American IPA and a Weissbier flavoured with lavender, mango and passion fruit. "I wanted people to look at the beer guide for Clarens, skim through it and say 'What?! I want to try this!'" says Jonathan, but it wasn't just a publicity stunt. There is a rule book at Three Skulls, but Jonathan loves to throw it out, adding spices to his beers, brewing unusual styles and above all keeping people guessing on what the brewery might put out next. "We will have flagship beers, but you can almost bet your house that there will always be something off-centre, something a little crazy," says Jonathan. "Three Skulls are never going to make the same thing all the time. Of course we will have our staples, but at festivals, especially if you want to taste something fantastic, look for the Three Skulls logo and I'm pretty sure we'll have what you're looking for."

Chilling the beer ready to fill the fermenters.

TASTING NOTES

THE SAUCE (3.2% ABV): This Belgian-style saison beer has a wheat beer-like appearance and a luscious creamy head. Orange peel notes on the nose draw you into a refreshing, summer beer with a touch of spice.

ACE OF SPADES (6.5% ABV): The use of de-husked Carafa Special malt gives the deep, deep colour of a stout without the excessive bitterness that roasted malt can often lend. That said, the stouty flavours are in attendance, with pleasant coffee notes and a rich, roasty finish.

Also look out for the Three Skulls entry-level beer, Gravedigger American Blonde Ale, and the more robust Golden Skull IPA.

Ask the brewer

What gives stout its dark colour?

"The base ingredient in beer is grain and this can be in the form of malted barley, wheat, oats, rye or any grain on the planet. Pale malted barley is roasted at maltsters to give it a darker colour which in turn provides for different flavours like coffee, chocolate or toffee. Stouts in particular use the darkest or black malts which have been roasted for the longest to give the brewer the darkest colour and the most intense roasty flavours."

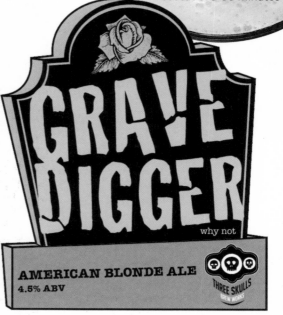

BREW-IT-YOURSELF
Gravedigger American Blonde Ale

80% Pale malt

7% Carafoam/Carapils

5.5% Light crystal

5.5% Vienna malt

Hop additions:

Centennial @ 60 minutes

Cascade @ 30 minutes

Three Skulls launched at the 2012 Clarens Craft Beer Festival.

SAB
The South African Breweries

THE SAB WORLD OF BEER

Welcome

Gambrinus: King of Beer

THE SAB WORLD OF BEER

Need to know...

Location: Gerard Sekoto Street, Johannesburg
Web: worldofbeer.co.za **Tel:** 011 836 4900 **Amenities:** Guided tours,
pub lunches, beer memorabilia shop, conferencing

If you needed proof that South Africa's beer culture is ready for launch, you only have to take a look around Johannesburg's Newtown district. There, in the city's revamped tourist quarter, near the illustrious Gramadoelas Restaurant and the eclectic exhibits of Museum Africa, sits what is definitely the city's most light-hearted museum, SAB's World of Beer. This homage to the amber nectar opened in 1995 to celebrate SAB's centenary and serves as a whirlwind lesson into the history, production and appreciation of beer.

The exhibits are delightfully tongue-in-cheek and at times borderline baffling in their silliness, perfectly portraying the down-to-earth nature that beer prides itself on. The 90-minute guided tour begins with a voice from beyond the grave as Charles Glass, founder of SAB's forerunner, the Castle Brewery, welcomes you. Audiovisual exhibits then take you through the early history of beer, beginning with an enjoyably cheesy 3D peek into ancient Egypt. Things then go local, with the slightly sour smell of sorghum beer filling the air as a video fills you in on the history and culture of traditional South African beer. There's a chance to taste the murky brew from a communal clay pot before delving into European beer lore. You're quickly transported back to South Africa though, with a mid-tour beer stop in a gold rush-era tavern and a walk through a mock-up 1960s shebeen.

Part two of the tour introduces novices and know-it-alls alike to beer's ingredients and gives an overview of the brewing process that's informative without being too technical. Even in the most science-laden parts of the tour, the sense of fun remains, with comments like "can you feel the heat? Well that wort certainly can as this is the hottest part of the process" emblazoned on the information panels. There's plenty of chance to munch on malt as you peek into copper kettles and press buttons to release the heady aromas of each stage in the brewing process. A video of what for many is the most mesmerising stage of a large-scale brewery tour rounds off the visit, with images of the never-ending bottling line flashing across a series of screens.

The tour naturally ends up in the on-site pub, where your ticket entitles you to two beers of your choice as you take in the brilliantly bizarre whirlwind tour of beer that has just been presented to you. It's not every country that can boast a museum dedicated to beer and the World of Beer is a perfect place to begin your education – welcome to Beer 101.

North West Province

BRAUHAUS AM DAMM

Need to know...

Location: On the R24 at Olifantsnek Dam, near Rustenburg
Web: brauhaus.co.za **Tel:** 087 802 5519
Amenities: Restaurant, beer tasting, off-sales

Every brewer has a story, but in the case of Brauhaus am Damm, the brewery itself also has a tale to tell. Described by brewer Imke Pape as "the Rolls-Royce of breweries", the 1 000-litre system is indeed a fine specimen of beer equipment, but the copper kettles are more than just a pretty face. This system was the lifeblood of one of South Africa's earliest microbreweries, much-loved Farmers' Brewery in Hattingspruit, KwaZulu-Natal. It helped realise the lifelong dream of a German expat, Otto Martin, who set up the brewery in 1993. It saw thousands of tourists and loyal locals pass through to sip on the oft-talked about Farmers' Draught and it was there in 2009 when the Farmers' Brewery closed its doors for the last time. But as Otto's son, Josef, was quoted in the most impassioned obituary you'll ever read for a brewpub, "the brewery is not dead".

It has been reincarnated in a grand setting on the edge of the Olifantsnek Dam near Rustenburg. Imke takes up the story where the Martin family left off: "Very good friends of ours, Walter and Christine Stallmann, went to Hattingspruit in 2008. The brewery had been closed for a while by then and

the beer they tasted was two years old, but it was the best beer they'd ever had!" Walter and Christine decided there and then that they wanted to buy the brewery, despite having no brewing knowledge or background. They headed home to try and get further backing for the brewery, which is where Imke comes into the story. "They sat here and said we are going to buy this brewery together. We said no – we don't know anything about brewing; no, we're not doing this – but, of course, here we are!" laughs Imke.

Challenges rained down – they had no premises, no brewer and a brewery sitting almost 500 km away, but gradually the solutions appeared. The first job was to move the brewery, an event that Imke remembers fondly. "We went down to Hattingspruit and labelled every part of the brewery. We also took thousands of photos because we didn't know where anything went and needed to know how to put it back together afterwards!"

The brewery was dismantled at the start of 2009 and placed into storage until task number two was tackled – finding premises for the new brewery. After looking around the Rustenburg region to no avail, Imke decided to sell a 10-hectare piece of the farm she was born on to the brewing consortium, making sure that the pub and restaurant would always enjoy uninterrupted views over the dam. In July 2009, construction of the impressive, airy building began, its expansive deck and vast windows all helping to make the most of the brewery's picturesque setting.

Now there was just one problem left to solve – the question of who was going to brew the beer. It was Imke who came to the rescue. "When we were dismantling the brewery I saw that this was a big thing and I wanted to be a part of it," she says. "I can cook but I didn't want to cook in a restaurant, so I decided to turn my hand to brewing. I started

Beer is pumped directly from the serving tanks to the bar above.

getting every book I could find on brewing and for two years I read, slept and drank beer. Then, when I finished the books I turned back and read them again!" With the theory part covered, it was time to get brewing. Imke started small – with a pot on the stove – before brewing with Heiko Feuring, a close friend who happens to be a qualified brewmaster, with whom she devised the Dunkel recipe that is one of Am Damm's flagship beers today.

But the beer education didn't stop there – Imke next headed for Europe, where she spent a week brewing and learning the all-important cellar work with Hanover-based microbrewery HBX. Next up was a gruelling fortnight in Vienna, brewing eight times on the same system that the Am Damm team had bought from Hattingspruit. "It was really, really intense," Imke recalls, clearly glad she doesn't yet have that hectic of a brew schedule. "I was finished afterwards!" But another mad brew session would follow a year later when Hanover brewer Klemens Schell visited Am Damm to help get the brewery running smoothly. Brauhaus am Damm then had three of their flagship recipes sorted – the Dunkel developed with Heiko, a Pilsner recipe from Hanover and the beer that started it all – the Farmers' Draught, which was bought from Hattingspruit along with the equipment.

The brewing is only part of it though – the hardest work comes afterwards, as Imke will tell you. "Brewers are the best paid cleaners in the world," she says, pausing for effect. "Well, when they get paid, that is! If you don't clean every single day it will bring trouble and then you are finished."

In November 2011, Brauhaus am Damm opened its doors, serving German-style beers and hearty food to match. In fact, the German backing is evident throughout – not only in the food and beer, but also in the hi-tech and über-organised cellar housing fermenters and shiny tanks from which the draught beer is pumped directly in this keg-free operation. Imke is rightly as proud of the equipment as she is of the beers and much of it is on show for patrons to inspect and admire. When she brews, she is out in the open for all to watch, although Imke is constantly surprised at how few people stop to ask questions or watch the work that's going into their pint.

Brauhaus am Damm's first year has been a big one, with an award at the Clarens Craft Beer Festival and their beers being embraced both by locals and Gauteng day-trippers. But there is much to do, with a basement sports bar due to open, seasonal brews to perfect, a yeast propagator to fathom and, of course, an annual Oktoberfest planned. But Imke, in her inimitable cheery manner, has no doubt that they'll achieve everything eventually, just as she achieved her goal to become a brewer. "If you want to do something badly enough," she says, "you will succeed, but you *really* have to want it."

Next to godliness: equipment sterilising in the spotless brewery.

REINHEITSGEBOT RULES

Brauhaus am Damm brew all their beers, with the exception of the Weiss, to the Reinheitsgebot or German Purity Law. Passed in Bavaria in the sixteenth century, the law states that only water, barley and hops can be used to make beers. Yeast is conspicuous in its absence from the list – back then brewers didn't know of its existence so it was not considered an ingredient in its own right.

TASTING NOTES

FARMERS' DRAUGHT (4.2% ABV): The beer that launched the brewery could be considered craft beer 101. Dry and mildly malty, it's a straightforward beer and an easy leap for a lager drinker.

BRAUHAUS PILSNER (4.8% ABV): Although unfiltered, like all of Am Damm's beers, the pilsner is a clear, amber-coloured pint. Subtle malty and fruity aromas and a slight honey sweetness make this not as dry as a pilsner can be.

BRAUHAUS DUNKEL (5% ABV): This classic example of the German dark beer uses five different malts. It's quite light in body though, with aromas of coffee and chocolate and a dry, roasty flavour.

Also look out for the full-flavoured light beer and the Weiss, both available in the warmer months. A Pilsner/Dunkel mix is available, with the latter's roast flavours cutting through the sweetness of the Pilsner.

BREWERS' PIZZA BASE

RECIPE COURTESY OF GREG CASEY, OWNER OF BANANA JAM CAFÉ

Thanks to a trio of shared ingredients – yeast, grain and water – there is no better accompaniment for beer than pizza. This recipe also uses beer as an ingredient in the base, just to make that perfect pairing even better.

Mix the cake flour, bread flour and salt in a bowl.

Heat the beer and water until tepid (not too hot or you will kill the yeast). Add the sugar and yeast and let it sit for a few minutes so that the yeast can start to react with the sugars.

Pour the flour mixture onto a clean work surface and make a well in the centre.

Pour the olive oil, beer and yeast mixture into the well and slowly start to mix the flour into the wet ingredients.

Knead the dough until smooth and silky, using the extra flour to keep the dough from sticking to the table. Once the dough is smooth, place it in a large bowl, cover and set aside in a warm place for 1½ hours.

Once the dough has risen to twice its original size, knock it down and divide the dough into 4 balls.

Let the balls rise for 30 minutes and then roll out the pizza bases using more flour so that they don't stick to the counter.

Preheat the oven to 230 °C.

Add desired toppings to your pizza – a suggestion that pairs well with Brauhaus am Damm's Dunkel (an excellent food beer) is pepperoni, artichoke, bacon and chilli.

Bake the pizzas for 10–15 minutes. For the best – and crispiest – results, use a pizza pan or pizza stone.

MAKES 4 PIZZA BASES

200 g cake flour
300 g bread flour
15 g salt
300 ml Brauhaus am Damm Farmers' Draught (or a similar lighter beer that won't colour the base or have too strong a flavour)
60 ml water
15 g sugar
1 x 7 g packet dry yeast
15 ml olive oil
Extra bread flour for mixing

CHAMELEON BREWHOUSE

Need to know...

Location: Chameleon Village, R104, Hartbeespoort
Web: chameleonbrewhouse.co.za **Tel:** 072 369 2309
Amenities: Light lunches, shopping, off-sales

"It took one sip and we were hooked" – that's how Amanda van den Berg sums up the beer awakening that started on a journey to Germany in 2006, a journey that led her and husband Ruaan to open the Chameleon Brewhouse six years later.

"We visited Germany as part of a European tour," explains Ruaan. "It was then that we tasted Weiss beer for the very first time in a small town called Weikersheim. We loved it and in the next town we went to we walked into a pub and asked for a Weiss. We were so stupid – we thought that Weiss was a brand name!"

Then Ruaan and Amanda realised that they couldn't get the beer made just a couple of towns away, but that each little town had its own brewery. It was this realisation that stirred something within. "We said we'd do anything to be able to have this beer at home – steal, borrow, import it … but when we came back I couldn't find anybody selling Weiss beer." There was only one option for Ruaan to get his Weiss fix – he decided he'd have to start making it himself.

Luckily the Wort Hog Brewers club was on hand to assist and after a few meetings Ruaan launched into all-grain brewing. Ruaan reckons he and Amanda must have "tasted" (or drunk) around 750 litres of homebrew over the next two years – a fact he recalls with a slightly embarrassed grin. But he's quick to add that it was all with good reason. "You have to brew as much as you can – that's how you learn the trade and that's how you learn from your mistakes."

The new passion also rekindled some old friendships in the form of André de Beer of the Cockpit Brewhouse (see page 159) and Stephan Meyer of Clarens Brewery (see page 215) – both old university buddies of Ruaan's. Their support is still evident around the brewery – Ruaan's boiler and mash tun came from Stephan, his hot liquor tank from André, and there's a lot of recipe-sharing love going around. The rest of the brewery though, Ruaan built from scratch. A mechanical engineer by trade, Ruaan hopes to turn the brewing into a full-time occupation one day. "Stephan says everyone must have a new career at 50," he laughs. "But of course we knew when we set it up that it wouldn't happen in a year."

André and Stephan also encouraged Ruaan to take the BJCP (Beer Judge Certification Program) test, an internationally recognised exam that qualifies you to judge beer in competitions. Although challenging, Ruaan encourages all brewers to take the exam as he did. "I've never learnt so much in such a short time as when I was studying for the BJCP. I think anybody in homebrewing or craft beer should do that exam so that you have the ability to recognise off-flavours before you present your beers to anybody."

It is usually Amanda who presents their beers to the public, in the cute little brewpub, perfectly placed in a setting frequented by tourists both domestic and international. "We were looking for a touristy spot," explains Ruaan but they ruled out their first choices: Pilgrim's Rest, Hazyview and Swakopmund (Namibia). "Our 16-year-old son did not take the relocation idea well!" says Amanda. But when it came to taking the premises at the Chameleon Village just north of the Hartbeespoort Dam the decision was two parts fate, one part luck. "We were here one day just for fun," Amanda recalls. "Through a series of coincidences we ended up meeting the landlord and before we left that day we'd already decided to take the unit." It's the perfect spot to enjoy a beer in the sun and an ideal family venue, its outdoor tables nestled among curio stalls and one-off home décor shops.

So what about the beers? Well, Chameleon offers a great range offering something for all palates. "In the last year-and-a-half I really started brewing nice beers – I hope I can say that," grins Ruaan. "They have won some awards." And did he ever re-create the beer that set the whole thing in motion? "Of course – it was the second beer I ever brewed!" says Ruaan of his Weiss named for the town where they first tasted it. They tested it out on German friends before launching it to critical acclaim at the 2012 Clarens Craft Beer Festival. But while Weiss was the beer that started it all, Ruaan and Amanda are certainly not stuck on one flavour. "We worked our way from the blonde to the Weiss and later to the APA," says Ruaan, "and now we're both addicted to hops."

Their hankering for hops might of course come from their other major source of inspiration – American brewer Sam Calagione of Dogfish Head Brewery. "Oh, we love him," Amanda enthuses.

TASTING NOTES

WEIKERSHEIM WEISS (4.7% ABV): Ripe bananas and bubblegum notes punch you in the nose, with the former following through on flavour in this, a lighter-bodied version of a classic Weissbier.

BLONDE ALE (4.5% ABV): Pale gold in colour with aromas of smoke, malt and a touch of grass, leading you into an easy-drinker with a dry, crisp, biscuit flavour.

ENGLISH BITTER (4.7% ABV): An almost savoury aroma of nuts and coffee. Smoky and dry but endlessly drinkable, it's the perfect partner for biltong.

PALE ALE (4.6% ABV): A hopful awakening with tropical fruits on the nose and a clean, grassy flavour. Enjoy it with a strong cheese like Gruyère.

STOUT (5% ABV): It's lighter in body than many stouts, but this beer doesn't scrimp on taste. It's full of bold coffee flavours, with a big, bitter finish.

I like cider but I ordered beer – why does my beer taste like cider?

"If you taste cider in your beer you are either drinking an American Light Lager-style beer where the aroma of green apples is acceptable or your beer has a bacterial infection. Another cause can be premature removal from the yeast. Both causes responsible for the off taste can be overcome by allowing the fermentation to complete and the practice of good sanitation to avoid infection. This characteristic in beer is called acetaldehyde."

"We read all his books, watch all his shows – we just haven't had the chance to taste his beers! He motivates you so much," she continues. "We close from Monday to Wednesday and sometimes it's difficult to get back into the swing of things on a Thursday, but if you watch an episode of *Brewmasters* you just feel like – yes, let's go to work tomorrow – let's go brew some beer!"

Amanda doesn't brew with Ruaan, but she's deeply involved in the brewery. Aside from running the pub itself she has a crucial role in the Chameleon Brewhouse. "I use Amanda as my tester for the first beer of each batch. She always has a very straight opinion of the beers!"

With five beers permanently on the repertoire, she has plenty to taste and might well have more to taste in future months. Ruaan plans to brew speciality one-off beers, including something extreme and out of the ordinary. And if you're not a fan of extreme beer, you know there'll always be a steady stream of the inspirational Weiss on tap – provided the locals don't drink him dry that is.

WATERZOOI

RECIPE COURTESY OF FRANC LUBBE, EXECUTIVE CHEF AT THE MOUNT GRACE

Serve with a Weiss beer, such as Chameleon's Weikersheim Weiss. Chef Franc says: "The crisp flavours of the Chameleon Weiss are always well suited for a Waterzooi, or any fish dish for that matter, provided that it is not too salty."

SAUCE

Begin by preparing a fish stock. Place the kingklip bones, onions, celery, garlic, wine, leeks, bay leaves, peppercorns and water into a large saucepan. Bring to the boil and simmer for 45 minutes. Strain the stock, place the liquid back over high heat and reduce to a strong fish essence. In a separate pan, reduce the cream by half. Add the cream to the fish essence and season with salt and pepper. Stir in the molasses.

STEW

Pour a generous helping of the sauce into a large saucepan and arrange the seafood and potatoes in the sauce. Cover with a lid and simmer for approximately 8 minutes until all the seafood is just cooked (be careful not to overcook and cause the seafood to become tough and rubbery). Drizzle the Pernod over the stew and carefully stir it in, avoiding breaking up the seafood.

Ladle the stew into a soup or stew bowl and top with the julienne vegetables, chives and tomato.

Serve immediately with a glass of cold Weiss beer.

FOR THE SAUCE
(MAKES 10 PORTIONS)

2 kg kingklip bones, roughly chopped
2 large onions, sliced
300 g celery, roughly chopped
1 garlic bulb, roughly chopped
500 ml dry white wine
300 g leeks, roughly chopped
3 bay leaves
10 white peppercorns
5 litres water
3 litres fresh cream
Salt and freshly ground white pepper
25 ml molasses

FOR THE STEW
(MAKES 1 PORTION)

3 medium-sized prawns, deveined
3 scallops in shell with roe
60 g portion of Scottish salmon
60 g portion of kingklip
3 clams in shell
3 mussels in shell
3 new potatoes, peeled and precooked
15 ml Pernod

FOR THE GARNISH
(MAKES 1 PORTION)

10 ml julienne of each red, yellow and green sweet pepper, soaked in ice water
10 ml julienne of leek, soaked in ice water
10 ml julienne of red cabbage, soaked in ice water
5 ml thinly sliced chives
10 ml tomato brunoise (diced tomato)

IRISH ALE HOUSE

Need to know...

Location: Jalapor Road, Broederstroom
Web: alehouse.co.za **Tel:** 082 464 9387
Amenities: Pub, pizzas, family friendly

Every craft beer culture needs a maverick brewer, a guy who would not only throw out the rule book, but would never deign to buy a rule book in the first place. In South Africa, that guy is Dirk van Tonder. Dirk sits at the helm of the Irish Ale House, probably South Africa's most rustic brewpub, sitting on a 4.5-hectare "beer farm" amid a network of dirt roads in Broederstroom.

Dirk's journey into craft beer began how most brewers start out – taking up the hobby of home-brewing. "I stumbled across it on the internet," says Dirk. "I skipped kit and extract brewing and went straight into all-grain and into kegs. Eventually I started annoying my wife in the kitchen, so we ended up buying the land here in 2004 – then I had plenty of space to brew without getting in the way."

The brewery is a small but shiny setup sitting in a one-room building, whose cement walls are washed with local sand to blend in with the dusty surrounds. Here Dirk brews, in his words, "whatever I can get my hands on". His flagship beer though is a blonde ale, generously hopped, unfiltered and carbonated only slightly. The recipe, he admits, changes depending on the grain and hops available, but it's a well-made brew that will satisfy any hankering for hops. This is particularly true when Dirk, a definite hophead, brews what he calls his "trailer trash blonde" – a similar recipe but one where he's heavy-handed with the Cascade (an American hop). A sole fermenter means he can only brew once every couple of weeks, but there are other craft beers from around the country permanently available, so there's no danger of an ale-free ale house.

Tastings take place in the Ale House proper, a larger version of the building housing the brewery, with rustic fittings and dim but atmospheric lighting.

Dirk likes to do things his own way, and that includes taking some of the brewing process outside.

Anglo-Boer War. Dirk is as passionate about the history side as he is about the beer and says that the Ale House is essentially a monument. "I had these relics that had been passed down in my family and I wanted to make a monument. But I thought – why build them another piece of granite? Why not build an ale house? The beer thing just happened and I thought – what a nice marriage."

There are no TVs and Dirk is proud of the fact that no sports game, however important, will ever be shown in his pub. It's a place for a tranquil sunset pint or a family afternoon munching on pizza and getting acquainted with Dirk's donkeys, which are as much a part of the brewery as he is. When Dirk is brewing, the donkeys are never far away. "They can smell the boil and they know they're going to get a good feed in a couple of hours – the spent grain is incredibly nutritious." And, of course, if there's ever a petrol crisis, Dirk would be one of few people who could still deliver beer. "I can just hitch on the donkey cart and be away!" he says.

This essence of stepping back in time is also the root of success behind Dirk's other baby, The Solstice Festival. Established in 2008, it is one of the country's oldest craft beer festivals and offers a totally different vibe to anything you'll find elsewhere. Bagpipes play, vendors sell chain mail and jester hats, and tipsy patrons pay to throw tomatoes at presumably equally tipsy participants. Dirk started the festival for two equally charming reasons: first, a simple love of beer and a desire to get the region's brewers together; second, to

The "Irish" part of the Ale House moniker refers not to any beers available or beer styles brewed here, but to a little-remembered piece of history that is close to Dirk's heart. His pub is part homage to beer and part homage to the Irish Brigade who sided with the Boers rather than the English during the

TASTING NOTES

ALE HOUSE BLONDE (4% ABV): Unfiltered and cloudy, Dirk's flagship blonde is a smooth and fruity beer, with a pleasant bitter finish. An assertive hop character will please lovers of the *lupulus* but isn't too overpowering for the uninitiated.

make a little extra cash so that he can fly his daughter over from Europe for an annual visit.

Speaking of Europe, I wondered if Dirk had any plans to visit Ireland, considering his historical interests and obvious passion for beer. It's obviously a question he's been asked many times before as his answer was quick and clear: "Oh no, I don't want to go there – I won't come back."

There's always something on tap at the Ale House, but until you get there, you're not quite sure what it will be.

Dirk describes his 4.5-hectare property as a "beer farm", though he also makes pretty awesome pizzas.

Mpumalanga

ANVIL ALE HOUSE

———— ————

Need to know...
Location: Main Street, Dullstroom
Web: anvilbrewery.com **Tel:** 073 168 6603
Amenities: Light lunches, beer tasting, off-sales

Fate often has a funny sense of humour. For instance, who would have thought that a painful back injury could have launched first a new hobby and eventually a successful brewpub serving a range of perfectly executed beers? As with other brewers in South Africa, Moritz Kallmeyer of Drayman's (see page 179) had a hand in the brewing career of Anvil Ale House's Theo de Beer. But rather than seeking out Moritz's widely respected expertise, you could say that Theo had greatness thrust upon him.

"I'd had a back op and Moritz did my rehab," Theo recalls. "He had me captive on a bicycle where you're pedalling like hell and not going anywhere, all the time yapping at my side about beer." By the end of the rehabilitation, Moritz had successfully converted Theo from a hobbyist winemaker into a homebrewer. This was over 30 years ago and Theo hasn't stopped brewing since.

It had always been just a hobby, but when a career change beckoned, Theo and his wife, Sarie, fancied starting a business in the hospitality industry – an industry they somewhat knew after years working in nature reserves. That's how Theo ended up with his first brewpub, Hops Hollow on the Long Tom Pass. "After the '94 election, the whole world wanted to come to South Africa and, of course,

Theo busy filtering his latest brew.

BEER FOR BREAKFAST?

No one bats an eyelid if you sip a flute of champagne for breakfast, so why not a glass of beer? We're not suggesting that you down a pint of stout with your cereal (though if it's milk stout, there is a certain logic ...) but certain beers do lend themselves well to light morning fare, in particular the Belgian Witbier. Its fine bubbles and subtle, fresh flavours of coriander and orange peel make the witbier (a spiced wheat beer) a perfect palate-awakener. Try it with scrambled eggs and smoked salmon – or in the case of White Anvil, swap salmon for the Dullstroom delicacy of smoked trout.

people would need accommodation. We wanted something that would set us apart from all the other places and that's where the brewery came in – we set about starting a guest house and brewpub – the total package."

Hops Hollow flourished, but Theo and Sari sold in 2008 with a plan to move to New Zealand and set up a brewery in that country's thriving craft beer sector. But fate stepped in again and with the world's economic crash that year, the De Beers felt their cash was just not enough to take the chance and instead opted to stay in South Africa.

"By that time we had sold the place lock, stock, and barrel – including the recipes. We literally walked out of there with our clothes!" says Theo, his face crestfallen at the memory. "We squatted for a year in a friend's flat and after looking around at our options we decided to do it all over again. In fact, when we started Hops Hollow, Dullstroom

was where we'd originally wanted to be." And that's exactly where they ended up with their second brewery, Anvil. Theo admits that the name is not as romantic as that of their first brewery, but there are solid reasons for choosing it. "My father was a latter-day blacksmith so I had this affinity for working with metal," he explains. "The other part of it is that the outline of an anvil is an iconic shape that people recognise immediately. The last and most practical reason is that with a name starting with A, we are listed first in directories!"

The brewery and pub sit on the edge of the town, a roaring fire in place for Dullstroom's notoriously cold winters and outdoor tables catering for the summer months. The range of beers likewise caters for all weathers, with a crisp and refreshing witbier brewed solely for summer and the roasty oatmeal stout helping to keep out the winter chill. Simple food is on offer to accompany the beer, including a superlative cheeseboard full of locally produced cheese and homemade chutneys. Theo also plans to have "brewer's table" dinners, where an outside chef will serve a special menu to diners in the brewery itself.

Opening another brewery in South Africa might not have been plan A, but it seems to have paid

TASTING NOTES

WHITE ANVIL (4% ABV): One whiff of coriander and you know that this is a Belgian witbier. Slightly hazy and light-bodied with flavours both fruity and dry.

BLOND ALE (4% ABV): Styled on a German Kolsch, the Blond is a light beer with a subtle, mildly fruity aroma and a finish that's dry but not overly so. A perfect summer sipper.

PALE ALE (4% ABV): An exquisite copper colour, this ale offers light aromas of granadilla yoghurt. Slightly sweet on the tongue, but a clean, bitter finish definitely leaves you wanting more.

BLACK ANVIL (4% ABV): A little lighter than some stouts, both in body and colour, this oatmeal stout delivers on flavour – look out for caramel, coffee and molasses.

Look out also for Anvil's Biere d'Saison, a Belgian-style beer with added spice.

off, with Anvil producing the same in three months as Hops Hollow patrons drank in a year. And Theo knows that now is the right time for another brewery. "In the last two to three years the craft beer scene in South Africa has taken off like a rocket," he admits. "When we opened Hops Hollow it was the seventh microbrewery in the country. Nowadays if there's a festival and there's anything under 20 breweries, then it's not really a festival. I think it's a fantastic road."

Ask the brewer

Some craft beers are cloudy – are they okay to drink?

"Cloudiness could be caused by the brewer choosing to keep the process as natural as possible, or the style of beer could have been developed as a cloudy beer. It could also be caused by a beer going off due to age or contamination. If you're confronted with a cloudy beer, do a sensory evaluation and if there are no funny aromas or bad tastes, it means you might just have struck gold. The brewer then has chosen to either do a secondary fermentation in the bottle and your beer will have everything in it that is supposed to be there or the brewer might have chosen not to filter and to clarify naturally. This prevents the life being stripped out of the beer in the process. Or it might be the style, which has developed over centuries due to necessity. Wheat was more readily available and cheaper than malted barley and wheat beers are always cloudy. What a poorer world this would have been without a Berliner Weiss or a Belgian Witbier!"

BEER, PEAR AND CHOCOLATE TART

RECIPE COURTESY OF SARIE DE BEER OF THE ANVIL ALE HOUSE

Roll out the puff pastry so that it is thin in the middle and slightly thicker towards the outer edge. Line a 25 cm pie dish with the pastry and leave in the freezer until you're ready to add the filling.

PEAR FILLING

Boil the water, beer, cinnamon, citrus fruits and pears for 20 minutes, or until the pears are just softening. Remove from the heat and leave the pears to cool in the liquid. When cooled, remove the cores and chop the pears. This sauce can be used for another tart – keep it in the freezer.

CHOCOLATE FILLING

Cream the butter and sugar. Add the eggs, flour and pecans, alternating each addition. Add the melted chocolate. Spoon half of the chocolate mixture over the pastry base.

Spoon the pear filling over the layer of chocolate, then spoon the remaining chocolate mixture over the top. Top with the flaked almonds.

Bake in a preheated oven at 180 °C for 50 minutes. The top of the tart will form cracks, like a quiche, but that's fine. Serve at room temperature as is, or with ice cream. This is quite a decadent tart, so rather cut small slices.

MAKES 1 TART

1 roll puff pastry

FOR THE PEAR FILLING

750 ml water

750 ml beer (a fruity blonde ale, such as Anvil Blond, is best, though a pilsner will also work)

1 stick cinnamon

1 orange, halved

1 lemon, halved

6 whole pears, peeled and with cores intact

FOR THE CHOCOLATE FILLING

115 g butter, at room temperature

115 g castor sugar

3 eggs

60 ml cake flour

100 g pecan nuts, coarsely chopped

225 g dark cooking chocolate, melted

60 ml flaked almonds

BREW-IT-YOURSELF

White Anvil
65% Pale malt
25% Unmalted wheat
10% Oats

Hop additions:
US 4/78 @ 60 min
US 4/78 and Saaz @ after the boil
Spices to your liking and naartjie peel
(or another citrus peel)

Free State

CLARENS BREWERY

Need to know...

Location: Village Square, Clarens **Web:** clarensbrewery.co.za
Tel: 082 901 4700
Amenities: Light lunches, beer tasting, off-sales

Strangely enough, it was a hankering to make cider that eventually led Stephan and Natalie Meyer to open a brewery. "It started 12 years ago," Natalie says. "We had an apple and cherry farm and started

Natalie pours a glass of the popular Clarens Red.

making cider, but we battled for about four years to get the cider sorted out."

Despite extensive reading and a cider-related research trip to Normandy, the cider just wasn't working out, as European producers used specific cider apples and the Meyers were using ordinary commercial apples. "We had to find our own way," explains Natalie, "which involved a lot of trial and error." Like other brewers, help was to be found within the homebrewing community and Natalie credits a Gauteng homebrewing club with the eventual success of their cider, claiming that they would "never ever have sorted it out without the help from the Wort Hogs". But while mingling with fellow hobbyist booze-makers, Stephan developed a sideline passion that would soon take over – brewing.

"We went to the Wort Hogs meetings for three years," Natalie recalls. "Stephan had never expressed an interest in brewing and then one day he just said 'I think I'll brew' and the beers were really good! We never knew that he had this talent so at the start we called the first brewery the Dark Horse Brewery."

Ask the brewer

I like butterscotch but I was told it's not a good flavour in beer – is that right?
"A butterscotch taste in beer is a result of diacetyl being produced in the fermentation process and the beer being racked off too quickly to allow the yeast to consume the diacetyl. The taste might be pleasant to some, however for true aficionados the prevalence of diacetyl in some styles of beer, such as a lager or pilsner, is considered a flaw, whilst in other styles, such as dark ales and stouts, it is considered acceptable."

Eric van Heerden, childhood friend and brewer at Triggerfish Brewing (see page 113), claims that "Stephan turns everything he does into a business", so it was only a matter of time before the brewery went commercial. First, however, the Meyers needed to get their cider production off the ground. After their first crop in 2002, Natalie and Stephan released their first commercial cider in 2005. "It was very difficult," admits Natalie. "We'd end up with a dozen different batches trying to figure out what worked, but then we'd have to wait until next year's crop to do it again." In the same year that the cider went on sale, Stephan started homebrewing, spurred on by another university friend, André de Beer from The Cockpit Brewhouse in Cullinan (see page 159). True to Eric's words, Stephan didn't delay in turning his latest hobby into a business and in 2006 the Clarens Brewery was launched.

"We thought we'd concentrate on the cider and just do a little bit of the beer, but it turned out to be the other way around," says Natalie of their first outlet in the town of the same name. Their beers were an instant hit, but the business didn't take off at the start, as Stephan explains: "People liked the beer, but we didn't make any money!"

A larger brewery followed, along with an outlet at the town's popular Clementine's Restaurant. Then, in 2008, Natalie and Stephan decided to make a go of it, renting their own premises tucked away in the corner of the Clarens village square. The brewery, supposedly for the short term, remained on the couple's farm while Stephan made a few upgrades. But thanks to a constant demand for the beer, dismantling and moving the brewery became unfeasible and it remained on the farm until 2012 when the brewery moved to a new and larger home a mere 100 metres from the original spot on the square.

"We were farming and brewing to 80% of what we should be doing and killing ourselves in the process," says Natalie. "So in 2011 we decided to take a larger space, enlarge the brewery and rent out our

Now that the brewery is based at the pub, patrons can watch Stephan brewing while they sip the spoils.

TASTING NOTES

CLARENS BLONDE (4.5% ABV): Biscuit aromas prevail in this entry-level beer. Pale straw in colour, it's an easy-sipper, ideal for sunny afternoons.

CLARENS ENGLISH ALE (4.5% ABV): A copper-coloured ale with delicate fruit aromas and a nice balance of malt and hops offering sweetness and bitterness in equal doses.

CLARENS RED (4.5% ABV): This ale's character has changed over the years, thanks to the ever-growing appreciation for hops in South Africa. The fresh aromas of granadilla and lychee instantly indicate American hops. It's light in body but full-flavoured.

CLARENS WEISS (4% ABV): Bananas and bubble-gum fill the nose. Perfect carbonation and flavours of ripe bananas, but with a dryness that provides the perfect backbone for extreme drinkability.

BELGIAN TRIPPEL (12.5% ABV): A definite sipping beer, this ale is a limited edition since it is matured for six months before bottling. It's a big, bold beer rich in fruity flavours and with a lightly smoky finish.

CLARENS STOUT (5.5% ABV): Deep, deep brown with a slight ruddiness. Like all the Clarens beers, it is light-bodied and easy to drink, with aromas and flavours of coffee and molasses and a bitterness that is not overpowering.

BELGIAN DUBBEL (7.5% ABV): A noseful of candi sugar and full-on fruit is followed up by a beer that is surprisingly dry on the palate. Think of toffee apples but with tropical fruits instead of apples – and in beer form! There's also a pleasing, almost bacon-like smokiness hidden beneath the fruit.

Also look out for the apple, berry and cherry ciders offering a contrast of sweet and tart flavours. There is also fruit juice on tap for kids and those who have to drive.

orchards." While away on a tasting trip to the UK, Natalie and Stephan decided they wanted to expand. Then, on arrival back in Clarens, a local landlord approached them saying he was planning a new building on the north side of the square and wanted the brewery to be in it. Clarens Brewery moved to its new home in 2012, just after the second Clarens Beer Festival. In its second year, the festival doubled in size and Natalie foresees it taking over the entire square in Februarys to come. Devised by Stephan and Natalie in 2011, the festival sees brewers from across the country coming together to pour pints – or tasters – of their craft beers. It has quickly come to be considered as the connoisseurs' beer festival, where people come to taste rather than drink. Since moving to new premises the brewery has seen a few other changes, including smart new labels and a couple of strong Belgian beers added to the drinks menu. In future you can expect to see more speciality beers rotating throughout the year and Natalie – the cider maker of the relationship – is working on plans for a Perry (pear cider) to add to the apple, cherry and berry versions. And of all the hobbies Stephan might have turned into professions, it seems that brewing was the one he was waiting for. "It's the nicest business we've ever had," he says as he runs back to the brewery to complete another batch of the flagship blonde ale.

THE DOG AND FIG BREWERY

Need to know...
Location: Klein Afrika Farm, Vaal Eden, Parys
Tel: 082 451 8634 or 083 628 8077
Amenities: Tasting room, off-sales

If you like your brewers to know their science, The Dog and Fig Brewery just outside Parys is the place for you. The five partners count between them two PhDs, two master's degrees and an honour's degree, all in chemistry. But more importantly, they share a love of beer and a determination to produce unusual beer styles from across the globe. In fact, it was researching world beers that got co-brewer Sean Barradas hooked on the amber nectar – though not necessarily drinking said beers. "I suppose my passion for beer started when I finished varsity in '92, when I started collecting beers," says Sean. "Initially I bought two of each so I could drink one and keep the other, but that got too expensive so a lot of them are still full." With 800 beers from around the world in his collection, you can imagine that some beer boffins would pay a great deal to sip some of those bottles, even if they are a couple of decades old. And it's surprising that they've survived, especially since Sean set up a beer appreciation club at work not long after he started his collection.

"There were about 10 guys and we'd meet to do a tasting at each other's houses," says Sean. "Then one of the guys, Johan [Huyser – one of the partners and The Dog and Fig's other brewer], brought some of his own beer to one of the tastings and it was brilliant. So one week we started brewing in someone's garage." It could have been an "aha" moment for Sean, but that early brew didn't go entirely as planned. He laughs when he thinks back: "It was terrible, like sour Champagne!"

It would be a few years before Sean attempted homebrewing again and he openly admits that between six buddies that were brewing they struggled to make any good beers for a while. Unperturbed, their combined love for beer saw them plan a local Oktoberfest event in 2004, with Gilroy's and SAB beers on tap, as well as their own beers. Speaking about his homebrew, Sean remembers how "people loved it, even though it was terrible!" Luckily, Sean and university friend Johan moved from kit brewing to full-grain in 2007 and even Sean admits that they finally started making some really good beers.

A year later the seeds that would grow into The Dog and Fig Brewery were planted, though Sean wasn't exactly a part of that momentous decision. "I was away in New York but my wife, Morné, was pregnant and couldn't fly. She was a little miffed! One night I called and she was having dinner at Johan and Michelle's place and they said they had big news for me, and that's where the whole concept of this brewery came from." Sean, Morné, Johan and wife Michelle were joined by Cathy Dwyer – all five employees at Sasol, though they had met much earlier at varsity. The university friends had long had the idea but needed a push to actually get the brewery off the ground – and it turned out that jealousy of one of their number living in up in New York was just the push they needed! And it's not just the partners that came from the University of Johannesburg – the brewery's name also has its roots at varsity. "At varsity, boys at that time were called dogs, girls were called figs, and although we went through a couple of names before deciding on this one, they all had dog and fig in them somewhere," says Sean.

Once the concept and the name were established, the beer ideas just started to flow. First was the ale and then Johan's preferred style – his job title of "stout director" refers to beer preference rather than body type. The most recent permanent addition to The Dog and Fig repertoire was their buchu beer, inspired by chef Philippe Wagenfuhrer. "He was tasting beers at the Magaliesberg Festival and he and said ours were all beautiful. He invited us for a food and beer pairing evening at Roots restaurant, but we had to come up with a fifth beer," explains Sean. With a brief that Chef Philippe wanted an African beer, the Dogs set about designing South Africa's first buchu beer. "The timing was such that we only had one opportunity, so we originally tried adding the

Sean pours tasters from The Dog and Fig range.

Ask the brewer

Does beer really give you a belly?

"Analyses on beer have shown that there is no fat in beer, so why is there this perception that beer drinkers suffer from beer bellies? It is more related to the traditions of the beer drinker. Typically, beer is consumed in bars and the food served in them is salty, making you want to drink more, which in turn makes you want to eat more! The food is normally fatty and greasy, which is obviously not good for the system. But a beer, all by itself, won't significantly affect your weight – in fact, beer typically has around half of the calories of an equal measure of wine. Beer actually has some health benefits when consumed in moderation, including lowering the risk of heart disease, helping reduce blood clots and increasing bone density."

buchu to Black Label to test how much we would need to add. What we wanted was to taste it but for it not to be overwhelming." Once the balance was right, Sean and Johan brewed an India Pale Ale, to combine a British beer style with an African flavour. The beer was an instant hit, though it's the easy-drinking Weiss that is The Dog and Fig's biggest seller.

It wasn't just the new beer that Chef Philippe inspired – he was also behind The Dog and Fig's unusual bottling procedure. "He said that our beers were too good to drink out of a bottle," says Sean. "So he suggested we put it in a bottle you can't drink out of." That's why The Dog and Fig's beers are so far only seen in Champagne bottles. While not a perfect procedure, the bottles are in keeping with The Dog and Fig's niche persona. Their beers are available at the brewery and one or two select outlets, though their fan base is growing as they appear at festivals around the country.

TASTING NOTES

WAFFERSE/WICKED WEISS (5% ABV): Banana aromas typical of the style prevail, though the somewhat smoky flavour is not traditionally found in a Weiss.

ALTERNATIEWE/ALTERNATIVE ALT (5% ABV): A brilliant copper-coloured beer topped with a gorgeous off-white head. Deliciously full-bodied with smoky flavours and a roast-malt aftertaste.

BALDADIGE/BOISTEROUS BUCHU (7% ABV): Traditional Africa meets the colonialists in this English IPA infused with buchu. It's both sweet and bitter in equal measures but finishes as clean as a sorbet palate-cleanser.

STEWIGE/STURDY STOUT (7% ABV): Johan's love of stout shines through in the cream of The Dog and Fig crop. Coffee aromas carry through to the palate where they meet with chocolate in this warming, robust beer.

Also look out for The Dog and Fig's Aardige/Agreeable Ale and the Sultry Saison.

MUSHROOM CONSOMMÉ

RECIPE COURTESY OF FRANC LUBBE, EXECUTIVE CHEF AT THE MOUNT GRACE

Pair with an Altbier, such as The Dog and Fig's Alternative Alt. Chef Franc says: "I found this beer to be full of earthy flavour and truffle notes on the nose, so to finish the dish off I would suggest a few drops of white truffle oil – it rounds off the earthy taste perfectly."

Mix the chicken stock and dried mushrooms and infuse over a low heat for 1 hour to obtain a strong mushroom flavour in the stock. Strain the mushrooms out of the stock, cut into julienne and reserve for garnishing. Place the stock in the fridge to cool.

In a mixing bowl, mix the egg whites, carrots, celery, leeks, onion, chicken mince, seasoning and wine together. Transfer the mixture into a saucepan and pour the cold stock over. Mix well for 5 minutes. Set over medium heat and bring to the boil. The egg whites and vegetables will form a foamy layer over the consommé after about 40 minutes of cooking. Scoop off the hard layer and discard. Skim any other fragments of debris left on the consommé. Strain the consommé through a muslin cloth. The consommé will now be clear.

Reheat the consommé just before serving. Ladle into soup bowls and garnish with the mushroom julienne and fresh herbs. Add a dash of truffle oil if available.

SERVES 4–6

1 litre chicken stock
150 g dried wild mushrooms
12 egg whites
100 g finely diced carrots
100 g finely diced celery
100 g finely diced leeks
100 g finely diced onion
250 g chicken mince
5 ml salt
5 ml pepper
100 ml dry white wine
Fresh herbs for garnishing
White truffle oil (optional)

KwaZulu-Natal

NOTTINGHAM ROAD BREWING COMPANY

Need to know...

Location: Off the R103, Nottingham Road, KwaZulu-Natal Midlands
Web: nottsbrewery.co.za **Tel:** 033 266 6728
Amenities: Pub, restaurant, tasting room, accommodation, off-sales

Some of South Africa's breweries have restaurants, some have pubs, but there are precious few where you can eat, drink and sleep without ever leaving the grounds. Nottingham Road Brewery is one of those few and it is very precious indeed. Founded in 1996, the brewery sits in the grounds of the Rawdon's Hotel, along the popular Midlands Meander tourism route. The often misty weather marries perfectly with the British-style beers served and the quaint and cosy pub in which you can enjoy them.

"It seemed like a place that needed to have draught beer," says Peter Dean, son-in-law of the hotel's owner. Originally from Australia, Peter moved to Nottingham Road in 1993 and, having seen the rise of microbrewed beer in his homeland, he soon suggested installing a brewery in the hotel. It started modestly, with a 30-litre homebrew set up in the basement. With Trevor Morgan, a retired SAB brewer as a mentor, Peter learnt to brew on a spectacularly small scale, grinding malt in a coffee

roaster when he graduated from extract to all-grain. "Halfway through our first brew there was a storm and we lost power," Peter says, remembering that they had to dump that first brew and keep people waiting a little longer to taste the beers. But once a test batch hit the taps of the hotel's bar it was obvious that the brewery would take off. In 1996, with Trevor at the helm, one of South Africa's earliest and longest-standing micro-breweries was born.

Deon Tegg was hired to manage the brewery in 2002 and took over as brewer in 2007, though his original foray into brewing, much like Peter's, was far from successful. "In my first month we threw away 3 000 litres," he admits candidly. "And in my second month we threw away 15 000 litres and shut the brewery for two weeks!" He recalls that beer – or an excess of it – was actually the cause of one 7 000-litre sour brew destined for the drain. After a particularly, let's say *enjoyable* Christmas party, Deon swore off beer for a while – not an ideal course of action for a brewer. "For the next month I didn't taste the beers and I didn't realise that the entire batch had been contaminated with wild yeast." His extreme honesty and openness – something you'll find over and over in the brewing world – continues with a comment that many wannabe brewers should always keep in mind. "Learning to make beer is easy," he says. "Learning how to clean up is the difficult bit!"

Luckily, Deon's brews improved and after four years heading up the brew house he trained a new brewer, Thokozani Sithole, and took on the role of brewery manager. Thokozani had a grounding in booze production thanks to a winemaking and distilling stint at nearby Born in Africa, though it was his position at the brewery that led to a not-so-curious rise in the number of friends he has. "Some of my friends have come to taste the beer and they loved it, especially the porter," he says. His personal favourite is the Whistling Weasel Pale Ale, perhaps in part because the beer's alliterative name has become his own nickname at work. "They say I look like a weasel because of my small head!" he grins, whistling as he gets back to his brew.

Nottingham Road's quirkily named beers are a constant talking point for those who come to taste

and drink here, but no one seems to remember how the names were thought up. "I still think the owners were all sitting in the pub and had had quite a few beers when they came up with the names," says Deon. "And I'm sticking to that!"

Ask the brewer

Do I need to tilt the glass when I pour beer, even if it's from a bottle or someone else's glass?

"This answer can change from keg to keg, but generally yes – you should always tilt the glass, at least at the start. Begin with a very small tilt, then after 100 ml you can see if you need to tilt more or not. If there is little or no foam keep glass straight, if there's lots of foam then tilt. DO NOT let the glass or beer touch the pouring nozzle or bottle."

TASTING NOTES

TIDDLY TOAD LIGHT LAGER (3% ABV): There are mild malt aromas on this not-too-fizzy lager. A dry, bitter finish makes it an easy-sipping session beer.

WHISTLING WEASEL PALE ALE (4.5% ABV): Nottingham Road's flagship beer has a mild hop aroma and a hint of toffee on the nose. It's a smooth pint with light fruity flavours.

PYE-EYED POSSUM PILSNER (4.6% ABV): A pale straw-coloured beer with a mild hop character. Bitter but not too much so, it's an incredibly drinkable pint.

PICKLED PIG PORTER (4.8% ABV): Mild aromas of caramelised sugar, toffee and smoke emerge from this chocolate-brown beer. True to style, it's a little lighter bodied than a stout, with rich toffee tones.

One story that everyone does remember is how the pig came to be more than just another beer label, becoming the emblem and mascot for the brewery. "Rawdon's had a black pig that was very cute when it was little and people used to feed it," reveals Deon. "Eventually its snout was level with the tables and we had to warn people to be careful because he might steal food from their plates." Notties' "Beware the Pig" slogan is now emblazoned on T-shirts and other memorabilia sold in the brewery shop, while the truck that Deon drives to festivals is easily recognised for its "Pig Rig" motif.

The Pig Rig is becoming more famous as the number of festivals balloons, though Deon admits that Notties' fame and history doesn't always go in their favour. "At the Clarens Craft Beer Festival everyone kept walking past me – they've tasted our beers and they wanted to taste something new. I now know exactly what SAB feel like!" he says. Having said that, one of the brewery's main goals now is to distribute their beers further afield, though first they're looking at ways to prolong the shelf life of the unfiltered and unpasteurised beer. Plans are afoot to use an all-natural, locally found preservative to up the shelf life from six weeks. If successful it will mean that after a decade and a half in the brewery business, beer lovers across the country will also have to make sure that they too "beware the pig".

THAI CHICKEN CURRY

RECIPE COURTESY OF KAREL JACOBS, EXECUTIVE CHEF AT HOTEL IZULU

Serve with a light lager, such as Nottingham Road's Tiddly Toad Light Lager. Chef Karel says: "The bitter taste from the beer balances well with the coconut cream and there's nothing better than to mix those two ingredients into a take on our famous local curry."

Heat the oil in a wok or large saucepan for a couple of minutes until the oil separates (it looks more liquid at this point). Add the onion and lemon grass. Fry for 3–5 minutes, until soft and translucent. Stir in the curry paste and cook for 1 minute, stirring all the time. Add the chicken pieces and stir until they are coated with the mixture. Add sugar, lime leaves, lager and coconut milk. Bring slowly to the boil, and then reduce heat and simmer, uncovered, for 15 minutes until the chicken is cooked. Stir the curry a few times while it cooks, to stop it sticking and to keep the chicken submerged.

While the chicken is cooking, strip the leaves from the coriander stalks, gather into a pile and chop very roughly. Taste the curry and add a little more curry paste and salt if you think it needs it. Stir half the coriander into the curry and sprinkle the rest over the top. Serve with Thai jasmine or basmati rice and a glass of cold Tiddly Toad.

SERVES 4

15 ml vegetable oil
1 small onion, halved and thinly sliced
1 stalk lemon grass, finely sliced
10 ml red Thai curry paste
4 boneless and skinless chicken breasts, cut into bite-sized pieces
5 ml brown sugar
4 lime leaves
300 ml Nottingham Road Tiddly Toad Lager
150 ml coconut milk
20 g fresh coriander

Visitors can view the copper kettles where Notties beers are boiled.

CHORIZO, SPINACH AND BEAN SOUP WITH PILSNER

RECIPE COURTESY OF KAREL JACOBS, EXECUTIVE CHEF AT HOTEL IZULU

Chef Karel says: "Cooking with beer is quite the challenge, especially if you cook it for too long – it can become bitter and overpower the rest of the ingredients. The pilsner has a fresh, crisp taste so you need to blend that into other flavours that don't take long to cook."

Heat the oil in a large pot. Add the onion and fry until translucent. Next, add the garlic and chillies and stir. Add the chorizo and cooking for 2 minutes. Add the tomatoes and pilsner, then all the beans and cook for about 5 minutes.

Using a potato masher, gently mash some of the beans. Add the spinach and cook for 5 minutes. Serve immediately.

If Notties' pilsner is not available, try substituting another pilsner.

SERVES 4–6

15 ml oil

1 onion, diced

3 cloves garlic, minced

3 dried chillies, crushed

½ chorizo, diced

1 can (400 g) chopped tomatoes

1 litre Nottingham Road Pye-Eyed Possum Pilsner

1 can (400 g) cannellini beans, rinsed and drained

1 can (400 g) butter beans, rinsed and drained

1 bunch fresh spinach

Salt and pepper

With hearty pies, beer biltong and, of course, Notties' four beers on tap, the pub at Rawdon's is the ideal place to escape the Midlands' misty weather.

OLD MAIN BREWERY

Need to know...

Location: Cnr Dennis Shepstone and Old Howick Road, Hilton
Web: rdmitchells.co.za/OldMainBrewery_9.ca
Tel: 033 343 3267 **Amenities:** Restaurant, beer tasting

Old Main might be one of the more recent additions to the KwaZulu-Natal (KZN) brew route, but the team behind it is not new to the beer scene. Rob Mitchells – no relation to the Knysna brewery – set up the Firkin Brewery in Durban in 2006. It ran for three years, but Rob admits that the rooftop of a mall wasn't the best spot for a brewpub. "People didn't seem to respect a brewery within a mall," says Rob, "although the concept was great." So Rob, a hugely successful name in KZN's food and beverage scene, has taken that concept and moved it to pretty Hilton, sitting in the Valley of a Thousand Hills, 100 km west of Durban.

Not only did he move the idea of the brewery, he also brought master brewer Paul Sims and assistant brewer Colin Ntshangase with him. Paul is another septuagenarian brewer who cut his teeth at SAB and has been pulled out of retirement to serve in the craft beer revolution. He supervises every brew, though you get the impression that the gungho and perpetually smiling Colin could take the reins if required. After covering the basics of brewing on a food technology course in Newcastle, Colin joined the Firkin team and has been working with Rob ever since. Having encountered a number of brewers that don't really drink beer, I put the question to Colin – his response is an even wider grin and a pat of his not huge yet not unsubstantial belly. Colin's jolly demeanour makes you want to linger longer at Old Main, as does the interesting eating setup. The brewery, rather than being tucked away behind closed doors, sits out

in the open in the restaurant, meaning you can watch Colin and Paul at work whenever they brew. It's a unique setup that would be a perfect setting for a food and beer pairing dinner among the fermenters – something Rob is looking into as the brewery grows.

Unusually for a brewpub, Rob allows Old Main's trio of beers to compete directly with SAB's products – and they're holding their own so far. "We want to give people the choice," says Rob. "Though, of course, we hope they'll choose our beers. For us it's about absolute passion for an artisanal product." As the brewery grows, beer fans can expect to find bottled beers on sale to take away and eventually the beers will be available in some of Rob's other establishments. But for the moment you can enjoy good beers in a cosy environment, surrounded by a group of gleeful guys clearly passionate about what they do.

Colin checks the quality of the brew.

TASTING NOTES

FOXX LAGER (4.9% ABV): A long-standing favourite from the Firkin, and Old Main's biggest seller, Foxx is an easy-drinking brew, slightly fruity and not too bitter.

1806 REAL ALE (5% ABV): The name has no real meaning, but Colin Ntshangase's favourite of the three is a very drinkable copper-coloured beer. Smoky, roasty and with a hint of spice, it's a light-bodied brew suitable for year-round sipping.

HONEY BADGER IMPERIAL STOUT (5.1% ABV): Although far from imperial, there are solid stout flavours here. A little light bodied, but filled with flavours of roasted malt and Irish coffee.

Diners can inspect Old Main's brewhouse up-close between courses.

Porcupine Quill Brewing Co.

Quills

South African Premium Ales

Karoo Red

www.porcupinequillbrewing.co.za

PORCUPINE QUILL BREWING CO.

Need to know...

Location: Old Main Road, Botha's Hill
Web: porcupinequillbrewing.co.za **Tel:** 031 777 1566
Amenities: Beer tasting, light lunches, deli, chef school, off-sales

While all of South Africa's brewers are enjoying riding the recent wave of beer appreciation, John Little is also helping to forge a new generation of brewers. His chef's school is located in the picturesque Valley of a Thousand Hills region west of Durban and on the syllabus alongside knife skills, baking and sausage-making is a relatively new addition – brewing.

"The students love it," says John. "Our second years who go over to the States to work sometimes even work at craft breweries over there when they're off. There's always a chance of one or two going down the brewery route and combining that with food, which would be great." The students certainly have chance to hone their food and beer pairing skills, with gourmet dinners and other events taking place throughout the year.

Visiting the Porcupine Quill Brewery is a full-on foodie delight, with an on-site cheesery, fresh produce from the student-run delicatessen, a constant supply of baked goodies straight from the oven and, of course, a range of unique, handcrafted beers. The brewery itself is a simple system that John imported from the United Kingdom when he started up back in 2010. He didn't follow the usual route of graduating through the homebrewing ranks before opening a commercial brewery, instead launching straight into all-grain brewing on a large-scale system. "I did a brewing course in Manchester," says John, "but more importantly I went and worked with commercial guys that had the exact same system as mine."

Soon enough John was back in South Africa, working on his own range of beers. First off the block was the very drinkable Kalahari Gold, followed quickly by a range of beers using ingredients from South Africa, the UK, Belgium and the USA. There are now 11 beers to choose from in three

With 11 beers permanently available, Porcupine Quill has one of the country's largest ranges.

hops make for tastier beers for sure." His brewery is actually designed to operate only using flower hops, John explains as his faithful dog Bacardi follows us from mash tun to kettle to bottle filler. There is no kegging facility here – all of the beers are bottle-conditioned, meaning the secondary fermentation which gives beer its bubble takes place in the bottle. Because of this you can expect a touch of yeast sediment in the bottle so careful pouring is essential. "Cans are nice," says a T-shirt in the Quills shop, adorned with cartoon boobs, "but real beer comes in a bottle."

different ranges including the extreme range, Dam Wolf. These are not brews for the faint-hearted, ranging from 8–9% ABV. "I like to do my own thing with regard to the beers, hence the Dam Wolf extreme beers," says John. His personal favourite is the Karoo Red from the flagship Quills range, though he admits that the 9% Yellow Eyes is great "if you're looking to get fired up." John promises exciting things to come at the brewery, including plans to age some of the higher alcohol beers in oak casks.

The entire Quills range already has a pretty idiosyncratic flavour though, largely owing to the use of whole flower hops where most breweries opt for pelleted hops. "We want to stay as close to Mother Nature as possible," says John. "It is more convenient to use pellet hops but flower

TASTING NOTES

QUILLS KALAHARI GOLD (4.5% ABV): A rich copper-coloured beer with a smooth, luxurious mouthfeel. Subtle flavours of brown sugar give way to a bitter taste, though not overwhelmingly. The use of American hops makes this a good companion to a Durban curry.

QUILLS NAMAQUA BLONDE ALE (4.5% ABV): It's dark for a blonde – like a redhead who prefers the term "strawberry blonde"! It's a great intro to hops, with peppery spice on the nose and a short, clean finish.

QUILLS KAROO RED (5.5% ABV): A deep russet-coloured beer with savoury aromas and a smoky, roasty flavour. Willamette hops give a faintly floral aroma.

AFRICAN MOON IMPALA LIGHT (5% ABV): The flower hops give a unique, spicy aroma to this beer, which has flavours of caramelised sugar and a long, bitter finish.

WOLF IN SHEEP'S CLOTHING (9% ABV): It's the colour of toffee and has the aroma of a freshly made crème brûlée, but this beer is not as sweet as you'd imagine, especially for one so strong in alcohol. There's a surprising roastiness that's well balanced with hops and the typical flavours imparted from a Belgian yeast.

Also look out for Quills Black Dog Bitter and Flat Tail Porcupine Ale, the African Moon Amber Ale and Black Buck Bitter, and the Dam Wolf Howl & Cry and Yellow Eyes.

SHONGWENI BREWERY

Need to know...

Location: B13, Kassier Road Shongweni Valley
Web: shongwenibrewery.com **Tel:** 031 7691235
Amenities: Beer tasting, light meals, off-sales

Sometimes the brewer goes to the brewery and sometimes the brewery comes to the brewer. In the case of Brian Stewart, the latter was very much the case. Although he had been happily making beer at home for 20 years, he had no plans to turn it into a commercial enterprise. Then a local brewery came up for sale and Brian is now making beer at one of KwaZulu-Natal's longest-standing breweries.

Shongweni Brewery was founded by British beer enthusiast Stuart Robson in 2006. A microbiologist by trade, Stuart had worked for various European breweries before setting up his own, smaller version not far from Durban. The beer range carries his surname, something that Brian is not going to change due to the label's loyal following. "Demand still exceeds supply," Brian grins, aware that the two brew-free months while he moved the 1 630-litre system put on further pressure from thirsty patrons. Luckily he didn't have to move the brewery too far – in fact, the equipment only had to travel 2 km down the road to its new home on Brian's duck farm.

Brian and Stewart were friends as well as neighbours and, after looking at the figures, in 2011 an offer was made. Following a few joint brews at its former home, the brewery moved down the road and Stuart moved back to the UK, leaving Brian to take the helm. The brewing schedule recommenced in June 2012 and luckily Brian had Johanes Mahlaba to ensure a smooth transition. Johanes had worked with Stuart Robson since the brewery's beginnings and brings an infectiously cheery demeanour along with his knowledge of the bottle-conditioned beers.

"Johanes is a huge boon," says Brian. "He is very committed and enjoys what he's doing." Johanes also has plans to design his own beer, once he's happy with the brewery's new layout and the changes that Brian has introduced to the process.

Brian has great ideas for the brewery, with a new beer, Durban Export Pilsner, already added to the brew sheet. A strong vintage stout is also in the pipeline and Brian has developed a cherry ale, which he admits has been particularly popular with the "fairer sex". Local restaurants are also looking to Shongweni, with Durban's dedicated craft beer bar, Unity, being the first to make use of the brewery's "Design-a-beer" facility, which provides restaurateurs with their own house beer. But it's not just the local market that enjoys Shongweni's beers – they were the first to distribute nationally and also the first to export their brews. "We definitely need to increase our fermenting capacity and conditioning capacity to keep up with demand," says Brian, speaking of both the local market and the export orders, usually 25 000 bottles each time being sent to the UK, Canada and the USA.

The future is looking rosy for Shongweni and Brian has no lack of plans, be they beery or otherwise. Duck dishes will one day be served at the brewery and a sample of his home-distilled grappa gives the idea that a liquor collection might not be too far behind the beer range. "The whole liquor industry is of great interest and I have a lot to learn," he says, the passion in his eyes assuring you that he won't delay too long in studying up.

SORGHUM BEER

Need to know...

Join an utterly authentic sorghum brewing experience in Zululand with Beyond Zulu Experience **Web:** zuluexperience.co.za; **Tel:** 079 583 2623.

Many people think that the homebrewing boom in South Africa is a recent phenomenon, one that has grown up alongside the craft beer explosion. But in fact, homebrewing has been happening on a large scale throughout South Africa for thousands of years – just with a different type of beer. Figures are essentially impossible to come by, but it's estimated that at least as much sorghum beer consumed in South Africa is made at home as that bought from commercial breweries. Unlike other beers, sorghum brews have remained virtually unchanged, never giving in to the temptations of filtration, carbonation and the like – consider it a living monument, and a useful one at that.

Called *umqombothi* by the Xhosa, *uTshwala besi Zulu* by the Zulus, *doro* by the Shona and *joala* in Tswana and Sotho cultures, there has always been more to this beer than a means to a good time. Rich in protein, vitamin B and a range of minerals, it is often referred to as a meal in a glass – well, in an earthenware pot. The beer is also still used in traditional practices, rituals and ceremonies, including coming-of-age ceremonies, weddings, funerals and when contacting the ancestors. Of course, brewing sorghum beer is also an excuse for a get-together and when Hlengiwe MaSimelane invited us to watch her brew, she knew there would follow a stream of uninvited – yet not at all unwelcome – guests the next day to sample her generations-old recipe.

To be fair, recipes tend not to vary too much from family to family, but they are handed down nonetheless from mother to daughter, for it is always the women who brew in traditional African culture. Hlengiwe lives in Nqolothi village in rural Zululand, a short drive from the miniscule town of Melmoth. Step one had taken place the night before – even measures of mealie meal and sorghum

Hlengiwe's uphiso was passed down from her grandfather.

malt were soaked overnight to begin the fermentation process. The following morning a fire was built in the homestead's courtyard and a hefty pot of water was slowly inching towards the boil – a lengthy process that brewers of conventional beers would likely lose their patience with.

But in rural Zululand, the pace of life is slow and while the water steadily heats up, Hlengiwe, talking through her tour-guide son Soka, shares some of the quirks and traditions that surround sorghum

beer. She tells us how people will drop in unannounced when they know beer is being brewed; how pretending to have left your hat behind is a common excuse to come back for more the next day, and how she'd had to cage the generally free-roaming chickens since the aroma of the boil brings them in search of what will later become their nutritious dinner – the spent grain. There's even time for a huge and hearty lunch of stewed meat and pap before the next part of the process occurs.

This is when the bubbling mixture from last night is gradually added to be boiled for the next hour. Although some of the equipment – like the large stick used to continually stir the mixture – is rudimentary, other items are intricately designed. The *ukhamba* – a communal clay drinking pot – was handmade by nearby artisans, the beaded *imbenge* (lid) adds a splash of colour and Hlengiwe's *uphiso* – a lesser-used individual drinking vessel generally reserved for senior males – was passed down from her grandfather.

Another hour passes while Hlengiwe works methodically and in near silence, only speaking when a new part of the process emerges or a titbit of *uTshwala* lore occurs. She tells of vessels smaller than *ukhamba*, known as *umancintshana*. The word translates as "stingy" and if beer is served to you in such a pot it's a sure sign that your host would like you to drink up quickly and leave. When the hour reaches its end, the mixture is decanted into an array of smaller vessels to cool, then returned to the large pot for fermentation. Unlike mainstream beer brewing, sorghum beer production doesn't dwell on the details. Measurements are vague – a pot here; a handful there – and temperatures depend largely on the weather. Once the brew is suitably cooled – "cool enough to touch it without burning yourself" – another measure of sorghum malt is added and the mixture is placed in a cool corner of the house overnight. While specific temperature control is not essential, there are some stipulations for fermenting sorghum beer – no onions, paraffin or oranges can be placed near the gently bubbling liquid, for they all impart unwanted flavours to the finished beer.

Decanting the brew, post-boil.

A day later the beer is strained and ready to drink, still in an active state of fermentation. Even commercially made sorghum beers only last for a few days, though Hlengiwe is not worried about any beer being wasted. Soon some of the 140 residents of Nqolothi, spread out through the hills, will descend to sip her brew and to leave imaginary hats behind.

TASTING NOTES

Sorghum beer has very little in common with its clearer, fizzier, better-known counterpart. It's a murky, opaque brew that is pinkish-grey in colour. A sour aroma unlike any other prevails, though the beer tastes better than it smells. Low in alcohol at 2–3% ABV, there is no kick to the beer, but its gritty texture and sour flavour make it an acquired taste.

In traditional settings, men will always drink first and the genders will often drink separately, sipping in a circle from a communal pot. Make sure the beer is stirred first with the brush-like *isigovuzo* – if not you might find yourself sucking on a mouthful of the skin that forms when the beer is left standing.

Placing the *imbenge* face up means you'd like another pour of the beer; face down signifies you've had enough. In less traditional settings, commercial sorghum beer is often swigged straight from the carton, though the sip-and-share custom continues, leaving you with a less-than-appealing soggy carton from which to drink.

ONES TO WATCH

The South African beer scene is expanding at such a rapid rate that we decided to feature some up-and-coming breweries alongside the established ones.

WESTERN CAPE

Cape Brewing Company
Paarl; capebrewing.co.za

There are some big names behind this Cape Wine-lands brewery, including Henrik Dunge from Swedish brewing company Åbro, wine giant Charles Back, Andy Kung from Fairview's Goatshed Restaurant and well-loved brewmaster Wolfgang Ködel, formerly of the V&A Waterfront's Paulaner Bräuhaus. The brewery will sit alongside the chocolatier, restaurant, glass-blowing studio and, of course, the wine tasting room at Spice Route, next to Fairview. CBC will produce a range of both top- and bottom-fermented beers, including lager, pilsner, IPA and stout – and yes, you will also be able to get your fix of Wolfgang's delectable Weiss.

Fraser's Folly
Struisbaai; bulldogbrewery.co.za

Fraser Crighton, a trained winemaker, started brewing when he moved from his UK home to South Africa, seeing it as the best way to get his beer fix. Expect traditional English styles, including the flagship English IPA from what will be Africa's southernmost brewery.

Gallows Hill Brewing Co.
Cape Town; gallowshillbrewing.com

Brothers Schalk and Christoff Marais have been homebrewing together since an overseas trip left them hankering for a greater range of beer styles. They decided to take brewing to a commercial level when they realised they weren't alone in their quest for something different in their pints.

While they don't plan to have flagship beers, certain styles will dominate, including India Pale Ales, porters and stouts. The Woodstock-based brewery will feature a tasting room and will be close to a number of restaurants.

Herold Beer
George; heroldwines.co.za

This established winery sits slap-bang in the middle of South Africa's only hop-growing region, so it makes perfect sense to add a brewery to the portfolio. A family-run enterprise, there's an unpretentious tasting room and meals are available. Brewer Nico Fourie has been experimenting with beer styles to find something unique to add to the Garden Route brew scene.

Honingklip Brewery
Bot Rivier; honingklip.co.za

Husband-and-wife team Mark and Analize ter Morshuizen are familiar faces in the Western Cape brewing world, thanks to their heavy involvement in the SouthYeasters Home Brewers Club. Their journey into beer began when they lived in Europe, something reflected in their flagship Belgian-style beers. The brewery is based on a family farm and will feature a tasting room with wonderful views over the Botriver valley. Light snacks will be available, as well as farm produce and a 4x4 trail for pre-tasting entertainment.

Karoo Brew
Montagu

Wayne Raath heads up this tiny brewery in the pretty town of Montagu. His trio of beers – Karoo Ale, Honey Ale and a Dark Roast Ale – are served in the Mystic Tin, a bar-bistro-B&B with eclectic décor and plenty of outdoor seating. Wayne is happy to show you his simple setup and the brewing process he learned from André Cilliers at the Sneeuberg Brewery in Nieu-Bethesda (see page 151).

Royal Capetonian Brewery
Stellenbosch

A group of Stellenbosch students have come together to realise their vision in this start-up brewery. As well as peddling their boutique beers, the team plans to sell brew kits, allowing customers to try brewing for themselves when not drinking Royal Capetonian's beers.

Saxon
Wellington

Roger Jorgensen is well known among boutique booze fans, although until now his name has not been associated with beer. "The Still Man" is renowned for his handcrafted vodka, gin and absinthe, but beer lovers will rejoice when they hear that he is also venturing into real ales. The project is in its early stages, but you can expect a range of bottle-conditioned ales inspired by the beers of England, Belgium and the USA, but with Roger's signature local twist.

South Cape Breweries
Mossel Bay; southcapebreweries.co.za

Brewer Johann Baker decided his homebrewed beers were too good not to share, so along with Jan van der Walt decided to turn his lifelong hobby into a business. The result is a pilsner, an ale and the flagship lager, all of which are being embraced by Mossel Bay locals. The beers are available around town and brewery tours are on the cards.

Stellenbosch Brewing Company
Stellenbosch

There's a lot of love, laughter and passion behind what will be a must-do stop on the Cape Winelands' burgeoning beer route. Longtime homebrewer Bruce Collins has travelled the world in search of great beer and has the IBD (Institute of Brewing and Distilling) diploma under his belt, as well as an apprenticeship with a US microbrewer. The brewery, set to be located at the Joostenberg Winery, will be run by Bruce, beer-loving wife Karen and fellow cerevisaphile, Herman Kruger. Bruce and Karen have been planning to open a brewery since they ventured across Karen's native USA in a craft beer-fuelled camping trip, while Bruce and Herman met over a pile of spare hops back in South Africa. Expect a creative range of beers featuring pumpkin, fruit and a whole lot of hops, as well as brewery tours, picnics and, of course, tasters in the tap room.

Woodstock Brewery
Cape Town

Sitting in a district that's set to become a must on the Cape Town beer circuit, Woodstock Brewery is the brainchild of André Viljoen. After nearly two decades in finance, André decided to launch a business in a field close to his heart – or at least his lips. The family-run operation will serve a range of beers incorporating Belgian, American and German styles in the beer garden and adjoining restaurant. There will also be a craft beer bottle shop and brewery tours will be available.

GAUTENG

Agar's Real Ales
Johannesburg

Brewing is in Michael Agar's blood. His grandfather brewed his own beer in the 1950s and 60s, though Michael admits "you couldn't drink it". Luckily, he is not experiencing similar problems with his own beers, which have proved an instant hit at festivals. Michael has been brewing since he finished varsity in 1984 and got a true beer awakening when he spent three years in the USA. The brewery will produce a range of styles including a German Kolsch, an American Amber Ale and a Belgian Saison named for his very proper white French Standard Poodle.

SMACK! Republic Brewing Co.
Johannesburg; smackrepublic.com

Expect funky branding and fresh, exciting beers from this trio of former homebrewers and self-described "hopheaded urban warriors". Homebrewing brought David Martin, Andrew Martin and Grant York together and their thirst for hops led them down the path to opening their own microbrewery. Their flagship beers – a Golden Ale, American Pale Ale, and a Weiss – will be on tap at the brewery, sitting SMACK bang in the centre of Jo'burg. The team is as passionate about reviving inner-city Jozi as they are about fighting for the rights of the artisanal beer drinker and their brewery will reside in the Arts on Main building, in the Maboneng Precinct.

Soweto Brewery
Soweto

Soweto's first brewery is in the very passionate hands of Vincent Lot Nkomo. His love of beer stems from a brewing stint while studying at hotel school and when kit brewing didn't hit the spot, Vince looked for all-grain inspiration. With Dirk van Tonder of the Irish Ale House (see page 205) as a mentor, Vince is ready to launch his lager, ale and light beer, all under the name "Sotra" – a slang term for Soweto. The brewery will have an attached pub, making it an exciting addition to Soweto's tourism scene, as well as a great intro to craft beer for locals.

The Keghouse Brewery
Randburg

Vincent le Roux is already well known in beer circles thanks to his Gauteng-based homebrew shop, The Beer Keg, so the leap to becoming a commercial brewer makes a lot of sense. Vincent started out wanting to learn how to distil, but on the journey he accidentally fell in love with beer and has never looked back. Once up and running, the shop and brewery will be in the same building and there will be a tasting room for sampling the blonde ale, APA and seasonal pumpkin ale.

NORTH WEST

Drostdy Brewery and Distillery
Wolmaransstad

Sitting in an offbeat corner of the North West province, the Drostdy Brewery is a worthy detour for a thirsty traveller. Pharmacist-turned-brewer Gert Jacobs makes a range of ales, all named for the various industries of the region. The brewery is based in the Drostdy Village, once the home of the town magistrate. The nineteenth-century buildings were razed in the Anglo-Boer War, but have since been rebuilt with a new – and many would say improved – purpose. Meals are available, as well as accommodation, just in case you have one too many. The beers are also available on tap around town.

Mogallywood
Maanhaarrand

When a couple who met at a beer festival later get married, it's no great surprise that they then go on to open their own brewery. It took Roeks and Lauran Griessel three decades to get around to opening their own brewpub, but Roeks was not new to the world of brewing, with his first homebrew hitting the fermenters in 1968. The Magaliesberg-based pub serves food (bookings essential) and there's accommodation available on the farm as well. Look out for occasional festivals or join in Roeks's hands-on brewing weekends.

MPUMALANGA

Hops Hollow
Long Tom Pass; hopshollow.com

Established in 2000, this brewery sits in a superbly scenic spot on the Long Tom Pass, making it the highest brewery in South Africa. Having changed hands since Theo de Beer – now brewmaster at Anvil Ale House in Dullstroom (see page 209) – the brewery was out of action when we visited, but keep an eye out for future beers. Accommodation and meals are also available.

KWAZULU-NATAL

Odyssey Craft Brewery
Durban North; odysseycraftbrewery.com

Father-and-son team Raymond and Ashton Barske started homebrewing in 2011, inspired in a large part by the Discovery Channel TV show *Brewmasters*. After one brew they were hooked and soon graduated from 60-litre batches to 700 litres. Thanks to Ashton's scholarship from the prestigious Siebel Institute of Technology, you can expect some unique brewing techniques to be employed. As well as year-round beers in a range of European styles, Raymond and Ashton will also brew a range of seasonal beers, including a warming cherry stout. Visit them for tasters and a brewery tour and join them on their journey into beer.

Standeaven Brewery
Alverstone; thestandeavenbrewery.co.za

This family-run brewery sits in a region that is fast establishing itself as a South African brew route, close to the Porcupine Quill (see page 237) and Shongweni (see page 241) breweries. Brewer Shaun Standeaven is a newcomer to brewing, but has a passion for beer that he's keen to share. The beer range includes a pilsner, an Irish Stout, an "African Pale Ale" and a Weissbier, all relatively low in alcohol.

OFF-FLAVOURS AT A GLANCE

Many of the aromas and flavours that are considered inappropriate in a beer are the result of organic compounds that have been created naturally during the brewing process. These are present in most beers, but if they are detectable to the drinker, it's generally a sign that something has gone wrong in the brewing process. There are exceptions, with certain "off-flavours" being appropriate in certain styles of beer.

NAME	CHARACTERISTICS	CAUSES	EVER APPROPRIATE?
Acetaldehyde	Green apples, cider	Removing from the yeast too soon; poor sanitation	Some light lagers, such as Budweiser, aim for a green apple aroma. A cidery taste is always inappropriate
Alcoholic	Hot, spicy flavour; prickling sensation. In extreme cases can be like paint thinner	High fermentation temperature; pitching too much yeast	To a tiny extent in strong ales and barley wine
Astringent	Gives a drying sensation in the mouth, often likened to sucking on a tea bag. Might have a vinegar-like flavour or aroma	Over-sparging, high temperature mash. Many causes that stem from mistakes in the brewing process	No
Butyric	Rancid, like baby vomit	Bacterial infection	No
Diacetyl	Butterscotch or butter; slick, oily mouthfeel	Removing beer from yeast too soon; low fermentation temperature; bacterial infection	Desirable in low levels in some ales, such as Scotch Ale, Stout and, to a lesser level, in Pale Ales
Dimethyl sulphide (DMS)	Cooked corn/cabbage/vegetal	Not boiling wort for long enough; keeping the kettle covered; bacterial infection	Low levels are expected in light lagers
Esters	Fruity aroma/flavour. Usually ripe bananas, but can manifest as pears or other fruit	High fermentation temperature; under-pitching yeast	Expected in Weissbier and some Belgian ales; generally inappropriate elsewhere

NAME	CHARACTERISTICS	CAUSES	EVER APPROPRIATE?
Light struck	Smells like a skunk that has just sprayed	A reaction to UV lighting; most commonly found in green or clear glass bottles	No
Metallic	Tastes like pennies or blood	Too much iron in the water; kettle made with unprocessed metal	No
Oxidation	Cardboard, sherry, rotten fruit or garbage	Oxygen getting into the beer, perhaps when transferring from one vessel to the next; too much headspace in bottled beer	No
Phenolic	Band-Aids, medicine chest, TCP, smoky, plastic. Can also manifest as a clove-like aroma/flavour	High levels of chlorine/chloramine in brewing liquor; using chlorine in sanitation processes	A clove-like aroma/flavour in Weissbier or Belgian Witbier is normal. Band-Aid or medicinal aromas are never appropriate
Solvent-like	Paint thinner; burning sensation on tongue	Wild yeast contamination, poor sanitation, high fermentation temperature, oxygenation, use of low-grade plastic in brewing process	No
Sour	Vinegary; noticeable sensation on sides of tongue and back of the mouth	Bacterial infection in the brewery; wild yeast contamination	Only in Lambic beers

GLOSSARY

ABV: An abbreviation for "alcohol by volume". This is the percentage of alcohol (ethanol) found in your beverage – the rest will be made up largely of water.

Adjunct: Something added to beer, normally another cereal, used in place of a certain amount of malt. Can be used to affect the colour, flavour or body of the beer or to save on costs.

Ale: A beer brewed with a top-fermenting yeast.

All-grain: A beer brewed with grain, hops and yeast with a mash. No malt extract (hopped or unhopped) is usually used. This term is generally used in homebrewing.

Bottle-conditioned: Using a fermentable sugar to carbonate the beer in the bottle. Used with many Belgian beers and in some South African micro-breweries. It's a traditional method and a natural way to carbonate.

Brewing liquor: The water used for brewing.

Brewpub: A bar that also brews its own beer, usually on the premises.

Chill haze: Excess proteins left over during the mash and boil will create a haze in the beer when it is chilled to below 1.6 °C. The beer will clear if allowed to warm up slightly.

Conditioning: A broad term used to describe various processes that can take place after fermentation. These can include lagering, bottle-conditioning and cask-conditioning.

Contract brewing: An arrangement where a brewing company will pay to produce its beer on another brewery's equipment. They might brew the beer themselves or employ the services of the in-house brewer. A way for a start-up to afford to launch a new brand without having to purchase equipment and premises.

Draught: Beer packaged in a keg and served on tap in a bar. It may or may not be pasteurised and is considered by many to be the best way to serve (or drink) a beer.

Dry hopping: Using hops in the fermenter, secondary fermenter or keg in order to infuse the beer with extra hop aroma and flavour.

Efficiency: The amount of sugars extracted during the mash. There are various types of efficiency throughout the brewing process, but all are essentially used to help determine the final alcohol content of the beer.

Extract brewing: Using dried or liquid malt extract to add fermentable sugars to your brew. No mashing is required in this style of brewing.

Filtration: Using a charcoal (or other) type of filter to sift out yeast, trub and proteins from the beer to make it clearer.

Grist: The malted barley after it has been crushed.

Hophead: A person who loves hoppy beers.

Hops: The cones (or flowers) of the *Humulus lupulus* plant, used to add bitterness, aroma and flavour to beer. Also helps to preserve the beer.

Hot liquor tank: A vessel for storing the water that will be added to the mash during the brewing process.

IBUs: International Bitterness Units. Measures the amount of bitterness imparted by the hops during the boil. Hopheads often look for beers that are above 50 IBUs.

Kettle: The vessel used to boil the wort.

Lager: A beer brewed with a bottom-fermenting yeast.

Lagering: A way to mature beer at near-freezing temperatures in order to produce a crisp, clean beer.

Lautering: The process of separating the wort from the grist after the mash. The vessel used for this is called the lauter tun, though homebrewers and small breweries might have a combination mash tun/lauter tun.

Liquor: See Brewing liquor.

Malt: A shortened term for "malted barley"– the base grains used to brew beer – which provide the fermentable sugars that turn wort into alcohol. These grains have been modified from their natural state in order to make the sugars easier to extract.

Mashing: The conversion of starches in the mated barley to sugars. This is the first step of the brewing process, once the malted barley has been crushed.

Mash tun: The vessel used to contain the grist at the start of the brewing process. This is where mashing takes place.

Microbrewery: A brewery that produces small volumes of beer. In South Africa at present there are no official parameters regarding the volume a microbrewery can produce. Also known as a craft brewery.

Mouthfeel: The perceived heaviness and texture of a beer in your mouth.

Off-flavour: A flavour – or aroma – that should not be present in a beer. Off-flavours can be caused by poor sanitation, bacterial infections and poor brewing practices among other things. Many of these compounds are always present in beer, but when a certain flavour reaches the human taste threshold, it becomes noticeable and undesirable.

Pitch: As in "to pitch the yeast". This simply means to add yeast to the wort – it doesn't mean it's being launched from some great distance.

Session beer: A lighter beer designed to allow the drinker to have several in one sitting.

Set mash: see Stuck sparge.

Sparge: Adding water to the end of the mash to get the last of the sugars from the grains. Will either be a fly sparge, where 75 °C water is added at same speed the wort is drained, or batch sparge, where the first runnings are drained and then the mash is refilled, re-circulated and the process is repeated.

Spent grain: The grains left after the mash. Usually sold to farmers for animal feed.

Stuck sparge: If the grains are crushed too finely or a lot of yeast is used without a protein rest, the sparge may become clogged during lautering. Among homebrewers this is commonly called a stuck sparge, while commercial brewers more often refer to it as set mash or stuck mash.

Trub: The yeast cells, hop residue, proteins and gunk left over after a brew. Will be at the bottom of the kettle as well as the fermenter.

Unfiltered: Beers that have not been filtered and, thus, will be cloudier with slightly more flavour.

Wort: The sugary liquid taken from the mash after the starches have been converted to sugars. It's pronounced "wert".

Yeast, top-fermenting: Refers to *Saccharomyces cerevisiae* (also called ale yeast), a yeast used in brewing. The yeast congregates at the top of the fermentation vessel, forming a layer of foam.

Yeast, Bottom-fermenting: Refers to *Saccharomyces pastorianus* (also called lager yeast). Unlike *Saccharomyces cerevisiae*, this yeast sinks to the bottom of the vessel during fermentation.

GENERAL INDEX

RECIPE INDEX